European and Transatlantic Studies

Springer-Verlag Berlin Heidelberg GmbH

Titles in the Series

B. Eichengreen, J. Frieden, J. v. Hagen (Eds.)
Monetary and Fiscal Policy in an Integrated Europe

B. Eichengreen, J. Frieden, J. v. Hagen (Eds.)
Politics and Institutions in an Integrated Europe

João Loureiro
Monetary Policy in the European Monetary System

Horst Entorf
Mismatch Explanations of European Unemployment

Stefan Immerfall (Ed.)
Territoriality in the Globalizing Society
One Place or None?

Dr. Iannis A. Mourmouras
Heriot-Watt University
School of Management and CERT
Edinburgh EH14 4AS
UK

Dr. Michael G. Arghyrou
Brunel University
Department of Economics and Finance
London, Uxbridge UB8 3PH
UK

Dr. Iannis A. Mourmouras has taught at the Universities of London, Southampton and Heriot-Watt, Edinburgh. Recently, he has been elected Associate Professor of Economics at the Aristotelion University of Salonica, Greece.
Dr. Michael G. Arghyrou is Lecturer in Economics at Brunel University, London.

ISBN 978-3-642-63118-4

Cataloging-in-Publication Data applied for
Die Deutsche Bibliothek – CIP-Einheitsaufnahme
Mourmouras, Iannis A.: Monetary policy at the European periphery: Greek experience and lessons for EU candidates / Iannis A. Mourmouras; Michael G. Arghyrou. Acting ed.: Jürgen von Hagen. – Berlin; Heidelberg; New York; Barcelona; Hong Kong; London; Milan; Paris; Singapore; Tokyo: Springer, 2000
(European and Transatlantic Studies)
ISBN 978-3-642-63118-4 ISBN 978-3-642-57032-2 (eBook)
DOI 10.1007/978-3-642-57032-2

Originally published by Springer-Verlag Berlin Heidelberg New York in 2000
Softcover reprint of the hardcover 1st edition 2000

Hardcover Design: Erich Kirchner, Heidelberg

SPIN 10725408 43/2202-5 4 3 2 1 0

Iannis A. Mourmouras
Michael G. Arghyrou

Monetary Policy at the European Periphery

Greek Experience and Lessons for EU Candidates

Acting Editor: Jürgen von Hagen

With 42 Figures
and 28 Tables

Springer

Μνημη παππου Γιαννη
I.A.M

Στην οικογενεια μου
M.G.A

Editor's Introduction

At long last, monetary union has dawned in Europe. Eleven member states now share the common currency, forming a larger EMU than many observers, who thought that monetary union would initially be restricted to the core countries of the European Union, expected. The next item on the EMU agenda now is the question how to bring the remaining members of the European Union into the monetary union.

I.A. Mourmouras and M. G. Arghyrou address this question from the perspective of Greece, and, with it, future European Union members such as Hungary and Poland. Their book presents a careful and interesting study of the Greek monetary policy experiences over the past 25 years. It demonstrates how Greece moved from an inflation-ridden economy characterized by rigid controls of the financial sector to an economy for which an independent central bank and inflation targeting are credible options.

The study is not only interesting in itself but also in that it bears important lessons for the development of monetary policy and institutions in the candidate countries of the European Union.

Jürgen von Hagen

PREFACE

This monograph proposes a coherent, novel monetary policy framework suitable for the European Periphery (Greece, CEE Transition Countries etc.) on the road to EMU. It particular, it aims at bridging a rather big gap in the existing literature on the theories and practices of monetary policies in Greece. Apart from the Annual Reports of the Bank of Greece, the standard reference on the topic during the late 1970s and 1980s has been the influential book by D. Halikias, *Money and credit in a developing economy: the Greek case*, 1978. However, Halikias did not address the European dimension of Greek monetary policy, nor could he possibly be concerned with the momentous monetary developments of the last twenty years, including three devaluations of the drachma, a switch of strategies from monetary targets to exchange-rate targets, the process of financial liberalization, the recent participation of the drachma in the Exchange Rate Mechanism of Europe, Greece's failure to be included in the founding members of EMU, and last but not least, the important institutional change towards granting independence to the Bank of Greece. It is in the light of the above developments that the book was originally conceived by one of us (I.A.M) back in the summer of 1996 and as such, the subject matter of the book is very much about these issues.

Various parts of the book have benefited from the constructive comments, discussions and detailed criticism made by a number of colleagues and friends. We would like to thank without implicating: Maria Asensio (European Institute, LSE), Tony Courakis (Brasenose College, University of Oxford), Richard Disney (University of Nottingham), John Driffill (University of Southampton), Vangelis Geraniotakis (Bank of Greece), Chris Gilbert (QMW, University of London), Sugata Ghosh (Cardiff Business School), John Grahl (QMW, University of London), Chris Martin (Brunel University), Triantafyllos Raftis (Aristotelion University of Salonica), Mark Schaffer (Director, Centre for Economic Reform and Transformation, CERT), Thomas Torrance (Heriot-Watt, Edinburgh), Chris Tsoukis (University of Hull), participants at a Lothian Foundation Conference on *A Central Bank for Europe* (November 1997) and an LSE Conference on *The Contribution of a Changing Greece to the EU* (March 1998). I.A.M would like especially to thank Theodore Vardas for numerous stimulating discussions on the Greek economy. Special thanks to Stelios Fountas (National University of Ireland) for very useful feedback on the theory of intermediate targets. This time, Vicky did not abstain from comment. Professor Jürgen von Hagen (University of Bonn), Editor of the *European and Transatlantic Studies Series*, has also made a number of helpful suggestions. We would also like to thank officials at the European Bank of Reconstruction and Development (London) for providing us with valuable material in relation to Chapter 7. One of us (I.A.M) would like to thank Gregoris Nicolopoulos and Charalambos Papademetriou, of *To Vima* and *Kathimerini* respectively for eagerly bringing into the public domain some nascent ideas that have been later fully developed in this book: the issue of how much independence should be granted to the Bank of Greece (published in *To Vima* in September 1994) and the prediction that the strong drachma policy would not stand the test of time (appeared in *Kathimerini* in January 1997 -- in March 1998 the drachma was devalued). Financial assistance from the British Council, the Royal Irish Academy and the University of London is gratefully acknowledged. Miss Neelam Patel has been generous with her time in providing effective proofreading of the whole book. Finally, we would like to acknowledge our gratitude to Professor Patrick Minford (Cardiff Business School) who embraced this project from the beginning with genuine interest.

I.A.M. *and* M.G.A.

July 1999, London.

BRIEF TABLE OF CONTENTS

Introduction 1

Part I: 1999 and the European periphery

1. The EMU Ins and the EMU Outs: Maastricht and beyond 7

2. Greece and the European Monetary Union: a bottle half-empty or half-full ? 31

Part II: An assessment of monetary strategies

3. Monetary developments in Greece: 1975-97 59

4. Recent Greek monetary policies 81

Part III: A new credible strategy

5. From intermediate targets to formal inflation targets in Greece 113

6. An independent Bank of Greece: An idea whose time has come 151

7. Summary and Lessons for EU candidates 188

Appendix Tables 199

List of Figures 202

List of Tables 203

Bibliography 205

ANALYTICAL TABLE OF CONTENTS

Introduction 1

1. THE EMU INS AND THE EMU OUTS: Maastricht and beyond

1.1. Introduction 7

1.2. On the feasibility of EMU in Europe 8

1.2.1. Nominal convergence 8
1.2.2. Real convergence 10

1.3. The Ins group and the Outs group 12

1.3.1. An evaluation 12
1.3.2 Ins and Outs: A brief engagement or a long *méssaliance?* 15
1.3.3. The Stability and Growth Pact 16

1.4. Monetary policy after 1999 19

1.4.1. Monetary policy within the EMU 19
1.4.2. Monetary policy and the EMU Outs 25

1.4.2.1. The Club-Med: A cautionary note 25
1.4.2.2. The would-be new EMU members 26

1.5. Summary and concluding remarks 29

2. GREECE AND THE EUROPEAN MONETARY UNION: a bottle half-empty or half-full ?

2.1. Introduction 31

2.2. The Greek economy: past performance and current position 32

2.2.1. 1980-94: the low growth period 32
2.2.2. Fiscal developments 40

2.3 Costs and benefits from EMU membership 43

2.4. The Greek Convergence Programmes: a deficit of credibility 44

2.5. What strategy for Greece? 53

2.5.1. Greece at the crossroads 53
2.5.2. Structural reforms 54
2.5.3. Fiscal and monetary policies 56

3. MONETARY DEVELOPMENTS IN GREECE: 1975-97

3.1. A brief account of monetary events 59

3.2. The process of financial liberalization 67

3.3. Money and credit aggregates 69

3.4. Interest rates 73

3.5. Exchange rates 77

4. RECENT GREEK MONETARY POLICIES

4.1. Introduction 81

4.2. Some preliminaries 82

4.3. Recent monetary strategies in Greece 84

4.3.1. The Greek experience with monetary targets 84
4.3.2. The *strong drachma* policy 90
4.3.3. The future of the drachma and the ERM-II 106

5. FROM INTERMEDIATE TARGETS TO FORMAL INFLATION TARGETS IN GREECE

5.1. Introduction 113

5.2. Inflation-targeting: theory and international evidence 114

5.2.1. Some theory 114
5.2.2. Inflation targets and the EMU Outs 119
5.2.3. International evidence 121

5.3. Inflation in Greece 127

5.3.1. Inflation developments 127
5.3.2. The main characteristics of Greek inflation 128

5.4. Main features and operation of an inflation-targeting regime in Greece 137

5.4.1. Why an inflation-targeting regime for Greece ? 137
5.4.2. Implementation and operation of inflation targets in Greece 140

5.4.2.1. Implementation of inflation targets 141
5.4.2.2. Operation of inflation targets 146

6. AN INDEPENDENT BANK OF GREECE: an idea whose time has come

6.1. Introduction 151

6.2. Central bank independence: A brief review of theories 153

6.2.1. The prototype model and some extensions 153
6.2.2. An optimal contract for the governor ? 155
6.2.3. Other recent contributions 156

6.2.3.1. Central bank independence in a public finance framework 156
6.2.3.2. Central bank independence, money financing and long-run growth 157

6.2.4. Some critical comments 157

6.3. The Bank of Greece: Past experience and current regime 160

6.4. How independent should the Bank of Greece be? 169

6.5. Independence and other associated functions of the Bank of Greece 172

6.5.1. Banking supervision 173
6.5.2. Debt management 177
6.5.3. Exchange rate policy 178

6.6. An independent and accountable Bank of Greece 178

6.6.1. Independence versus accountability? 178
6.6.2. Institutional arrangements towards an independent Bank of Greece 180
6.6.3. How to secure the accountability of an Independent Bank of Greece 184

Annex: Assessing the recent Bill 2548/97 186

7. Summary and Lessons for EU candidates 188

Appendix Tables 199

List of Figures 202

List of Tables 203

Bibliography 205

INTRODUCTION

On May 2, 1998, at the Brussels European Summit, the leaders of EU governments finally chose the eleven founding members of the Economic and Monetary Union in Europe (EMU). In essence, they followed the European Monetary Institute's recommendations (based on the Maastricht convergence criteria) regarding the first wave of countries which should adopt the common currency, the *euro*. This first group of EMU participants includes Austria, Belgium, Finland, France, Germany, Ireland, Italy, Luxembourg, the Netherlands, Portugal and Spain, that is to say all current EU members, with the exception of Greece which did not manage to meet the Maastricht criteria, and the three countries which preferred to stay out on their own wish, namely, Denmark, Sweden and the United Kingdom (see Table 1 below). The Brussels summit has also confirmed that the conversion rates to be used for the transition to the euro will be the ERM central rates which prevailed on the 1st of May 1998. Thus, on the 1st of January 1999, national currencies of the eleven founding members and the euro became alternative expressions of what is economically the same thing. From the same date, the European Central Bank (ECB) started to conduct common monetary and foreign exchange policy in euros. On January 1, 2002, the ECB will begin issuing euros and start exchanging national currencies with euro notes and coins. During the transitional period 1999-2002 when exchange rates will be irrevocably fixed, new public debt issues will be denominated in euros, something that would aim in enhancing the liquidity and depth of the euro financial market. According to the provisions of the Maastricht Treaty, the ECB will enjoy political and economic independence in the conduct of common monetary policy and its primary objective will be the maintenance of price stability. It will also have the exclusive right to issue currency, manage the exchange reserves of the members' central banks, formulate discount rate policy, set reserve requirements and implement the European exchange rate policy designed by the European Council. Those countries staying out of the EMU (the Outs), are expected to enter into a new ERM agreement with the euro to prevent any competitive devaluations that would harm the EMU members (the Ins). The relation between the Ins and the Outs is now one of the major economic and political issues in Europe, as it is far from clear that all the Outs will be able to join the EMU by 2002, and hence this relationship might be enduring. On the other hand and on the fiscal policy front, the Dublin Summit (December 1996) accepted essentially Germany's Stability and Growth Pact which aims at guaranteeing fiscal discipline within the EMU. As a result, there can be no longer fiscal policies *à la carte*. The rationale behind the Stability and Growth Pact is that some fiscal co-ordination will be required in order to avoid the possibility of a conflict between a (common) monetary policy and non-coordinated national fiscal policies.

For good or bad, all the above changes are of paramount importance for the European continent and the rest of the world. By deciding to launch the euro, European

Table 1

	Inflation	**Fiscal position of General Government (% of GDP in 1997)**		**Long term interest rates**	**ERM participation**	**EMU founding member**
	Jan-98	**Budget Deficit (+) or Surplus (-)**	**Public Debt**	**Jan-98**	**May-98**	
Maastricht Reference Value	2.7	3.0	60.0	7.8		
Austria	1.1	2.5	66.1	5.6	yes	YES
Belgium	1.4	2.1	122.2	5.7	yes	YES
Denmark	1.9	-0.7	65.1	6.2	yes	NO
Finland	1.3	0.9	55.8	5.9	yes	YES
France	1.2	3.0	58.0	5.5	yes	YES
Germany	1.4	2.7	61.3	5.6	yes	YES
Greece	5.2	4.0	108.7	9.8	yes	NO
Ireland	1.2	-0.9	66.3	6.2	yes	YES
Italy	1.8	2.7	121.6	6.7	yes	YES
Luxembourg	1.4	-1.7	6.7	5.6	yes	YES
Netherlands	1.8	1.4	72.1	5.5	yes	YES
Portugal	1.8	2.5	62.0	6.2	yes	YES
Spain	1.8	2.6	68.8	6.3	yes	YES
Sweden	1.9	0.8	76.6	6.5	no	NO
UK	1.8	1.9	53.4	7	no	NO
EU15	1.6	2.4	72.1	6.1		

Source: European Commission

Nominal convergence among EU Member States

governments have crossed the Rubicon. However, it is fair to say that for a number of EU countries, national pride was at stake and by fiddling some of the figures and ignoring others, and writing post-dated cheques on the distant future, they managed to get on board. Furthermore, the selection of the reference values in the Maastricht rules has been criticized quite vividly as there is no robust theory behind them, except perhaps of the fact that they represent the average performance of the EU members during the 1970s and 1980s. Nevertheless, beyond any disagreement regarding the relevance of the Maastricht numerology blueprint, it is widely accepted that nominal convergence might be a necessary but not a sufficient condition for the success of the EMU project. That will certainly require a higher degree of real convergence among European countries.

On the other hand, Greece is the only EU country which clearly wanted but failed to join the euroland in 1999. All Greek governments during the 1990s have categorically stated that their main aim has been EMU participation. Most of the Greek political parties and the overwhelming majority of Greek people have enthusiastically embraced the prospect of participation at EMU. In the light of the above, the obvious question that arises is the following: *what went wrong for Greece during the 1990s?* We do not intend in this brief introduction to provide an answer to the above simple but quite important question. We attempt to do so in chapters 2 and 4 of this book. The bottom line of our answer is that successive governments during the 1990s (from both the wings of the political spectrum, left and right), although aware of the main causes of the problems of the economy and their remedies, instead of making the sensible thing, i.e. start initiating some hard choices, chose the easy option of postponing the much needed adjustment policy reforms. The end result is that Greece is now running out of time.

Here, instead, we would rather raise and answer a more fundamental question than the above, namely: *what are the reasons behind the whole-hearted support by the Greek people for the EMU project?* Part of the answer can be found in Figure 1. Following the restoration of democracy in 1974, in the second part of the 1970s, and in particular during the 1980s, Greek governments proceeded to a reckless consumption-oriented fiscal expansion which led to two-digit inflation rates, low growth rates, high budget deficits and an explosive public debt. This unwise policy turn, together with the erosion of the public sector by a number of militant trade unions, contributed significantly to the poor macroeconomic performance during that period. It is not then perhaps a surprise that Greek people look at the euro as a way out of the three times devalued, inflation-prone drachma. It is not a surprise that Greek people look at EMU as a credible alternative to failed Greek governmental policies over the last twenty years, as a means of achieving fiscal and monetary discipline and securing a stable currency. That, together with the enormous cash injection through EU transfers aimed at improving the economy's infrastructure (see Figure 2 which reveals that only for the period 1994-99 Greece will receive a sum of more than 17 billions ECU which, on a yearly basis, represent approximately about

Figure 1

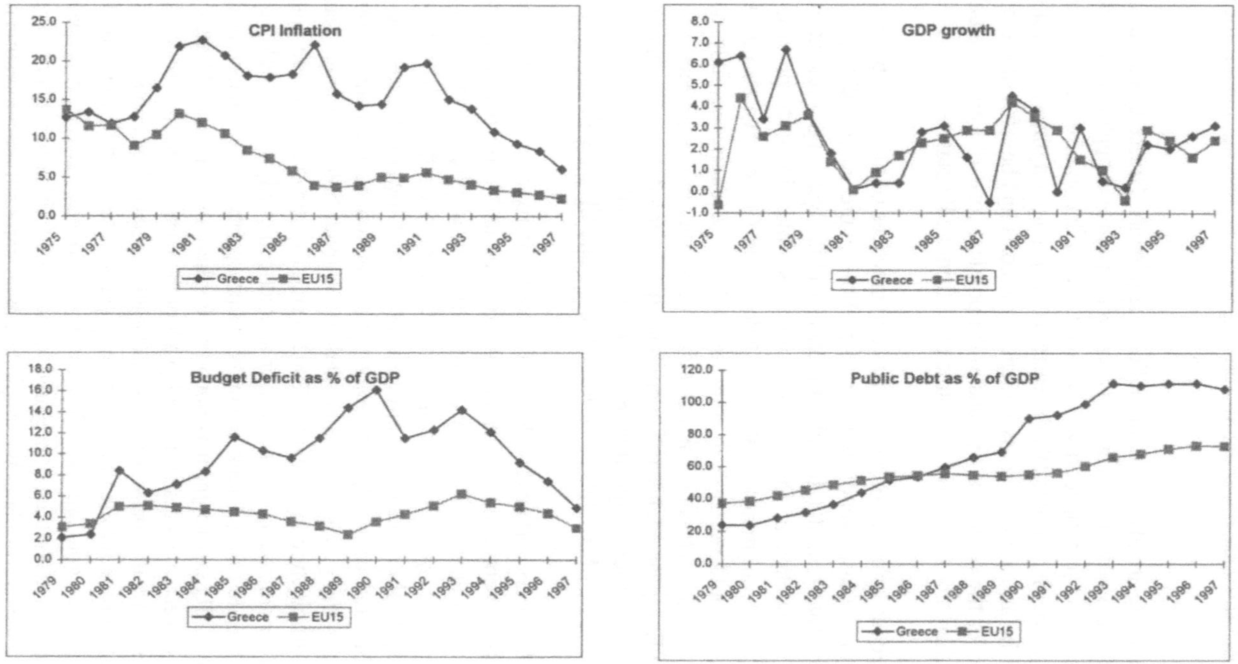

Source: European Economy No 64, Statistical Appendix

Greek economic performance at a glance: the safety of the bottom

5% of Greek GDP) are the economic driving forces behind the support for the EMU project.

In addition, there are also powerful political arguments. Greece is a small country in the Balkans that needs friends as she was never fortunate enough in having the best of neighbours. EMU participation will help the consolidation of democracy and secure somewhat its borders (especially the eastern ones). To put it differently, for Greece at the core of the argument is an assessment of the costs and benefits of standing alone. The danger for the country is obvious as the political costs of standing alone may be far greater than any short-term economic costs from EMU participation.

This book focuses mainly on the theories and practices of monetary policies adopted in Greece in the last twenty years or so and the future course of Greek monetary policy on the road to EMU. It is about monetary objectives, targets and instruments in Greece in the context of Europe. Our aim is twofold: firstly, to provide a critical assessment of recent monetary strategies adopted in Greece. We also try to explain why Greece should not rush to join the ERM-II; secondly, we fully develop an alternative credible strategy for achieving price stability in Greece on the road towards the European Monetary Union. It should be noted that our proposed strategy is far from being country specific; on the contrary, it could well be applied, *mutandis mutandis*, to other EMU Outs countries in Europe and EU candidates.

All in all, it appears certain that despite Greece's failure to be included in the eleven founding EMU members, the country will continue its bid for becoming the twelfth EMU participant in 2002. It is now clear that substantial progress in the fiscal field is a condition *sine qua non* for nominal convergence of the Greek economy. Furthermore, a salient feature of any genuine attempt towards making the economy more flexible and achieving real convergence should be the active promotion of competition in the goods and labour markets. Without bold adjustment reforms, the drachma's participation in the euro in 2002 is an uncertain event. Equally importantly, even if EMU participation is one way or another achieved, without bold adjustments in the supply side of the Greek economy the prosperity of the country in the highly competitive EMU environment is doubtful. Furthermore, one should also be aware that even if Greece manages at the end to adopt the euro, uncertainty may still be with us. This is because the fundamental issue (largely neglected by economists so far) for the whole of Europe for the years to come might well be the following question: *even if the EMU project goes ahead, is the euro irreversible and therefore for ever?* This is a hard question and we are not prepared in this book neither to attempt to provide an answer nor even to speculate. We might, however, entertain the temptation of quoting the well-known historian and self-proclaimed pro-European (writer of the authoritative book *Europe: a history*, 1996) Professor Norman Davies: "The lack of democratic accountability has not been properly addressed...Political integration has been stalled, while economic integration with deep political implications has been driven forward, but with few of the necessary arrangements to manage it effectively...

Figure 2

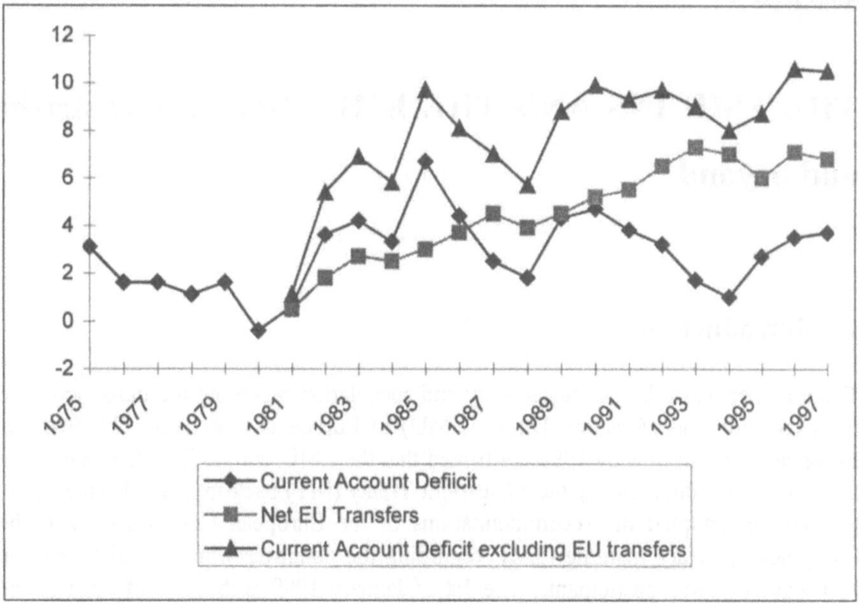

Current Account and EU Transfers in Greece (% of GDP), 1975-97

Source: European Economy No. 64, Statistical Appendix and Bank of Greece, Monthly Statistical Bulletin (various editions)

At some point (perhaps as a result of a dispute over the level of interest rates) that process will grind to a halt. And nobody will have the means to break the impasse), neither the European Commission (which is the servant of the Council of ministers) nor the Central Bank, which will be independent, nor the toothless European Parliament".

Chapter 1

THE EMU INS AND THE EMU OUTS : Maastricht and beyond

1.1. Introduction

The long period of doubts, uncertainty and speculation regarding the introduction of the Economic and Monetary Union (EMU) in Europe is now over. The Brussels European Summit of May 1998 confirmed that the EMU will be launched according to the time schedule laid by the Maastricht Treaty (MT) back in 1991. Furthermore, the Summit adopted the recommendations of the European Commission and the European Monetary Institute (EMI) regarding the countries which should form the first wave of EMU participants. The 1st of January 1999 is the date of birth of the new currency, the euro, and of the EMU which includes eleven out of the fifteen members of the European Union (EU). The MT was the last in a series of attempts to promote monetary integration in Europe which started immediately after the collapse of the Bretton Woods system in August 1971. It followed the short-lived Snake Arrangement in the mid-1970s and the creation of the European Monetary System (EMS) in 1979. However, the EMU project is much more ambitious, simply because it involves the abolition of national currencies and their replacement with the euro. According to the MT, the sole responsible for the conduct of monetary policy within the EMU will be the European System of Central Banks (ESCB) with the European Central Bank (ECB) being its centre point. The role of the national central banks (CBs) will be limited to the execution of the ECB policy guidelines and the promotion of financial stability in individual countries. For good or bad, these changes are of paramount importance. By deciding to introduce the single currency in 1999, the European governments have crossed the Rubicon. Hence, a new economic reality has been created in the continent and that would affect, in various ways, both the EMU Ins as well as the EMU Outs. Furthermore, it will certainly affect the economic policy of those countries which aspire to become EU members at the turn of the century.

For the countries belonging to the first group, out of which a few were heavily criticized for the methods they used in order to gain EMU qualification, the real challenge may still lie ahead. That would be to prosper within an economic environment most of which so stubbornly attempted to join. On the other hand, for Greece, the only EU country which, despite the economic progress achieved in the 1990s, wanted but could not join the EMU in 1999, the major policy objective will be to gain EMU participation in the foreseeable future. Finally, for the countries which stayed out of the EMU on their own wish, the main task will be to assess the post-1999 experience of the Ins and accordingly, judging by their own standards, decide if and how long they will remain outside the Union.

This chapter aims to address a number of interrelated issues relevant to the above topics. The assumption is that as Greece will have to continue its bid for EMU participation after 1999, knowledge and understanding of the external environment, will both be vital factors for the success of the whole effort. Its remainder is organized as follows: In section 1.2 we examine the feasibility of the EMU in the context of the Maastricht criteria and real convergence. Section 1.3 is dedicated to an evaluation of the Ins and the Outs, the future relations between the two groups of countries and the role of the fiscal discipline within the EMU. Section 1.4 refers to the future monetary policy of the EMU Ins and the EMU Outs after 1999. Finally, section 1.5 offers a summary and some concluding remarks.

1.2 On the feasibility of EMU in Europe

1.2.1. Nominal convergence

The Maastricht Treaty made the admission of a country in the EMU conditional upon the fulfillment of the well known criteria of nominal convergence. These include a low inflation rate; low long-term nominal interest rates; a low budget deficit; a sustainable public debt to GDP ratio; and exchange rate stability for two years prior to the admission of the country to the EMU[1]. Finally, EMU participation presupposes the adjustment of central bank legislation in a way compatible with the statutes of the ESCB.

[1] More specifically, the inflation rate should not be higher than the average rate of the three lowest inflation countries of the Union by more than one and a half percentage units; the long-term interest rate on public bonds should not exceed the average interest rate of the three countries with the lowest inflation rate by two percentage units; the national currency should not depreciate by a percentage greater than the one allowed by the "normal band of fluctuation" as defined by the ERM mechanism for two years prior to the introduction of the EMU; the public deficit should not be above 3% of the country's GDP or, in case it is higher, its deviation from the reference value should be small, declining or of temporary nature; and public debt should be less than 60% of the country's GDP or, in case it is higher, it should present clear improvement dynamics. With regard to the exchange rate criterion, the MT did not specify what was meant by the term exchange rate stability. The relevant provision is that successful EMU applicants should keep their currencies movements within "the normal band of fluctuation" without specifying which band (e.g. ±2.5% or another one) was meant. That has given rise to various legal interpretations, some of which put the validity of the criterion into question (see National Institute of Economic Review 1996, Artis 1996).

The aim of the Maastricht criteria is twofold: First, to operate as a self-discipline mechanism for some individual countries which seem reluctant to introduce necessary macroeconomic adjustments by themselves, i.e. encourage and help authorities in these countries to promote unpopular economic reforms with as little social reactions as possible. Second, and perhaps more important, to prevent any monetary and economic instability of the EMU (i.e. to exclude from the EMU those countries whose economic fundamentals are not consistent with a fixed exchange rate regime) and ensure that the economic structure of the EMU will be such that large asymmetric shocks will be avoided. In other words, the Maastricht criteria can be seen as a screening mechanism designed to make the EMU a low-risk project for low-inflation countries; speed up necessary structural adjustments in countries which, for the one reason or another, seem reluctant to proceed to such adjustments by themselves; and to promote structural homogeneity among European economies[2].

Inflation convergence is necessary for reasons relevant to market rigidities: wages, contracts and other costs do not adjust instantly to changes of market conditions. Unless inflation convergence has taken place, the producers of high-inflation countries will face competitiveness problems at the early stages of the EMU. The welfare cost caused by the adjustments which would then be necessary would be much higher in comparison to the cost caused under a flexible exchange rate regime. Exchange rate stability is justified, among others, on grounds of efficiency and credibility gains: a stable exchange rate is easily observed by the public and operates as a signaling mechanism towards agents. It signals the commitment of authorities to low inflation and moderates inflation expectations. The criterion referring to interest rates addresses the issues of national default risk and expectations about future inflation, exchange rate fluctuations and fiscal policy: within the EMU interest rate differentials will reflect different probabilities of national default which have to be minimized by all countries prior to their accession to the Union. In addition, a low long-term interest rate accompanied by a low inflation rate and exchange rate stability reflects market expectations for low inflation in the medium-term future. Such expectations reflect the fact that agents are convinced that the exchange rate of the currency is in equilibrium and at a maintainable level whilst nominal depreciations as well as expansionary fiscal policies are not expected. This is closely linked to the criteria of small budget deficits and national debt. The presence of countries with fiscal problems in the Union may oblige the ECB to deviate from its inflation-averse policy. More precisely, admitting a country in the Union whose government runs a high public debt might have inflationary consequences for the whole Union. If, for instance, investors feel that there is a default risk in a country-member of the EMU, they may suddenly want to sell bonds which may result in a dramatic drop in their prices. If the ECB feels obliged to buy these securities in order

[2] For a more detailed discussion on these issues, see Eichengreen (1993).

to prevent a crisis in the bonds market, the exchange of bonds for money may eventually engineer inflation in the Union as a whole.

The question that arises of course, is whether these criteria are likely to lead to the achievement of their targets and promote the future stability of the EMU. Academic discussion on the Maastricht rules has been quite vivid. First of all, it should be taken into consideration that the rules described above represent policy guidelines which were not derived using specific theoretical arguments (see Buiter, *et al* 1993). The arbitrary selection somehow of the reference values is the reason behind the interpretation clause incorporated in the MT according to which the European Council had to decide which of the candidate countries for EMU participation had met the criteria[3]. However, going further than the numerology issue, some economists have put into question the whole philosophy of the Maastricht Treaty[4].

1.2.2. Real convergence

Beyond the disagreements regarding the appropriateness of the Maastricht blueprint for nominal convergence set by the MT, consensus seems to emerge on the view that such convergence might be a necessary but surely not a sufficient condition for the success of the EMU project. That will certainly require a higher degree of real convergence among the European economies. The latter is defined as the equalization of real per-capita income and productivity rates. Within the context of the EU, a country is considered to have achieved real convergence when the per-capita income of her citizens is equal to the 80% of the Union's average. At present, productivity and income differences across Europe are far from being negligible (see Table 1.1). The MT has not set any specific criterion relevant to real convergence. However, its importance for the success of the EMU is undeniable. Real convergence, in the sense of poorer countries catching up with the rich ones is desirable. Poor countries would like to achieve it in order to improve the welfare standards of their citizens. Richer countries would like to see it happening in order to avoid levying their tax payers in favour of others or seeing the ECB adopting accommodating monetary policies to smooth regional recessions (see section 1.4 below). Finally, in a world of open economies where interaction among countries is significant, trading with rich partners is always a motive to invest more, to develop economies of scale and achieve a higher level of production. That being the case,

---

[3] See, however, Arrowsmith (1995) who argues that the selection of the reference numbers is not entirely arbitrary. They represent the average performance of the members during the 1970s and 1980s. 60% is the level at which national debt is stabilized if a country runs a 3% deficit with an annual GDP growth of 5%.

[4] For example, the collection of essays edited by Patrick Minford (1992) takes a consistently *eurosceptic* attitude towards the Maastricht Treaty and further integration in Europe.

Table 1.1

	in ECU	in PPS
Austria	118.6	107.1
Belgium	113.1	111.5
Denmark	144.1	116.0
Finland	105.2	97.2
France	115.0	106.8
Germany	124.9	110.0
Greece	**50.8**	**65.9**
Ireland	84.3	98.1
Italy	91.9	103.8
Luxembourg	182.3	167.1
The Netherlands	109.9	107.4
Portugal	45.7	68.3
Spain	65.0	77.0
Sweden	122.9	100.1
United Kingdom	84.6	95.9
United States	118.9	142.5
Japan	157.5	118.7

Gross Domestic Product at market prices per head of population (1996 figures, EU15=100)
Source: European Economy No 64, Statistical Appendix

the important question is how achievable is real convergence in the context of the EU.

The EU based its convergence policy on two pillars: The first is the direct financial transfers which it provides to her members and in particular the less developed ones. These transfers have followed a strong increasing pattern over the years and in particular since 1985 when the Delors Packages I and II (especially the latter) allocated massive sums of money to some member states. The second is the MT which was expected to re-orientate national economic policies towards structural adjustments. It would appear that both these choices are in the correct direction. However, convergence cannot be guaranteed only because of the existence of transfers and the MT. The experience of the Delors Package I is illustrating. As

Figure 1.1

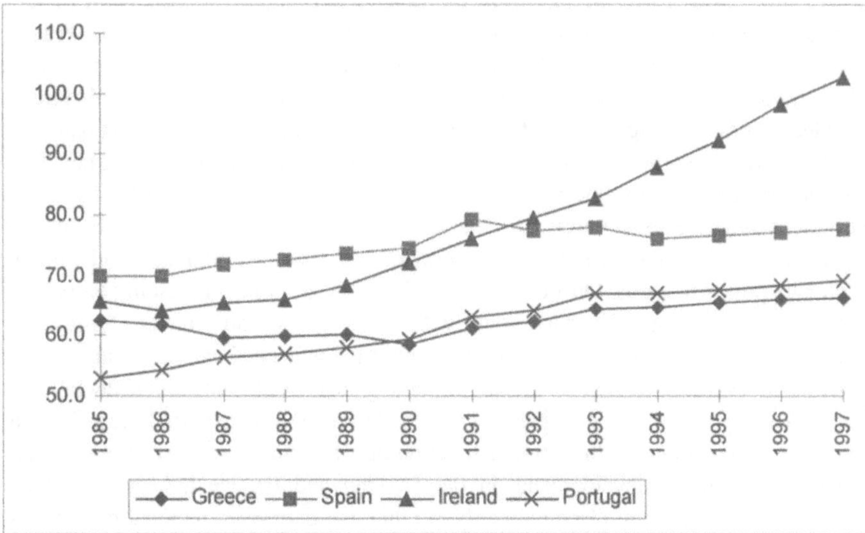

Income convergence in the Cohesion countries (GDP per head in PPS, EU15=100)
Source: European Economy No 64, Statistical Appendix

Figure 1.1 suggests, some of the recipient countries improved their economic performance (Ireland and Spain being the most successful), some others did not (Greece being the least successful). It appears that for a certain period EU transfers increase the government's disposable income. It seems however that they do not always increase production. In case they are allocated to private and public consumption purposes only they lead to higher external and public deficits which raise welfare temporarily but in the medium-term hinder, instead of facilitating, the growth of the economy.

1.3. The Ins group and the Outs group

1.3.1. An evaluation

The years which followed the signing of the MT saw a lively debate regarding the feasibility of introducing the EMU in 1999. In the context of this debate, a number of British and German politicians, but also some of the officials of the Bundesbank, expressed, for different reasons, the view that despite the improved macroeconomic performance, it might have been better to postpone somehow the whole venture and not to proceed to EMU in 1999. On the other hand, under the leadership of key European politicians, including the German Chancellor Kohl and the French President Chirac, the Brussels European Council of May 1998, adopting the early 1998 reports of the European Commission and the European Monetary Institute, decided that the starting date of EMU will be the 1st of January 1999[5]. That date, the existing ERM central exchange rates between participating currencies turned into conversion rates, so that the national currencies and the single currency, the euro, became alternative expressions of what is economically the same thing. From the same starting date, the ECB has been conducting (common) monetary and foreign exchange policy in euros. On January 1, 2002, the ECB will begin issuing euros and start exchanging national currencies with euro notes and coins. During the transitional period 1999-2002 when exchange rates will be fixed, new public debt issues will be denominated in euros, something that would aim in enhancing the liquidity and depth of the euro financial market. During the same period the ECB will support efforts to ensure the smooth functioning of a money market in euros, and monitor changeover developments in the banking and finance industry. National currencies will remain in place until July 1, 2002, the date when national bank notes and coins will lose legal tender status.

Obviously, the most important issue which had been addressed by the reports of the Commission, the EMI and the heads of states of the EU who met in Brussels, was the selection of the founding members of EMU. From the economic point of view, two approaches could be used in trying to identify them. The first is the Theory of Optimum Currency Areas (TOCA). The second is the Maastricht numerology. As far as the TOCA is concerned, this advocates that members of a successful EMU should have a high degree of price and wage flexibility as well as high capital and labour mobility. In addition, participants should have similar production structures in order to cope better with adverse supply and demand shocks. The natural question that arises is whether the EU is an Optimum Currency Area or not. According to a number of studies the answer to the above question turns out to be negative[6]. However the same studies suggest that some of the EU member countries have all the characteristics required in forming an Optimum Currency Area. In particular, these countries are the following: *Austria, Belgium, Denmark, Germany, Luxembourg, the Netherlands and possibly France and the UK.* From that point of view, these are the countries which should have formed the first wave of EMU participants.

---

[5] Here we should mention that the two documents (i.e. the reports of the European Commission and the one of the EMI) do not make identical reading. More specifically, the report of the EMI gives only a hesitant "go-ahead" message while emphasizing the need for further fiscal and structural adjustments in the EU countries (for further discussion on this point, see section 1.4.2.1).

[6] See e.g. Eichengreen (1990), Canzoneri and Rogers (1990), Bayoumi and Eichengreen (1993), De Grauwe and Vanhaverbeke (1994), von Hagen and Neumann (1994).

Regarding now compliance with the Maastricht criteria, the picture is as follows: the period 1995-97 saw a strong effort on the part of most EU countries, and in particular those which have been regarded as favourites to be initially among the Outs group, to qualify for the EMU in 1999. This effort primarily consisted of a more active fiscal consolidation policy mainly expressed through privatizations, cutting of public expenditure and raising public revenue. However, a number of objections were raised with regard to some of the methods used to achieve fiscal convergence. Specifically, countries like Italy, Spain but even France have been accused that they employed "window-dressing" practices, i.e. measures which provided them with an one-off improvement of their pubic finances but will not have any structural effect on their public deficits. It was quite clear that as the European Commission had previously judged that Denmark, Ireland and Luxembourg (i.e. countries with public debt in excess of 60%) were meeting the debt requirement, this criterion would be given a rather flexible interpretation. But with respect to the rest of the criteria, and in particular the deficit one, a vivid discussion was taking place as to whether the so-called "creative accounting" measures should have been accepted and, more importantly, how should they have been assessed when the European Council decided which countries should be in the first wave of entry in the EMU 1999[7]. After all, that was the burning question. The dilemma was the following: either a hard-core EMU would be created, incorporating those countries whose economies have displayed a prolonged fiscal and monetary discipline. That would have obvious stability advantages but it might polarize the EU for some time; or a softer EMU would be introduced incorporating countries which have recently initiated economic policy reforms but their fiscal situation is not yet quite sound. Such a development would have political advantages but also some highly undesired economic risks (see section 1.4 below)

Finally, the Council, based on 1997 actual figures, decided that the first wave of EMU participants should include *Austria, Belgium, Finland, France, Germany, Ireland, Italy, Luxembourg, the Netherlands, Portugal and Spain*, i.e. all EU members with the exception of *Greece*, which, despite the economic progress she achieved in the 1990s, did not manage to meet the Maastricht criteria, and the three countries which stayed out on their own will, i.e. *Denmark, Sweden* and the *United Kingdom.* All eleven countries which form the first wave of EMU participants met the criteria referring to inflation and long-term interest rates. On the other hand, the objections regarding the one-off fiscal measures mentioned above were not taken into consideration, therefore they were also judged to have met the deficit criterion. Finally, for a number of reasons mentioned in section 1.4.2.1 below, the European Council decided on a flexible interpretation of the debt criterion, so public debt stocks exceeding the threshold of 120% of GDP did not prevent countries Belgium

[7] Masson (1996) however does not restrict criticism to these measures only. According to him, most of the EU countries approached the Maastricht criteria the wrong way, i.e. they attempted to increase public revenue without placing emphasis on a reduction in expenditure.

and Italy to join the EMU. However, this came at a cost for some of the rest EU members. More specifically, Germany insisted on, and finally secured, a fiscal arrangement (i.e. the Stability and Growth Pact) which aims to guarantee that the euro will be as strong as the DM (see section 1.3.3 below).

1.3.2 Ins and Outs: a brief engagement or a long *mésalliance*?

The relation between the two groups of countries is one of the major economic (and political) issues in the EU, as it is far from clear that all the Outs will be able to join the EMU by 2002, and hence this relationship might be enduring[8]. Furthermore, this relation will certainly affect those countries which will be included in the next EU enlargement (see section 1.4.2.2 below). These countries, will be regarded (and asked to behave) as being members of the Outs group, therefore the relation under consideration acquires an extra element of importance. The basic aim of the plan is the achievement of greater convergence between the Ins and Outs; and to ensure the monetary and economic stability in both groups. The underpinnings of the plan are the following: First, countries outside the single currency should pursue certain domestic policies towards meeting the convergence criteria *(reinforced convergence)*. Their economic performance will be monitored closely by the Ins. If the Outs persist to run excessive budget deficits, then they could loose some structural funds and the Council can make "when necessary, non-binding recommendations". The central banks of the Outs will not be subject to the jurisdiction of the ECB and they will retain their powers in the area of (national) monetary policy. However, they will be in close co-operation with the ECB. Second, the Outs are expected to enter into a "new ERM" arrangement with the euro. The idea here is that abandoning restrictions altogether could be interpreted by the markets as an admission that these economies are not robust enough for EMU participation, thus leading to credibility problems (see Arrowsmith, 1995); and that ERM-II participation would prevent any competitive devaluations which might harm the Ins.

One of the novel features of the proposed system is that the ECB would play a prominent role in the functioning of the mechanism. In particular, although central rates against the euro will be determined jointly by individual countries and the ECB, it is proposed that the latter should have the ultimate role in setting the rates, ERM bands and the right to limit levels of intervention. On the other hand, the ECB and the central banks of other out countries can suspend intervention if this were to be in conflict with the primary goal of maintaining price stability. This is going to be quite an important change which would enhance the independence of the ECB beyond that foreseen in the MT. In the old ERM, parity changes were often delayed for too long

[8] The MT refers vaguely to the matter implying that a system similar to the EMS will continue to operate for the member states with a derogation after 1999 without, however, making any specific reference.

due to political reasons which involved "national pride". In the new ERM the ECB will have the freedom to intervene and change the parities "in a timely fashion" in order to avoid significant misalignments. By giving the ECB a key (and less politicized) role in changing the parities of non-EMU countries, it is hoped that the new arrangements will help in enhancing the efficiency of the system.

With regard to the band of fluctuation, there existed two scenarios before the Dublin Council. According to the first one, wide bands (up to 15% or even more) would be used. On the other hand, a system with narrower bands (up to 2.5% or even less) had been proposed along with an optional membership. In view of the lessons of 1992-93 EMS crisis and the different economic performances among the Outs, the European Council has opted for the first option *(flexibility)*. Although the actual band was not officially announced, the Dublin draft states that it will be "relatively wide, like the present one". However, it will be allowed to countries outside *euro* with a good convergence record to strengthen further their links with the *euro* by moving into a narrower band. Finally, it has not been yet specified whether an Outs country must be a participant of the new ERM for a specific period prior to admission in the EMU. However, although it seems that due to British and Swedish insistence participation in the new ERM will be optional *(non-coercion)*, countries outside the EMU will be expected to join the system.

1.3.3. The Stability and Growth Pact

It is quite clear that after 1999 the EMU Outs pursuing EMU participation (i.e. Greece and the would-be new EU members) will continue their fiscal adjustment effort with an aim to meet the Maastricht fiscal criteria. On the other hand, the Outs who did not join the EMU on their own wish (i.e. Denmark, Sweden and the United Kingdom) will most probably follow the fiscal policy which they believe suits best their national economic interests. However, as far as the Ins are concerned, there can no longer be national fiscal policies *à la carte*. The point is that there has to be a certain degree of fiscal coordination, otherwise the EMU may be threatened by a possible conflict between a common monetary policy and national fiscal policies. A fiscal relaxation aiming to moderate a national recession could endanger price stability and the stability of the euro in international financial markets. The question which then arises is what can be done in order to avoid such a conflict of policy objectives.

The TOCA, for example, suggests that if markets rigidities exist, a possible solution to the issue raised above could be the delegation of fiscal policy to an independent Union body which could face shocks by means of transferring funds from the Union's budget to the members hit by a recession[9]. However, although it

[9] Such as view has been adopted by the MacDougall Report (EC, 1977), and Begg and Wyplosz (1989).

is expected that the degree of fiscal coordination in the EMU will definitely increase (Masson 1996), politically speaking, complete fiscal centralization is, at least for the time being, highly unrealistic. But even if that was a real possibility, it is not clear that it would be the best way to proceed. The reason is that evidence from some countries where specific regions are considered handicapped and are heavily supported by public money shows that transfers to the supported areas tend to acquire a permanent character without resulting to any improvement. It might therefore be the case that centralization can operate as an obstacle to structural adjustment.

Excluding centralization as a solution, the important issue is the sustainability of the discretionary character of national fiscal policies. Clearly, there are certain limitations in this field. If, for example, the interest rate on government debt exceeds the growth rate of the economy, the evolution of national debt tends to become unsustainable. But, on the other hand, causality runs both ways as the risk premium incorporated in the rate of interest on government debt is a positive function of the public debt stock. In other words, if a country enters such a vicious circle and continues to record public deficits, it runs the danger of a public debt crisis. The important question which subsequently arises is the following: what will be the impact of EMU on national fiscal policies? It seems that there are two views here. The first opinion is that the EMU will lead to smaller public deficits. As Eichengreen (1993) has argued, the borrowing ability of a government is a function of its ability to raise taxes in the future. Under conditions of reasonable capital and labour mobility, governments who realize that increased borrowing today may eliminate the tax base tomorrow will follow a more disciplined fiscal policy. The second opinion suggests that the EMU will lead to higher deficits because within the EMU interest rates on national bonds will not reflect the true default risk. This view is based on the argument that the ECB will most probably "bail-out" an EMU member which faces a debt crisis, otherwise events might lead to a major financial crisis for the whole of the Union. This would then create a moral hazard problem as in the event of national recessions, EMU members will have an incentive to proceed to a fiscal relaxation. This, in turn, will compel the ECB to finance the expansion, either through direct monetization or open market operations. This would contribute to high growth rates of money supply, a deterioration of inflation expectations and, eventually, a high level of actual inflation in the EMU and a soft euro in international financial markets.

There is no theoretical reason to believe that one of the two effects presented above is stronger than the other. Of course, empirical evidence suggests that countries which participated in the EMS present a higher degree of fiscal discipline[10]. Nevertheless, given the high stakes involved in the EMU project, if a cooperation mechanism which eliminates the moral hazard problem mentioned

[10] Lamfalussy (1989) claims that countries who participate in schemes of monetary integration tend to present small budget deficits.

above could be devised, it might be wise to implement it[11]. A solution could be an explicit institutional arrangement which would prohibit the ECB to bail-out EMU members. A second solution is the creation of rules which will not allow national debts to exceed certain limits. Both these provisions are incorporated in the Maastricht Treaty. However, in view of the fact that it is not clear that these measures alone will lead to smaller budget deficits[12], a third solution could be the combination of fiscal rules and the existence of a sanction mechanism against those countries who violate them. Such a solution has been proposed by Germany in the context of the Waigel proposal in December 1995 for the signing of a new Stability Pact. The main point of the German proposal was that in case a member country of the EMU runs a budget deficit higher than 3% of GDP, it should be fined by an amount equal to 0.25% of its own GDP for each unit in excess of the 3% threshold. Also, Germany proposed the creation of a Stability Council whose aim would be to coordinate the fiscal policies of EMU members.

The proposal for a stability pact aimed at guaranteeing fiscal discipline within the EMU was motivated by the fear that some of the "soft currency" countries could be admitted in the Union in 1999. It effectively represented an insurance policy that the euro will be as strong as the DM. In addition, Germany claimed that the demographic pattern in Europe is such that the forthcoming pension payments will represent a serious burden on government budgets. The German views acquired many supporters in other low inflation, low debt countries as the countries of the highly indebted *Club-Med* initiated an all-out effort to join the first wave of EMU participants in 1999. The German idea was accepted in principal by the ECOFIN meeting in Dublin in September 1996 but the numerology proposed by the European Commission in October 1996 was different than the one of the Waigel proposal as it involved smaller fines. In addition, the Commission proposed that no fine should be imposed in "temporary and exceptional circumstances".

The major point of controversy between Germany and the countries which disagreed with her lied exactly in the field of definition of "temporary and exceptional circumstances". Eventually, a compromise was achieved in the Dublin summit of December 1996. Counties with a budget deficit in excess of 3% of GDP will be automatically exempted from sanctions if they have experienced an annual fall of their GDP of at least 2%. In cases where GDP has contracted between 0.75% and 2% the ECOFIN will have to decide whether the fall was due to exceptional circumstances or not. The abruptness of the contraction will be taken into

---

[11] This, however, is not an opinion shared by all economists. Buiter and Kletzer (1990) have argued that the rise of interest rate in a monetary union following the fiscal expansion of some countries may create a distribution-based but not an efficiency-based argument for intervention and fiscal cooperation.

[12] See Buiter and Kletzer (1990), Begg *et al* (1991), van der Ploeg (1991), von Hagen (1991) ,Wyplosz (1991), Buiter W., Corsetti G., Roubini N. (1993), Allsopp and Vines (1996), von Hagen and Eichengreen (1996).

consideration during the decision process. Finally, sanctions will be imposed on countries who violate the 3% threshold in years when GDP has contracted by less than 0.75%. The fine which will be paid moves on a sliding scale from 0.2% of GDP to a maximum 0.5%. The compromise achieved in Dublin was regarded to be closer to the German wishes. That was rather expected in view of the fact that Germany had been threatening for some months to abandon negotiations with the rest EU members and negotiate it alone with the EMU participants after 1999. That threat raised important political issues for some of the Outs countries. They thought that it would be better to accept an agreement closer to the German views now instead of having no say on the subject after 1999. Finally, in order to mollify public opinion in countries like France and Italy, EU leaders agreed to name their agreement as "Stability and Growth Pact", a concession which is not expected to change the character of the deal.

1.4. Monetary policy after 1999

1.4.1. Monetary policy within the EMU

In this chapter we have extensively referred to the issue of common European monetary policy with going into any detailed discussion. We aim to do this in this section. For instance, what will be the objectives of the ECB ? How these objectives will be pursued ? What will be the role of national central banks in the new regime?

Monetary policy in the EMU will be conducted by the ESCB, a federal organization constituted by the ECB and the members' national central banks. The former will be responsible for the design of monetary policy and the latter will implement it according to the ECB's guidelines and instructions. The primary target of the ESCB is clearly defined by the MT to be the maintenance of price stability. The ESCB is also to promote a smooth operation of the payments system and contribute to the prudential supervision of credit institutions and the stability of the financial system. Without prejudice to these targets, the ESCB is to provide support to the rest of the general policies of the Union. There is no reference to lender of last resort facilities. The ECB is empowered with the design and conduct of the EU-wide monetary policy but the responsibility for banking supervision is left with national authorities[13]. In order to pursue these objectives the ECB will have the exclusive right to issue currency, manage the exchange reserves of the

[13] Grahl (1997) provides a detailed account on the potential problems which might arise from the proposed separation of the ECB functions, namely on the one hand monetary policy and banking regulation and supervision on the other. On the same separation issue, see also Goodhart and Schoenmaker (1995).

members' Central Banks, formulate the discount policy, set reserve requirements and conduct day-to-day foreign exchange intervention through open market operations. Finally, the participation of the EU in international monetary arrangements is left to the European Council which, after consulting the officials of the ECB, will reach final decisions.

Monticelli and Vinals (1993) suggest that all the above define a general institutional framework but leave a number of important issues unsettled. To a certain extend, that was unavoidable because although in 1991 the principles of the ESCB had to be made clear in order to send the appropriate signals to economic agents, a certain degree of flexibility had to be maintained in order to approach the establishment of the EMU in the most efficient way. However, as time passes the issues which were not addressed in 1991 are now calling for a clarification. The first issue on which a decision had to be taken was that referring to the conversion rates used to transform national currencies into euros. This was by no means a formality as three alternative solutions had been proposed (see De Grauwe, 1996a).

The first solution was to make no announcement at all and leave the markets decide on the issue. In that case, the conversion rates would be the market rates prevailing on 31/12/1998. This solution would ensure full credibility and would guarantee that speculative attacks during the transition period between May 1998 and January 1999 would be avoided as the national central banks of the Ins would not be obliged to defend any particular parity. However, under such an arrangement, serious misalignments could occur if for one reason or another market rates deviated substantially from their equilibrium values during the transition period. The second solution was to announce the conversion rates along with the announcement of the first wave of EMU participants. The advantage of this solution was that, provided that the markets regarded the announced rates as credible, exchange rate stability would prevail during the transition period. The disadvantage was that if the markets were not to perceive the rates as being credible, they could subsequently challenge them. Finally, a third solution which had been proposed was the so-called Lamfalussy rule, named after the first President of the EMI who has suggested its adoption. According to this proposal an announcement could be made prior to 1999 stating that the conversion rates would be equal to a weighted average of the market exchange rates observed in 1996, 1997 and 1998[14].

[14] According to Lamfalussy, such an announcement could be made any time before 1999 and could then be applied retroactively. The rationale behind Lamfalussy's rule was to achieve a compromise between credibility (necessary to avoid serious misalignments during the determination of the conversion rates) and stability (necessary to avoid exchange rate turbulence during the transition period between the announcement of the INS and the introduction of the euro on 1/1/1999).

The decision finally reached in Brussels was that the conversion rates to be used for the transition to the euro will be the ERM central rates which prevailed on the 1st May 1998 (see Table 1.2). To a great extent, this decision reflected the fact that the markets did not react by putting any currency under pressure when in March 1998 the European Commission and the EMI proposed the formation of a large EMU. This was largely interpreted by the heads of states of the EU members as a signal that the markets were convinced that none of the currencies which would form the euro was fundamentally overvalued, therefore there was no danger of any speculative attack during the transition period[15].

Having settled that issue, the main challenge for the ECB still lies ahead. More specifically, taking in mind that the primary objective of the ESCB is the maintenance of price stability in the EMU, the question is what could be done in order to establish and maintain an inflation-averse reputation for the new organization. Three factors are now introduced into the discussion. The first factor is the success of the national central banks in reducing inflation prior to the establishment of the EMU. That target was largely achieved and its importance was to convince agents that as national monetary authorities are "hard-nosed", their successor in the conduct of monetary policy, the ESCB, will also be so. The second factor refers to the political and economic independence of the ESCB. It is true that the MT has institutionally ensured both forms of independence for the new system[16]. However, institutional arrangements alone cannot guarantee price stability[17]. The ESCB has to work hard in order to establish an anti-inflationary reputation and in that sense the choice of a suitable monetary policy strategy is quite important. There are two alternatives with regard to that strategy: the first one is that the ECB should adopt a money supply target[18]. Issing (1994) provides a guide to the reasons arguing in favour of such a choice. The first is the success of

---

[15] In fact, the March 1998 revaluation of the Irish punt against the DM by 3% was decided with this consideration in mind.

[16] The MT provisions prohibit officials of the ESCB to receive instructions from officials of the Union, national governments or other agents ; prohibit national governments and the governing bodies of the EU to pursue intervention in the decisions of the ESCB; establish the secrecy of the proceedings of the meetings of the Governing Council; define an eight year non-renewable term office for the members of the Executive Board and a five year term office for the Governors of the national central banks; prohibit the arbitrary discontinuation of the services of the officials of the ECB and the Governors of the central banks on the part of national governments and the European Commission ; prohibit privileged treatment of the Union or member states or local governments in credit and overdraft facilities; prohibit the ECB or national central banks to bail out national debts ; prohibit the ESCB to participate in issues of debt of any kind of national governments, local governments public enterprises of any country and in general any body controlled by the EU or its member-states. However, in order to establish the ability of the ESCB to perform open market operations the Maastricht Treaty does not prohibit transactions involving such securities in the financial markets.

[17] This point is extensively discussed in chapter 6.

[18] Intermediate monetary targets are further discussed in chapter 4.

Table 1.2

	Austria	Belgium	France	Finland	Ireland	Italy	Luxembourg	Netherlands	Portugal	Spain	Germany
Austria	1	0.3411	2.0977	2.3143	17.4719	0.007107	0.3411	6.2441	0.0686	0.0827	7.0355
Belgium	2.9316	1	6.1498	6.7847	51.2211	0.020834	1.0000	18.3055	0.2012	0.2424	20.6255
France	0.4767	0.1626	1	1.1032	8.3289	0.003388	0.1626	2.9766	0.0327	0.0394	3.3539
Finland	0.4321	0.1474	0.9064	1	7.5495	0.003071	0.1474	2.6981	0.0297	0.0357	3.0400
Ireland	0.0572	0.0195	0.1201	0.1325	1	0.000407	0.0195	0.3574	0.0039	0.0047	0.4027
Italy	140.715	47.999	295.183	325.657	2458.557	1	47.999	878.643	9.658	11.6372	990.002
Luxembourg	2.9316	1.0000	6.1498	6.7847	51.2211	0.020834	1	18.305	0.2012	0.2424	20.6255
Netherlands	0.1602	0.0546	0.3360	0.3706	2.7981	0.001138	0.0546	1	0.0110	0.0132	1.1267
Portugal	14.5696	4.9698	30.5633	33.7186	254.5595	0.103540	4.9698	90.9748	1	1.2049	102.5050
Spain	12.0918	4.1246	25.3655	27.9842	211.2671	0.085931	4.1246	75.5030	0.8299	1	85.0722
Germany	0.1421	0.0485	0.2982	0.3289	2.4834	0.001010	0.0485	0.8875	0.0098	0.0118	1

The EMU Ins: official bilateral conversion rates*

* as decided by the Brussels Summit of May 1998

Source: Financial Times, 3 May 1998

the approach so far. Having in mind the German experience, he argues that there is no reason to change a strategy which has proved successful in the past. Second, it should be kept in mind that the establishment of the EMU is currently regarded by many European citizens with fear and uncertainty. The ESCB will need to inherit as much credibility by its predecessors as possible i.e. it has to convince agents that it will be as inflation-averse as the Bundesbank which sets money supply targets (see Table 1.3). In other words, in the context of the EMU, the main benefit from such a monetary strategy is its continuity with the German way of conducting monetary policy. Finally, as long as many other important decisions relevant to economic policy will continue to be decided by national governments in a decentralized level, a clear money supply target will allow governments to adjust their policies accordingly and promote coordination of actions[19]. However, the effectiveness of a common monetary policy targeting money supply in delivering price stability crucially depends on a number of prerequisites, not least the maintenance of money demand stability. According to a number of economists (see De Grauwe 1994c, Kenen 1995), the main problem with monetary targeting at the European level is that the concept of Europe-wide money targets is not a clear one and it needs to be explained and understood by all in order to be credible. According to this view, if the ECB opts for a money supply targets, it may face difficulty in delivering price stability or deliver it at the expense of a higher short-run output cost[20]. Based on this argument, a large number of influential European economists has argued in favour of a generalized inflation targeting both for the ECB and for national CBs of the Outs countries[21].

Finally, a third factor which might be associated with the ability of the ECB to avoid external interventions (and consequently with its anti-inflationary credibility) refers to the personality which will head the new organization. In other words, in the context of a project of a such a large scale like the EMU, do personalities really matter or not? This issue recently made the headlines after the controversy which erupted between Germany and France regarding the duration of the term in office of the first president of the ECB. Although opinions are split on this issue, in our view the answer is that to a certain (non-negligible) extent, personalities do matter, especially in terms of signals send to the markets, because irrespective of their individual views and abilities, the image of personalities also depends on the reputation of the institutions from which they are coming. This is especially true in the case of appointments for institutions like the ECB which have no policy tradition of their own. The argument is exactly equivalent to the one mentioned above regarding the issue of monetary strategy and its continuity with the German way of conducting monetary policy. Therefore, it is not clear to us that the deal

---

[19] In fact, the ECB finally adopted Europe-wide money supply targets supplemented by an inflation target.

[20] Issing (1994) however believes that the stability of money demand will not be seriously affected by the introduction of EMU.

[21] The advantages of this strategy are thoroughly discussed in chapters 5 and 6.

Table 1.3

Exchange rate targets (ERM participation)   Austria, Belgium/Luxembourg, Denmark, Greece, Ireland, Italy, Netherlands, Portugal,
Exchange rate targets /ERM participation supplemented by other targets   France (broad money supply targets), Spain (inflation objectives)
Monetary targets   Germany (M3)
Inflation targets   Finland, Sweden, United Kingdom

Monetary policy strategies in the European Union before the introduction of the euro
Source: Central Bank Reports, European Economy

reached at Brussels was the best think which could accompany the announcement for the introduction of the euro[22].

To turn now to another issue, due to the systematic risk present in contemporary economies a non-distortionary regulation of the European financial is considered necessary in order to guarantee the existence of financial stability (see Giovannini 1992). There are two points related to this: first, the organization of an efficient payments system within the EMU and second the supervision of commercial banking. The MT defines the promotion of the former as one of the objectives of the ESCB. Towards that direction, the integration of the interbank payment systems is considered necessary and it is already under way. With regard to the latter, whether the ESCB should undertake sole responsibility for banking supervision is a debatable subject. The ECB could be more efficient in providing supervision due to economies of scope developed by the gathering of information about banks necessary for the implementation of monetary policy. Also, co-ordination of national authorities in order to achieve this task will be practically difficult and prawn to external influences. On the other hand, it is feared that too many operations concentrated in the hands of the ECB will increase the range of possible interventions and will reduce its efficiency in attaining the primary object, i.e. price stability (see Arghyrou and Mourmouras, 1998).

[22] In Brussels it was decided that after four years in office, Mr. Wim Duisenberg (the Dutch candidate supported by Germany and most EU countries) will step down in favour of Mr. Jean Claude Trichet who was the French candidate for the post.

Finally, another important issue relevant to the operation of the ESCB is the question of its accountability[23]. Delegating monetary policy to the ESCB is subject to the criticism of leaving such an very important matter in the hands of some appointed technocrats. From that point of view, accountability could ensure the consistency of its policies with the aims of the Union and the wishes of the public, especially during periods of major unexpected shocks. However, that would increase the scope for external interventions and the probability of following non-optimal policies. The MT does not specify to whom the ESCB is accountable. Also, there are no articles referring to explicit procedures through which the performance of the ESCB will be assessed[24].

1.4.2. Monetary policy and the EMU Outs

1.4.2.1. The Club-Med: a cautionary note

Given the high stakes involved in the EMU project and the sceptical views which had been expressed by a number of observers and institutions (including the Bundesbank) regarding the formation of a large EMU, the decision to admit in the first wave of EMU participants a large number of countries might seem surprising and perhaps too risky. However, there are a number of reasons which might explain the rather generous interpretation given to the Maastricht criteria by the European Council. These include the following: First, all EU countries achieved a substantial degree of nominal convergence during the period 1991-97. As the wording of the Maastricht Treaty allowed more than one interpretation, these countries had strong economic, legal and political arguments during the subsequent negotiations. Second, and perhaps more importantly, prior to the selection of the EMU founding members, there were doubts whether Germany itself would be in position to meet the 3.0% deficit target. In view of the late 1998 German general elections, this fact, along with the political capital which the German government had invested in the creation of EMU, obliged Germany to ascent to a flexible interpretation of the deficit criterion.

Without any doubt, the EMU is a project bearing considerable economic risks. The initial choice of the countries will probably be a vital factor with regard to the credibility and stability of the euro and consequently the success of the EMU during its crucial introduction period. The situation being so, we believe that on

---

[23] The importance of the accountability issue is one of the arguments adopted by those economists arguing in favour of the adoption of inflation targets for the ECB. For further discussion on this point, see chapter 5.

[24] The MT states that the ECB is obliged to publish a quarterly report on the activities of the ESCB and an annual report on the developments of monetary policy and issues relevant to it; the President of the Council of Ministers and a member of the Commission have the right to attend the meetings of the Governing Council without being eligible to vote during decision taking; and the European Parliament may invite the President or the Executive Board to be heard by some of its committees.

the delicate point of its introduction every care should have been taken in order to maximize the possibilities of success and this could only be achieved if the first wave of participants included the countries which have shown that they have the capacity to achieve fiscal discipline and the ability to retain a strong currency for a long time. As a result, although we believe that countries like Italy, Portugal and Spain which have relatively recently initiated fiscal correction policies should have been encouraged to continue their effort, we also believe that they should not have been admitted in the EMU in 1999 because they might undermine the credibility of the single currency. It is also our opinion that it would have been both for the benefit of the EMU and these countries if they had stayed out of the EMU, or a new ERM arrangement with narrow bands of fluctuation, until they had achieved a better degree of nominal *and* real convergence.

There are two kinds of arguments behind this view. The first one refers to the fiscal imbalances characterizing some of the countries of the *Club-Med*, and in particular Italy. The second refers to the distinct structural differences which exist between the South European economies and those of the European North. As far the stability of the euro is concerned, the dangers of including in the EMU heavily indebted countries were earlier discussed in the context of our reference to the Stability and Growth Pact, therefore the arguments will not be repeated here. With regard to the second point, a large EMU incorporating countries which may be subject to asymmetric real shocks may have negative implications for the *Club-Med* countries in the following sense: assuming that the ECB will not be willing to relax its monetary stance, within the framework of the EMU, or a narrow banded ERM-II, the only way available for countries with lower productivity rates than the EMU average to address problems of their real exchange rate in the short-run will be to follow appropriate fiscal and incomes policy. In addition, such policies should be quite firm in order to bring quick results. In other words, given the competitiveness gap which exists between the European North and the European South, and also in view of wage and price rigidities, there is a danger that the welfare implications of the EMU for these countries could be, indeed, very serious. On the other hand, on the assumption that the EMU were introduced in 1999 including the hard-core countries only, we believe that the South European countries should have been given a solemn promise that in case they continued their effort to correct fiscal imbalances they would have been admitted in the EMU in 2002, provided that in the meantime no serious upheavals of the euro would have taken place. That would be helpful because it could retain public support for EMU which is essential for the completion of the reforms currently under way.

1.4.2.2. The ERM-II, the EMU Outs and the would-be new EMU members

We end this chapter with a brief reference to the prospects of future monetary policy in the EMU Outs group. For the time being, these include the current EU members which stayed out of the EMU on their own wish (Denmark, Sweden and the United Kingdom) and Greece. However, here one should also consider those countries which will be included in the next EU enlargement, i.e. *Cyprus* and some of the transition economies (i.e. *the Czech Republic, Estonia, Hungary, Poland and Slovenia)*[25]. In the medium-term future, these countries will most probably be regarded (and asked to behave) as countries which prepare for EMU participation.

To begin with, one might notice that neither of the two groups mentioned above is completely homogeneous. In the monetary field, this fact is reflected in the differences among the inflation rates in the countries of the two groups (see Table 1.4). As far as the first group is concerned, the difference is between Greece and the rest three countries whose public finances stand on a sound basis and their economies present great similarities with those of the hard core of the EMU. On the other hand, it is quite clear that the economy of Cyprus is in much better position compared to the remaining five Central and Eastern European (CEE) countries which have recently started accession negotiations with the EU. In fact, one might say that the Cypriot economy is in better shape than the Greek one as Cyprus currently meets all the criteria of nominal convergence set by the Maastricht Treaty[26].

Speaking now in relation to the future monetary strategy of the EMU Outs, it seems very probable that, with the possible exception of the United Kingdom, these countries will join the ERM-II. For the time being, this certainly applies for Greece and Denmark whereas the Cyprus government has already announced that after 1999 the Cyprus pound will remain pegged to the euro. However, it is not quite clear that ERM-II participation would be advantageous for the economies of these countries and will suit their economic fundamentals[27]. The point is that given the existing productivity differentials and the macroeconomic imbalances characterizing some of the current and future Outs (and especially those of the transition economies),

---

[25] According to the decisions reached at the European Summit of Luxembourg in December 1997, the future enlargement of the EU will take place in two steps. The first will involve the six countries mentioned above. These countries have already started accession negotiations with the EU. The second step will include the rest of the transition countries (i.e. Bulgaria, Latvia, Lithuania, Romania, Slovakia), whose economies were not judged to be ready for the beginning of accession negotiations. Finally, in Luxembourg it was also decided that at some stage in the future the Turkish application for EU membership will be considered. However, for the time being, the economic situation of this country, combined with its rather poor human rights record and its problems with Cyprus and Greece, imply that the accession of Turkey in the EU will not take place in the foreseeable future.

[26] The opinion of the European Commission on the application of Cyprus was issued in June 1993 and among others it stated the following: "In regard to economic aspects...the adoption of the *Acquis communautaire* by Cyprus will pose no insurmountable problems...The economy of the Island has demonstrated an ability to adapt and seems ready to face the challenge of integration, provided that the work already started on reforms and on opening up to the outside world is maintained".

[27] The advantages and disadvantages of ERM-II participation are further discussed in great detail in chapter 4 in the context of our discussion on the prospects of Greek monetary policy after 1999.

and also taking into consideration the probability that the euro will follow an appreciating pattern during the first stages of its introduction[28], participation in the ERM-II could well imply an overvaluation of some of the Outs' national currencies. The problems created by such an overvaluation are well known and thoroughly documented in the economic literature: under such conditions the entire credibility of monetary policy rests on the maintenance of an unsustainable exchange rate which necessitates the use of high interest rates and continuous intervention in foreign exchange markets. These high interest rates tend to attract portfolio inflows of short and medium term nature which, in turn, tend to jeopardize the anti-inflationary character of monetary policy by increasing liquidity while, at the same time, damaging the external sector of the economy. The realization that some of the Outs currencies are overvalued could then lead to speculative attacks which could produce a forced devaluation or even a forced exit from the system (see also De Grauwe, 1996b). This is largely the unfortunate tale of the 1992-93 EMS crisis[29]

Table 1.4

	1991	1992	1993	1994	1995	1996	1997
Current EU members[1]							
Denmark	2.4	2.0	0.4	1.8	2.1	2.1	2.3
Greece	19.8	15.0	13.8	10.8	9.3	8.3	6.0
Sweden	10.3	2.2	5.7	3.0	2.4	1.2	1.6
United Kingdom	7.5	5.0	3.4	2.5	2.6	2.8	2.3
Future EU members[2]							
Czech Republic	52.0	13.0	18.0	10.0	8.0	9.0	8.4
Cyprus[1]	5.0	6.5	4.9	4.7	2.6	3.0	3.6
Estonia	304	954	36	42	29	24	10.6
Hungary	32	22	21	21	28	22	18.3
Poland	60	44	38	29	22	19	15.9
Slovenia	247	93	23	18	9.0	10	9.1

CPI Inflation in the EMU Outs (% per annum)

[1] *Source: European Economy No 64, Statistical Appendix;* [2] *Source: Begg (1997), p. 35*

[28] For a justification of this view see chapter 4 (section 4.4.3).

[29] Artis (1996) agrees on this point. He claims that the ERM crisis of 1992-93 showed that in the absence of sufficient convergence, a narrow band can cause serious misalignments which unavoidably lead to speculative attacks exchange rate crises.

and there is no reason to believe that history will not repeat itself in the case of ERM-II, especially if participation to the latter is to involve a narrow band of fluctuation.

If such conditions ever materialize, the negative implications may not be restricted to the Outs group only. In fact, the ECB could find itself in front of an unpleasant dilemma, i.e. either to allow a repetition of the 1992-93 events or to intervene in international money markets to an extent incompatible with its target of maintaining price stability. The latter point is straightforward. As Gros and Thygesen (1992) have argued, to the extent that the Outs include a large number of countries or a single influential one, the prevention or handling of an exchange rate crisis might require extended intervention in euros to support some of the Outs' currencies. This could imply that by assisting the national banks of the Outs to defend the agreed ERM-II parities, the ECB might contribute to an increase in liquidity in Union level which could produce inflationary pressures. Certainly, the possibility of conflicts of interest of this kind cannot be ruled out, especially in view of the 1992-93 experience (the events of 1992 involving the sterling pound and the refusal of the Bundesbank to lower its interest rates is one characteristic example). In fact, a number of observers (see e.g. Arrowsmith 1995) have taken the view that such conflicts of interest between the ECB and the national central banks of the Outs could be more pronounced than the ones which appeared in the context of the old ERM arrangement.

1.5. Summary and concluding remarks

This chapter has addressed a number of interrelated issues relevant to the establishment of an Economic and Monetary Union (EMU) in Europe and the creation of a European Central Bank (ECB). According to the decisions of the Brussels Summit in May 1998 Greece will have to continue its bid for EMU participation after 1999 and hence, knowledge and understanding of the external environment, will both be vital factors for the success of the whole effort. In the light of the decisions of the Brussels Summit, the first wave of EMU participants includes all EU members with the exception of Greece and the countries which stayed out of the EMU on their own wish (i.e. Denmark, Sweden and the United Kingdom).

Whether the decisions taken at Brussels were the optimal ones regarding the success of the EMU project is a rather debatable subject. What is certain is that economic issues were not the only ones which were taken into consideration. Furthermore, there is little doubt that in addition to nominal convergence, the future stability of the EMU will require a higher degree of real convergence among the European economies. The countries which joined the EMU delegated monetary policy to the European Central Bank whose primary objective is the maintenance of price stability.

The ECB will also play a key role in the ERM-II arrangement. The rationale behind ERM-II is to help the Outs maintain a low rate of inflation and enhance the credibility of their economic policies and avoid competitive devaluations. However, it appears that the ERM-II suffers from a number of problems at both the theoretical and the practical level. More specifically, given the existing productivity differentials and the macroeconomic imbalances characterizing some European countries, some of the Outs could end with overvalued currencies, especially if the euro is to follow an appreciation pattern after 1999. Under such circumstances, speculative attacks cannot be ruled out and, in that case, the possible conflict of interests between the ECB and national central banks of the Outs could lead to a repetition of the 1992-93 crisis. Therefore, to foreshadow what follows in the remaining chapters of this book, an alternative monetary strategy for the Outs could take the form of a direct inflation targeting monetary regime, involving, perhaps, an inflation target slightly higher than the inflation rate prevailing in the EMU. As we will argue later in the context of our discussion on Greece[30], such a policy could reduce the degree of the interdependence between the ECB and the Outs countries and may prove to be more effective both in terms of inflation progress and output loss.

---

[30] See also our discussion on inflation and the EMU Outs (chapter 5, section 5.2.2).

Chapter 2

GREECE AND THE EUROPEAN MONETARY UNION: a bottle half-empty or half-full ?

2.1. Introduction

As we have seen in the previous chapter, Greece is not alone within the group of the EMU Outs countries. However, there is one important difference between Greece and the other three countries, namely that Greece did not stay out of the EMU on her own wish. In fact, Greece was the only EU country which did not meet any of the criteria of nominal convergence set by the Maastricht Treaty. It is not that Greece did not make any effort to gain EMU qualification in 1999. All Greek governments in the 1990s have categorically stated that they aim at EMU participation as soon as possible and they pursued this objective by means of three stabilization/convergence programmes. The question which then arises is how hard did Greece try to be among the EMU Ins in 1999 or, in other words, why the did convergence programmes fail to secure an EMU place for Greece. This is an issue which has to be addressed in two levels: first, the economic background which accompanied the introduction of the convergence effort back in 1991; second, the nature of the policies followed in the 1990s. The above being as they may, the pressing question which is now faced by Greek policy makers is what economic measures should be taken so that Greece is admitted into the EMU in the foreseeable future. In other words, what economic strategy should Greece adopt in order to achieve EMU participation by 2002 ? Obviously, the answer is conditional upon an assessment of the reasons which prevented Greek entry in the EMU in 1999.

The present chapter is concerned with the above issues. Its remainder is organized as follows: Section 2.2 refers to macroeconomic performance and the main guidelines of Greek macroeconomic policy over the last twenty years. Special emphasis is placed on fiscal policy as monetary developments are examined in detail in chapters 3 and 4. Section 2.3 presents briefly the main arguments in favour and against EMU participation. Section 2.4 examines in some detail the convergence programmes which have been applied by the Greek governments in the 1990s. Finally, in section 2.5 we advance a number of proposals regarding the future strategy of Greek economic policy in relation to EMU participation.

Figure 2.1

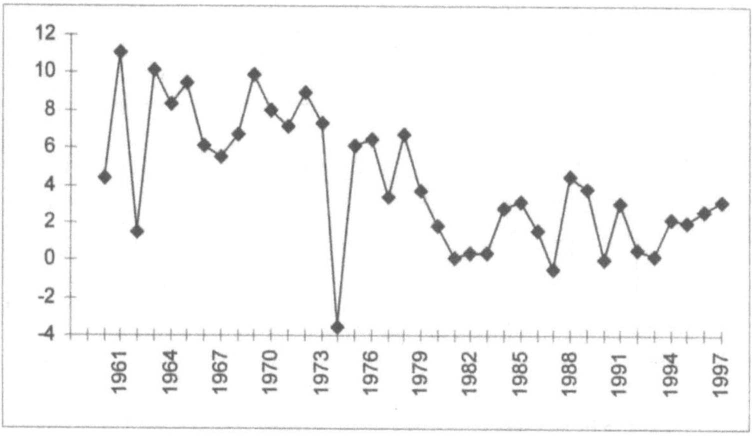

Real GDP - Annual growth rate

Data Source: European Economy No 64, Statistical Appendix.

2.2. The Greek economy: past performance and current position

2.2.1. 1980-94: the low growth period

Greece entered the second part of the 1970s with a particularly promising economic record established during the first post-war decades. However, things took an increasingly unpleasant turn thereafter. It is beyond our scope to provide a detailed assessment of the reasons behind the disappointing performance of the Greek economy in the last twenty years or so. Here we restrict ourselves in highlighting a number of important points. Above all, it is quite imperative to refer to the impressive antithesis which characterizes the growth performance of Greece during the period 1960-97 (see Figure 2.1 and Table 2.1). Between 1960 and 1980 Greece was the fastest growing economy in Europe and the second in the OECD area behind Japan. In contrast, during the 1980s the country dropped to the last place in both areas. Only recently, after 1990, Greek governments initiated a genuine effort to reverse the situation. However, considerable imbalances still remain.

The post-1975 deterioration of Greek macroeconomic performance coincides with developments in four important fields affecting the Greek economy. These are (a) the fundamental change in the international environment expressed by a world-wide

Table 2.1

Period	GDP growth	Inflation (CPI)	Unemploy-ment	Budget deficit	Public Debt	Current account
1961-73	7.5	3.5	4.6	N/A	17.7	-2.4
1974-80	4.7	14.9	2.1	2.3	21.2	-1.4
1981-90	1.6	18.3	6.4	10.4	53.1	-3.6
1991-97	1.9	11.8	8.5	10.2	106.5	-2.8

Main economic indicators in Greece
Data Source: European Economy No 64, Statistical Appendix.

slowdown; (b) a major turn in the field of Greek fiscal policy towards fiscal expansion, initiated in 1975 and strengthened in the 1980s; (c) changes in the field of Greek politics: since the fall of dictatorship in 1974 the Greek economy has been subject to the (previously non-existent) effect of political business cycles; (d) the accession of Greece to the EU.

As far as external influence is concerned, it is only fair to say that the international recession which followed the two oil shocks has, not surprisingly, contributed to the Greek growth slow-down. With regard to the impact of EU participation, some economists such as Giannitsis (1988, 1993) have argued that the accession of the Greece in the EU and the increased competition caused by the globalization of the international economy was a major shock for domestic producers because it reduced considerably effective protection against imports, thus leading to an increase in the volume of the latter. Consequently, the inadequately prepared industrial sector of the Greek economy did not manage to adapt to the new competitive conditions. As a result industrial production fell, de-industrialization occurred and the economy experienced a reduction in its growth rate.

Although the above arguments are clearly not irrelevant[1], they seem to be rather unconvincing in explaining completely the total collapse of the growth process which appeared in Greece after 1980. In fact, it would appear that the reasons

[1] For econometric evidence in support of the opinion that EU participation has had a statistically significant impact on the volume of Greek imports from EU countries (see Arghyrou 1999b).

behind the stagnation which hit Greece should also be sought within the country and not in exogenous factors only. There are a number of arguments which offer support to this view. First the recession of the Greek economy has lasted much more than the recession in Europe. Second, there are countries with economies similar to the Greek one, e.g. Ireland, Portugal and Spain, which achieved very satisfactory growth rates during the 1980s and the early 1990s (see Larre and Torres, 1991). Third, the accession of Greece in the EU did not eliminate completely state protection in favour of Greek firms, at least not before 1990 (see Arghyrou 1999b).

Therefore, it seems that Greek governments of the last twenty years have significantly contributed to the aggravation of the crisis caused by the international recession by making a number of serious policy errors. This opinion has been expressed by the world's leading economic organizations on many occasions[2] and a number of economists which have dealt with the subject (see, among others, Papademos 1990, Larre and Torres 1991, Tsoukalis 1993, Alogoskoufis 1995, Halikias 1993, 1996, Arghyrou 1999a and the references therein). The consensus is that since the mid-1970s, and in particular during the 1980s, Greece followed an economic policy mix which on the one hand created serious macroeconomic imbalances; and on the other aggravated existing and created new microeconomic distortions. In particular, there is wide agreement on the view that between the period 1975-90 Greece proceeded to a consumption-oriented fiscal expansion (see section 2.2.2 below) which was in contrast to the mainstream of economic developments in Western Europe. In order to finance this expansion Greek governments relied increasingly on internal and external public borrowing. The increasing EU transfers also contributed. However, despite higher public revenues, deficits and national debt continued to compound (see section 2.2.2 below). Government intervention in the markets of goods, labour and capital increased through the imposition of new controls and limitations as well as the donation of credit facilities and subsidies to firms whose competitiveness was declining. In the monetary field, opting for flexibility in the conduct of monetary policy, a crawling-peg exchange rate policy was introduced in order to maintain the competitiveness of Greek exports and cope with current account problems. The Bank of Greece (BoG) increased domestic credit to the public sector but credit-rationed the private one.

The consumption oriented fiscal expansion implemented after 1975 was justified on the grounds of two objectives. First, the achievement of a re-distribution of income in favour of the lower-income classes. Second, the achievement of a higher level of national income through a higher level of aggregate demand. With regard to the first objective, there is little doubt that prior to 1975 the Greek society was characterized by significant income inequalities, hence one might suggest that there was a moral case for undertaking an income re-distribution effort. However,

[2] See OECD Economic Surveys of Greece 1993, 1995, 1996, OECD Economic Outlook and European Economy, Annual Report for various years.

it is not quite clear that the fiscal policy followed after 1975 succeeded in reducing income inequalities[3]. Regarding the second objective, it is widely acknowledged that the policy-mix implemented by Greek authorities failed to meet the objectives set by the authorities.

As mentioned above, the fiscal expansion undertaken by Greece during the period of 1975-90 was largely financed by monetary accommodation (mainly in the form of increased credit to the public sector) as well as increased public borrowing. Under the assumption of an upwards sloping aggregate supply curve, the output implications of a money-financed fiscal expansion would have be studied within a Barro-Gordon (1983) set-up. Money-financed deficits would have positive output implications provided that they remain unanticipated by the private sector. Under rational expectations, anticipated monetary accommodation of expansions would give rise to higher inflation expectations and, ultimately, higher actual inflation, without any long-run output gain. In fact, by leading to higher inflation, money-financed budget deficits may be harmful to long-run growth due to the well-documented costs of higher inflation in which they result[4]. On the other hand, bond-financed expenditure may involve expansionary effects of a more lasting nature provided that the anticipation of future interest payments to bond holders causes positive wealth effects on private consumption (see Blinder and Solow, 1973). However, such effects may well be offset by crowing-out effects[5] and the real costs implied by higher future

---

[3] Sarris and Zografakis (1995) argue that income inequality declined during the period 1974-81 but did not decline during the 1980s.

[4] Economists like Okun (1975), Carlton (1982), Feldstein (1983) and Romer (1996) have suggested numerous channels through which inflation can affect long-run growth in a negative way. In addition to its standard "shoe-leather" and "menu/indexation" costs, inflation distorts the tax system and results in sub-optimal investment and savings' decisions. Furthermore, since individual prices are not adjusted on a continuous basis, even anticipated (steady) inflation can change relative prices and disrupt the operation of the price mechanism as an efficient guide to the allocation of resources. These costs are even higher under conditions of unanticipated (unsteady) inflation: increased uncertainty may affect the rate of growth of the economy in a negative way by means of reducing long-term investment spending. Empirical findings provided by economists like Fisher (1991, 1993) and Barro (1995) are consistent with the views presented above. All in all, as the Bank of England (1996, p.1) has put it, "inflation generates uncertainty as to how far it will go, how long it will last and what actions will ultimately be needed to bring it under control. That uncertainty distorts savings and investment decisions, which tend to place excessive weight on the short-term; and it obscures the relative prices signals that are necessary to efficient resource allocation. So, it damages long-run economic performance".

[5] There are two channels through which bond-financed deficits can cause crowding out effects. The first is related to portfolio adjustments. An increase in the stock of bonds may necessitate a similar increase in interest rates to maintain equilibrium in the bond market. The second is related to money market adjustments. Given a certain level of nominal money, increasing prices caused by higher public expenditure would lead to a reduction in real money stock and an increase in interest rates which would crowd-out private consumption and investment

inflation rates resulting from bond-financed public expenditure expansions[6]. The above arguments seem to be quite relevant in providing insights behind the reduction in the rate of growth of the Greek during the period of 1975-90, a period charachterized by mounting fiscal imbalances which contributed to high inflation rates and the crowding-out effects implied by the reduction in private investment spending (see Figure 2.2).

A second channel through which harmful, largely unanticipated inflation appeared in Greece after 1975 is related to the elements of surprise behaviour on the part of the Greek governments in the external sector of the economy. More specifically, in an effort to push exports and recover the declining competitiveness the Greek economy, on two occasions in the 1980s (January 1983 and January 1985) Greek governments proceeded to two substantial devaluations of the drachma against the US dollar. However, in the absence of other measures aiming to stabilize the expectations of the private sector, the traditional Keynesian demand-management policies implemented by the Greek authorities both in the internal and the external sector of the economy, together with the escalator clauses embedded in the wage-indexation ATA scheme passed by the parliament in 1982[7], resulted in mounting external imbalances (see Figure 2.3), higher equilibrium inflation rates and higher unemployment (see Figure 2.4) and, ultimately, lower growth rates : Recent empirical evidence emerging from the application of various time-series methodologies (see Arghyrou 1998, 1999a) suggests that in the Greek case, there is no statistically significant causation pattern running from public expenditure (and public consumption in particular) to national income. In contrast, as Halikias (1993, 1996) argues, the expansionary policy followed after 1975 increased inefficiency in production and public administration, reinforced market rigidities and distortions and eliminated the dynamism of the Greek economy by weakening the forces of competition. The accommodating monetary policy of the BoG, together with the increasing EU

[6] Sargent and Wallace (1981) have argued that if the increase in interest rates resulting from a lax fiscal policy is enough to lead to a real interest rate higher than the rate of growth of the economy, expectations will be created that the government's solvency condition will be violated in the future as the central bank will be obliged to resort to higher future seignorage than what would otherwise have been the case. Higher inflation expectations would then lead to higher actual inflation and higher inflation costs similar to those earlier mentioned. Finally, a bond-financed budget deficit would have no expansionary effects at all (not even in the short-run) if the Ricardian Equivalence Hypothesis were valid. The latter, adopted by a number of neoclassical economists (see e.g. Barro 1974), suggests that the aggregate private sector does not consider public bonds as part of its wealth because it realises that increased public borrowing will ultimately result in increased taxation. In anticipation of this event, agents increase their savings, something which offsets the expansionary impact of higher public spending.

[7] The wage-indexation ATA scheme stayed in place for 10 years before being abolished in 1991.

Figure 2.2

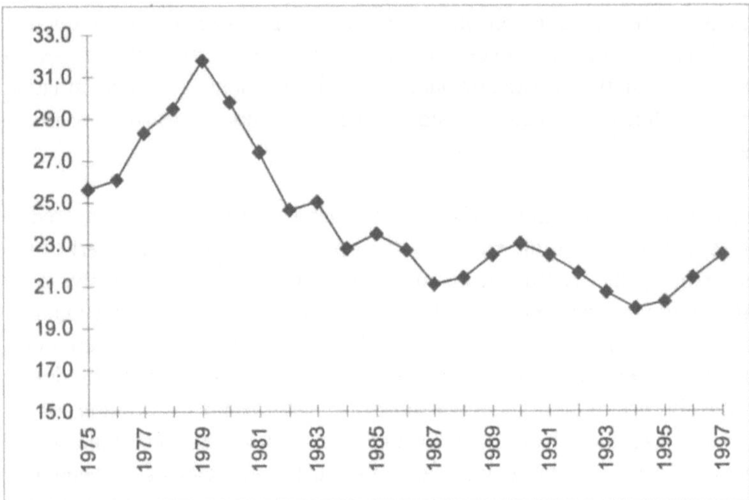

Gross fixed capital formation (% of GDP)

Data Source: European Economy No 64, Statistical Appendix.

Figure 2.3

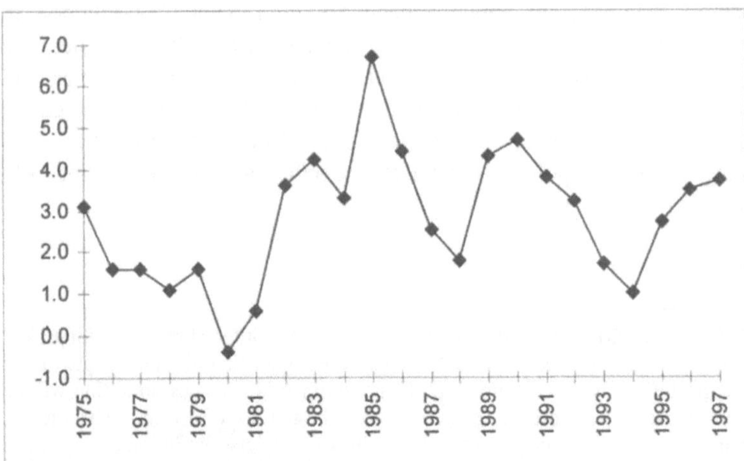

Current Account deficit (% of GDP)

Data Source: European Economy No 64, Statistical Appendix.

Figure 2.4

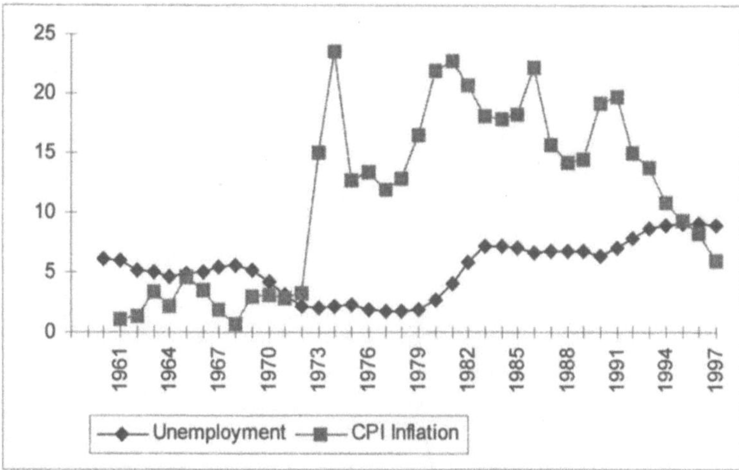

CPI inflation and unemployment Rate
Data Source: European Economy No 64, Statistical Appendix.

transfers allowed the government to maintain for a whole decade increasing budget deficits which led to a rising and finally explosive public debt (see Alogoskoufis, 1995). It seems therefore that the crawling peg exchange rate policy did not help the Greek economy. In the 1980s, despite falling oil prices, a number of trade indeces suggest that the competitiveness of the Greek producers in many sectors declined (see Arghyrou 1999b). The private sector and foreign investors did not fail to notice the worsening of the macroeconomic perspectives of the country and responded by reducing investment spending. All in all, the end result was a prolonged stagflation.

The above developments were clearly reinforced by the political developments which followed 1975. The influence of politics over the economy is not a phenomenon observed in Greece only. In fact, it is a common characteristic of Western democracies and it has been extensively debated in economic literature. After 1975, the year that democracy was restored in Greece, one notices that during election years, or/and one year before, the budget deficit deteriorates (see Figure 2.5) as a result of shortfalls of public revenue and overruns of public expenditure (see Christodoulakis, 1994). Typically, the fiscal overshooting is accompanied by even looser monetary policies (see Figure 2.6). The role of trade unions in this process has also to be emphasized. Taking advantage of their power, unions in Greece have exhibited a behaviour of rather high demands. This "unions militancy" gave rise to unjustified wage demands, disruptive strikes and social security protection that led in turn to wage inflation and the failure of the economy to move to structural

Figure 2.5

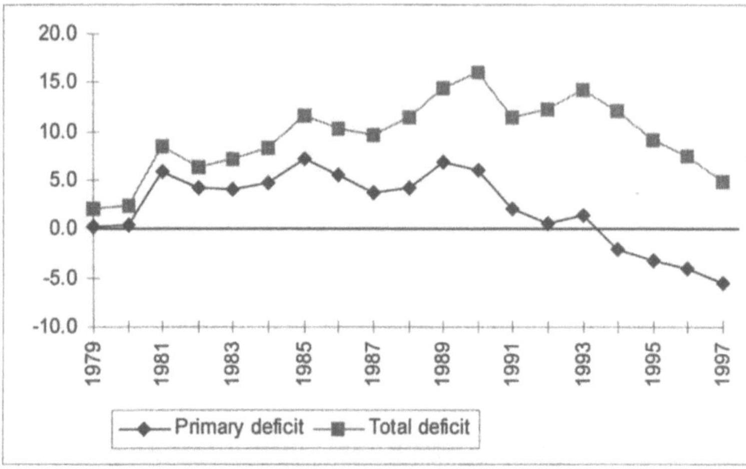

Primary and total budget deficit (% of GDP)
Data Source: European Economy No 64, Statistical Appendix

Note: Years of general elections: 1977, 1981, 1985, 1989, 90, 93

Figure 2.6

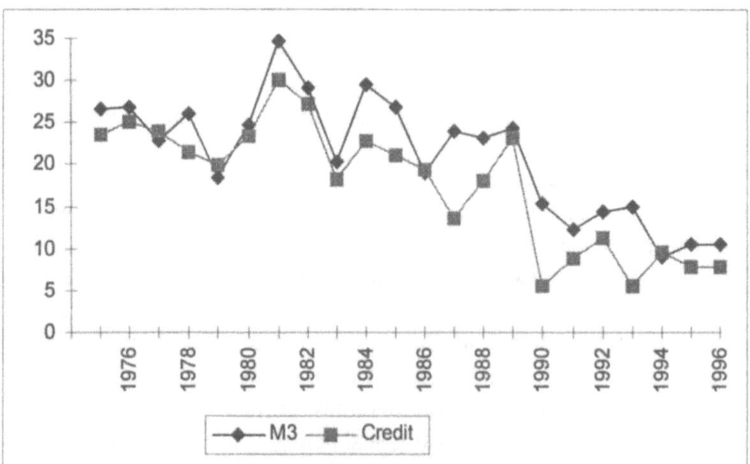

Money supply (M3) and credit growth (annual % change)
Data Source: Bank of Greece, Monthly Statistical Bulletin (various editions)

Note: Years of general elections: 1977, 1981, 1985, 1989, 90, 93

adjustments[8]. It has also been a decisive factor for the unwillingness of domestic and foreign investors to invest in the country.

2.2.2. Fiscal developments

One of the main characteristics of Greek economic policy prior to 1973 was the strictly observed fiscal discipline. Governments endeavored to follow sound public finance policies. Public revenues were always higher than public consumption and any (small) budget deficit was the result of public investment expenditure. As a result of this prudent fiscal stance, gross public debt in 1973 was equal to 16.1% of GDP, significantly lower than the European average (35.7%). The first signs of a change in the field of fiscal policy appeared just after the restoration of democracy in 1974. The change of political regime was accompanied by an increase in state intervention in the Greek economy. The period 1974-80 saw the first major nationalizations, including those of Olympic Airways and the Commercial Bank of Greece (the second largest bank of the country). Furthermore, the first generous increases in nominal and real wages took place. As a result of the increase in public revenue, public finance remained in control but the budget deficit increased slightly reaching the level of 2.4% of GDP in 1980. Public debt started rising and by 1980 it had reached the level of 28.8% of GDP.

However, the turning point for fiscal affairs in Greece was 1981. In view of the general elections of that year the conservative government initiated a fiscal and monetary expansion aiming to remain in office. Greece experienced a significant increase in public expenditure, mainly caused by an increase in employment in the public sector and an increase in pensions and salaries as well as a stagnation of public revenues caused by the official reduction in tax rates and the unofficial overlooking in collecting taxes (see Christodoulakis, 1994). Nevertheless, this expansion did not save the conservatives from an electoral defeat and the socialists succeeded them in power. But in spite of accusing their predecessors for having left behind them what they called "scorched earth", due to ideological positions and pre-electoral commitments the new government continued and intensified the public expansion by hiring new personnel for public administration and state-owned firms as well as increasing the level of minimum wages and pensions by 40%. In addition, the system of automatic indexation of wages and pensions (ATA) to the price level was introduced which resulted in high and permanent inflation rates throughout the 1980s[9]. In November 1983, after the abandonment of the short-lived Arsenis

---

[8] According to data from the International Bureau of Employment, between 1983 and 1993 Greece was the second country among the EU members as regards the number of strikes. The average number of strikers per 1000 workers was 195.2 second only to Spain (204.1). The relevant figure for Germany was 7.6.

[9] Mourmouras (1997a) develops a theoretical model that predicts the inflationary effects of widespread escalator clauses, even in the absence of shocks.

Stabilization Programme[10], the government adopted a new five-year Economic and Social Development Plan (1983-87). This aimed to resume the economic development of the Greek economy by means of supply side policies where the state would play the major role. Within that context the government created the Organization for Enterprises Restructuring (OAE). The new organization proceeded to the nationalization of a large number of private firms which, due to a number of reasons related to increasing labour cost, adverse economic developments, bad management strategies and the accession of Greece to the EU, had lost their competitiveness and were at the brink of bankruptcy. In addition, the authorities proceeded to the nationalization of some firms which did not present financial difficulties as well as to the foundation of many new public enterprises and institutions which were also financed by the public budget.

Having under its control such a vast number of enterprises and in the light of the forthcoming European Parliament elections of 1984 as well as the general elections of 1985, the government continued its policy of hiring new personnel *en mass.*

Figure 2.7

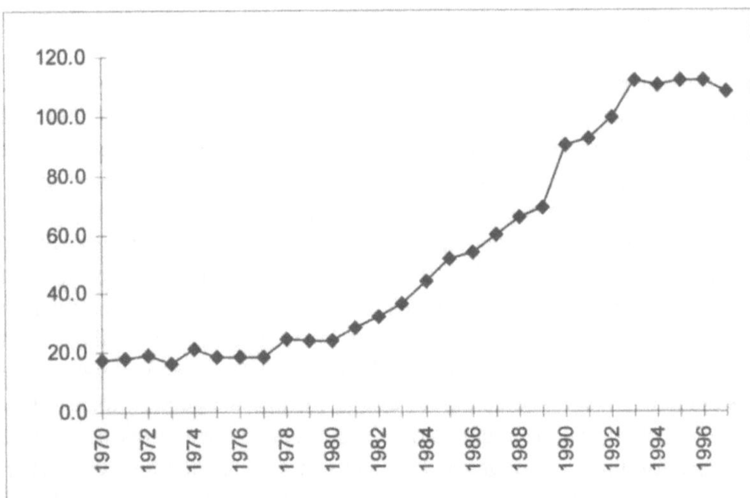

Public debt (% of GDP)

Data Source: European Economy No 64, Statistical Appendix.

[10] The Arsenis Stabilization Programme (named after the then Minister of National Economy Mr. G. Arsenis) was introduced in January 1983 after a current account crisis in 1982. Its main provisions lie in the field of monetary policy (see chapter 3). With regard to fiscal policy, it involved a set of measures aiming at a reduction in public spending and an increase in public receipts. In reality however, very few of the planned measures were actually taken as the programme lasted only for eleven months (January-November 1983).

Furthermore, in 1983 authorities proceeded to a reform of the national pension system which increased dramatically the number of persons entitled to pension rights and lowered the retirement limit to 23 full working years for men and 17 years for women. In order to finance the above described expansion, Greek governments proceeded to a significant increase in public borrowing and (to a lesser extent), intaxation. As a result, deficits and national debt continued to compound (see Figures 2.5 and 2.7).

By 1985 the Greek economy was facing a new current account crisis. After the elections of 1985 the government, under the leadership of a new minister of National Economy Mr. K. Simitis, was obliged to introduce a stabilization programme initially planned to cover the period 1986-87. With regard to fiscal and incomes policy, the programme involved the total freezing of nominal wages above a certain level in both the private and the public sector and the adjustment of the remaining wages according to the projected, rather than observed, rate of inflation (excluding the impact of import prices). It also included a set of measures aiming to cut public expenditure (through the reduction in public employees, the closure of some loss-making public firms, the abolishment of some tax allowances etc.) as well as an increase in public revenues mainly through the reduction in tax-evasion and the imposition of an once-for-all tax on company profits and self-employment incomes and rents. The stabilization effort produced some positive results and in 1987 the primary deficit of the government budget fell to 3.7% of GDP in comparison to 7.2% in 1985. However, in spite of the tougher fiscal stance the overall budget deficit deteriorated further. That was mainly the result of increasing interest payments, which had already acquired a self-propagating mechanism, and expenditure overruns by public corporations. As a result, public debt continued to increase. Furthermore, much of the improvement in the field of primary deficit was due to a reduction in public investment spending (see Figure 2.8), a fact which reduced even further the percentage of the latter in total public outlays and represented a further blow to the already outdated public infrastructure of the country. These facts obliged Mr. Simitis to propose the continuation of the stabilization programme. However, in view of the general elections of 1989 his proposal was dismissed and he resigned. A new, unprecedented fiscal and monetary expansion followed. In view of the unwillingness of the authorities to raise taxes during an election year, the government resorted once again to borrowing. As a result, in 1989 the primary and overall deficit of public budget reached record levels and it would not be an exaggeration to say that as a result of the fiscal policy of 1988-89 and the political instability which prevailed in 1989-90, Greece faced the danger of national bankruptcy in 1990-91 as suggested by Alogoskoufis and Christodoulakis (1991). This fact obliged Greek policy makers to realize how important is to correct fiscal imbalances in order to create healthy economic conditions. Since 1990 both parties which have ruled the country have followed a more restraint policy in the fiscal front. This effort has produced some positive results and with the exception of 1993 the primary deficit has been

Figure 2.8

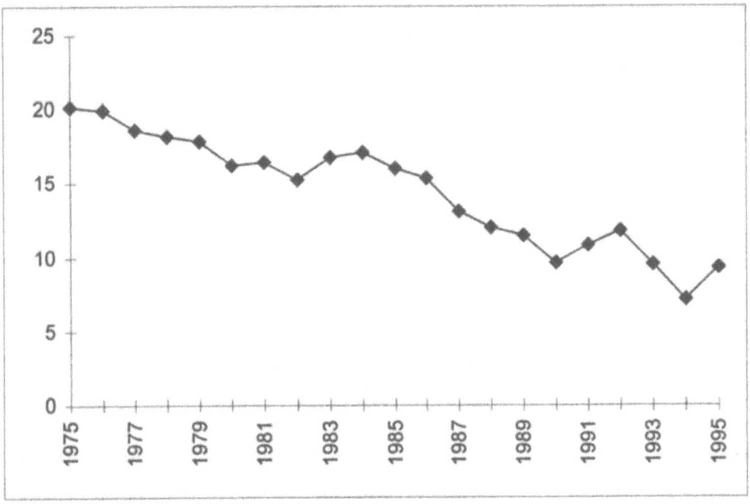

Public investment as % of total public outlays
Source: International Financial Statistics, CD 09-97

declining (see section 2.4 below). In fact, since 1994 increasing primary surpluses have been recorded. However, neither the PSBR which includes interest payments nor the public debt have declined impressively. Over the last three years the latter has taken values well above the threshold of 100% of GDP. This shows that despite the increasingly restrictive fiscal policy which has been followed during the 1990s the imbalances created during the 1980s are very deep and the creation of healthy fiscal conditions will be a long and hard process.

2.3. Costs and benefits from EMU membership

The obvious disadvantage of participating in a Monetary Union is the abolition of national monetary discretion. That was indeed one of the points emphasized by the Theory of Optimum Currency Areas (TOCA) which was pioneered by the paper of Mundell in 1961. The loss of monetary independence implies the abandonment of certain options to cope with unexpected adverse economic events. For instance, in the event of a demand shock or a current account crisis, a devaluation of the national currency can no longer be employed. A second argument against EMU membership is the loss of seignorage as a means of financing public deficits and servicing public debt (see Giavazzi, 1989). Countries which use seignorage as a means of financing public deficits will have to resort to higher taxation or a reduction in government expenditure which might reduce welfare in the country. Finally, under no circumstances one should ignore the political cost accompanying the EMU. For citizens of countries with a long national history as well as economic and political tradition, the loss of monetary independence may be considered as a blow to the national sovereignty of the countries involved. Without any doubt, governments which will ignore such feelings and go ahead with EMU plans unavoidably undertake a significant political cost[11].

As far as the main arguments in favour of the EMU are concerned, the first to be mentioned is the elimination of all transaction costs involved in converting one national currency into another. At the macroeconomic level these costs are rather small[12]. At the microeconomic level, however, they might represent a non-negligible amount for economic agents who enter transactions involving currency conversions. Another argument in favour of the EMU refers to the gains which are expected to follow the elimination of exchange rate risk. The reduction in uncertainty accompanying the adoption of a single currency will lower the real interest rate in the economy because agents will discount future cash flows using a lower rate. The reduction in the real interest rate could also exercise a positive impact on the rate of growth of the economies of the participating countries. Finally, another argument in favour of monetary integration is associated with the credibility gains for governments prone to inflationary polices. The argument here is that within the context of a monetary union, a country with a high inflation culture like Greece may borrow credibility from the central bank of a partner (or the Union's central bank) enjoying an anti-inflationary reputation.

2.4. The Greek Convergence Programmes: a deficit of credibility

Since 1991, the year that the Maastricht Treaty was signed, most of the Greek political parties have declared categorically that they support the participation of the country in the third stage of the EMU. This position is also shared by the overwhelming majority of Greek people. Recent public opinion surveys conducted by Eurostat have shown that among the countries of the EU, Greek citizens are the warmest supporters of the EMU project. This euro-enthusiasm is motivated by politics rather than economics. In Greece it is widely believed that apart from the possible economic benefits, EMU participation will operate as an extra guarantee for

---

[11] The EMU might involve other categories of economic cost which are less highlighted in the literature. These refer to the short-run inflation-unemployment trade-off and the worsening of economic conditions if participating countries present differences in labour market flexibility or different growth rates.

[12] In the case of the EMU Gross and Thygesen (1990) argue that these gains will be between 0.25 and 0.50% of the EMU's GDP. The corresponding figure suggested by the European Commission (1990) is 0.3-0.4%.

the security of the country's eastern boarders. In brief the prospect of EMU participation is widely regarded as unique opportunity to apply policies which could allow the Greek economy to catch-up with the rest of Europe. Furthermore, the broad support of this cause creates conditions for the implementation of these policies with the minimum possible social reaction.

As argued in the previous sections, at the dawn of the 1990s the Greek economy found itself in an extremely dangerous position. Since then, in the light of the Maastricht criteria and under pressure from the rest of the EU countries, Greek governments undertook an effort to achieve EMU participation. This has taken the form of three convergence/stabilization programmes: The three-year Medium Term Adjustment Programme (MTAP) 1991-93, the Convergence Programme (CP) 1993-98 and the Revised Convergence Programme (RCP) 1994-99. It is important to say that in view of the fact that these programmes aimed at EMU participation by 1999, they were designed by the Greek economic authorities with an aim to be approved by the European Commission. The latter gave its consent in all three cases and monitored its implementation.

The MTAP 1991-93 passed by the then newly-elected conservative government in 1990 included measures such as an increase in taxation, a cut in public expenditure, a reduction in recruitment in the public sector, an increase in the VAT rates, the abolition of the ATA system and a number of pension rights, an increase in the prices of public utilities, and the announcement of a privatization programme. It was also accompanied by new legislation which aimed at increasing labour market flexibility and reforming the problematic pension system of the country. Finally, in the field of monetary policy, it involved the intensification of the process of financial liberalization which had been introduced in 1987 and the continuation of the strong drachma which had been introduced in 1988. The targets set by the programme were rather optimistic and their fulfillment presupposed a radical tightening of fiscal and monetary policies as well as a fast implementation of structural reforms and in particular privatizations. However, in spite of the fact that the situation stopped deteriorating in many fields, there is little doubt that the implementation of the programme was not as drastic as the emergency of the situation required and the improvement was not the one expected. There are a number of reasons explaining this less-than-expected progress. The main ones were a shortfall in public revenue during 1991-92, largely attributed to a deeper than expected recession, the fall of tourist revenue, the persisting tax-evasion, the weaknesses of the tax-collection services and the failure to reduce employment in the wider public sector. Furthermore, the privatization programme was not taking place at the speed which was expected and the process of deregulation in the goods and labour markets was not as quick as envisaged. Of course, it is true that the MTAP coincided with the Gulf war and the war in ex-Yugoslavia which had a negative impact on the Greek economy. However, the government of New Democracy has been criticized by many economists home and abroad for its attempt to compromise economic and political aims, for reneging on their pre-electoral commitments and for its failure to promote as actively as they should the strict corrective measures they had promised to implement[13].

In view of the rather slow progress described above, a new minister of National Economy, Mr. Manos, was appointed in 1992. He discontinued the MTAP and launched a new stabilization effort, the CP 1993-98, whose aim was to lead Greece to meeting of the Maastricht criteria by 1999. This was to be achieved through the reinforcement of the structural and institutional reforms and a more active pursuit of macroeconomic adjustment. More specifically, the programme involved a cutting of public consumption and an increase in public investment, the speeding of privatization, a reform of the tax system to curb tax-evasion, new cuts of pension rights and an increase in social security contributions. In the monetary field, the plan involved the continuation of the policy of strong drachma, the future participation of the Greek national currency in the ERM, the abolition of the remaining obstacles in the field of capital movements, the discontinuation of monetary accommodation of public expenditure and the granting of a higher degree of independence to the BoG. These measures, combined with a high increase in indirect taxes on petrol and other goods of low income elasticity in August 1992 as well as some further interest rate capitalization, achieved some positive results. Nevertheless, in 1993 the main economic indicators did not improve according to the convergence plan (see Table 2.2). To begin with, in spite of the fact that credit to the private sector was tight, money supply (i.e. M3) grew at a rate above 15% compared with the target band of 9% to 12%. However, the major set-back was the overshooting of the fiscal targets which was mainly due to a large shortfall in budget revenues and to a small overrun in expenditure. As a result, like the MTAP, the CP 1993-98 proved short-lived and was consequently revised.

The reasons for the failure of the MTAP and the CP are rather common. Above all, it would appear that there was no organized plan to promote the promised reforms and, more importantly, there was not enough political will to implement them in the face of a strong social reaction[14] against the stabilization policy, particularly from the highly politicized labour unions of the public sector[15]. Of course, it is only fair to say that Mr. Manos in 1993 and his predecessors in 1990-92 were unlucky in the sense that their stabilization efforts coincided with the EMS crisis of 1992-93 which brought a turmoil in the financial markets and contributed to a

[13] For a collection of papers referring to this subject see Kollintzas and Bitros (1992).

[14] According to data from the International Bureau of Employment, in 1993 the number of strikers reached 1.5 million workers which cost 20 million lost working hours. That has definitely contributed to the contraction of GDP by 0.5% which took place that year.

[15] See Mourmouras and Su (1995a) for a theoretical model that predicts the effects of polarization (in terms of restricting policy reforms) upon the success of public debt stabilization programmes.

Table 2.2

	Planned	Outcome
Annual growth rates		
GDP real prices	2.0	0.2
Unemployment	9.8	8.6
Private consumption deflator	12.6	13.8
Compensation per employee	10.5	8.1
Per cent of GDP		
Current account balance	-2.1	-1.7
General government		
Net borrowing	8.6	14.2
Primary surplus	5.1	1.4
Debt	107.5	111.8

The year 1993 performance of the Convergence Programme 1993-98
Source for planned values: OECD Economic Survey of Greece, 1992-93, p. 49
Source for outcomes: European Economy No 64, Statistical Appendix.

strong recession in Europe. Also, both programmes faced exogenous political constraints in the form of intragovernmental disagreements related to foreign and economic policy which finally led to the resignation of the conservative government and to the general elections of 1993. However, these facts alone cannot stand as convincing explanations for the rather over-cautious attitude displayed in advancing the promised reforms and especially the planned privatizations.

The socialist government which emerged from the 1993 elections, largely thanks to an anti-austerity, anti-privatization pre-electoral campaign, decided to continue, after all, the nominal convergence effort initiated by the conservatives and was committed to EMU participation in 1999. However, as the fiscal performance of 1993 had invalidated the CP 1993-98, the new government prepared the RCP 1994-99 whose target was explicitly defined to be the fulfillment of the Maastricht criteria by 1999 and the reconstruction of the Greek economy. The RCP was divided in two sup-periods (1994-96 and 1997-99) and its three main targets were set to be fiscal consolidation, lower inflation and the improvement of the supply side of the economy through the realization of new public and private investment. During the first sub-period (1994-96) the RCP placed emphasis on fiscal consolidation, lowering inflation and accelerating public investment, largely to be financed from funds provided by the Delors Package II. In the second sub-period (1997-99) it was expected that the beneficial impact of the improvement realized in the first sub-period would set in motion private investment. As a result, although fiscal and monetary policy would remain restrictive, higher GDP growth rates would be achieved. Fiscal consolidation was expected to be achieved, once again, through an increase in public revenues and a reduction in public expenditure. The former involved an increase in the revenues from direct and indirect taxes. These were planned to take place through the widening of the tax-base, i.e. taxation of incomes which were not subject to taxation in the past, an increase in corporate tax rates, a reinforced attempt to curb tax evasion, the abolition of a substantial number of tax exemptions, the privatization of some state-owned enterprises and the introduction of shares of some state monopolies into the Greek and foreign stock exchanges. Public expenditure was planned to be declining by 0.5 % annually until 1999 through the granting of only modest nominal wage increases to public sector employees, the limitation of hiring new personnel, the privatization of state-owned firms and the reduction in spending in all levels of public administration through a reorganization of their administration. In the monetary field, the RCP involved the continuation of the strong drachma policy and the accession of the drachma to the ERM of the EMS in the middle of 1996. It also involved modest increases for the growth of nominal money supply and domestic credit.

During the period of its implementation (i.e. 1994-1997), the RCP achieved some undeniable stabilization progress which has been recognized by all international economic organizations. During the last four years the growth rate of the economy recorded modest but accelerating increases, mainly due to the recovery in public and private investment; inflation declined substantially and by the end of 1997 it had reached its lowest level over the last twenty years (6% as opposed to a 20% inflation rate in 1990); unemployment has stopped increasing and has stabilized at the level of 10% of the labour force; and Greece has achieved a certain degree of nominal (inflation and interest rate) convergence with the rest of the EU (see Table 2.3). However, in contrast to what was supported in 1994 when the RCP was passed, Greece did not manage to achieve EMU participation in 1999 as it did not meet any of the Maastricht criteria by the end of 1997. The main area where things did not go according to plan was inflation where, despite the substantial reduction in the rate of growth of prices, there has been a significant overshooting of the targets set by the RCP. There has also been a less pronounced but still important overshooting in the field of the general government public deficit, mainly caused by the failure of the government to deliver the planned reduction in public consumption (see Table 2.3). Other areas where important deviations between the

Table 2.3

	1994	1995	1996	1997	1998	1999
GDP growth at constant prices	1.1	1.2	1.7	2.6	3.0	3.5
Outcome	**2.2**	**2.0**	**2.6**	**3.1**	**3.4**	
Private consumption growth	1.2	1.3	1.7	1.7	1.8	2.0
Outcome	**1.5**	**1.6**	**2.2**	**2.1**	**1.8**	
Public consumption growth	0.0	-0.5	-0.5	-0.5	-0.5	-0.5
Outcome[2]	**3.5**	**1.5**	**1.4**	**0.6**	**-0.6**	
Private investment growth	2.5	0.9	3.5	6.8	8.4	10.1
Outcome[2]	**0.6**	**5.3**	**11.0**	**9.4**	**n.a.**	
Public investment growth	6.0	8.0	9.5	11.0	12.0	14.0
Outcome[2]	**0.2**	**7.4**	**14.9**	**18.0**	**n.a.**	
GDP deflator	10.7	8.0	6.3	4.0	3.6	3.3
Outcome	**10.1**	**9.3**	**8.9**	**6.7**	**5.5**	
Private consumption deflator	10.8	7.9	6.1	3.9	3.5	3.3
Outcome	**10.8**	**9.3**	**8.3**	**6.0**	**4.8**	
Real disposal private income	2.9	-1.1	-1.2	-0.7	1.4	2.5
Outcome[3]	**1.2**	**2.9**	**3.1**	**3.2**	**0.9**	
Real unit labor cost	0.5	-0.5	-0.5	-0.7	-0.8	-0.9
Outcome	**1.6**	**1.8**	**1.1**	**0.6**	**-2.2**	
Change in the parity of drachma against the ECU	7.5	3.0	1.0	0.0	0.0	0.0
Outcome[4]	**7.2**	**4.0**	**0.5**	**0.0**		
Long-term interest rate	19.5	15.6	11.0	8.5	7.6	7.2
Outcome	**19.0**	**17.3**	**14.0**	**9.3**	**8.5**	

The Revised Convergence Programme of Greece, 1994-99 [1]

Table 2.3 (continued)

	1994	1995	1996	1997	1998	1999
GDP deflator in EU	3.0	2.9	2.7	2.6	2.6	2.6
Outcome	**2.6**	**2.9**	**2.6**	**1.9**	**1.8**	
GDP growth in EU	1.2	2.0	3.0	3.4	3.6	3.6
Outcome	**2.9**	**2.4**	**1.6**	**2.4**	**1.7**	
Long term interest rate of EU member states	6.9	6.8	6.7	6.4	6.4	6.4
Outcome	**8.2**	**8.6**	**7.3**	**6.5**	**4.9**	
Borrowing requirements of general government (% of GDP)[6]	0.7	2.9	4.3	5.1	5.4	6.1
Outcome	**2.1**	**3.2**	**4.1**	**5.6**	**6.7**	
Interest payments on public debt (% of GDP)	13.9	13.6	11.9	9.3	7.8	7.0
Outcome	**14.2**	**12.4**	**11.5**	**10.5**	**9.2**	
General government debt (% of GDP)	112.1	115.2	115.3	113.4	109.3	103.4
Outcome	**110.4**	**111.8**	**111.8**	**109.5**	**108.7**	
Current account balance (% of GDP)	-2.9	-2.5	-2.2	-2.0	-1.8	-1.8
Outcome	**-1.0**	**-2.7**	**-3.5**	**-3.7**	**-2.4**	
Unemployment (% of labor force)	10.1	10.4	10.2	9.7	8.9	7.9
Outcome	**8.9**	**9.1**	**9.0**	**8.9**	**9.4**	

The Revised Convergence Programme of Greece, 1994-99 [1]

Table 2.3 (continued)

	1994	1995	1996	1997	1998	1999
Private sector's average propensity to save (% of disposal income)	22.1	20.2	17.9	15.9	15.6	16.0
Outcome ***(private gross saving, % of GDP at market prices)***	**28.6**	**25.1**	**25.0**	**23.3**	**19.8**	

The Revised Convergence Programme of Greece, 1994-99[1]

[1] *Source:* " The Greek Economic Convergence Program", Bank of Greece, Economic Bulletin, November 1994. *Source for outcomes:* European Economy No 64, Statistical Appendix. Outcomes referring to 1998 represent provisional estimates.
[2] *Source:* Bank of Greece, Economic Bulletin No 9 (March 1997).
[3] Percentage change of real compensation per employee, total economy (CPI deflator).
[4] The Revised Convergence programme planned the accession of the Drachma to the ERM in 1996. This target was not met.
[5]*Source:* International Financial Statistics, Yearbook 1997
[6] Excluding interest payments, excluding revenue from privatization.

targets set by the RCP and the actual values taken by the variables include the current account deficit (whose widening size had assumed worrying dimensions); and increases in nominal and real wages and labour costs.

As Greece failed to be included in the first wave of EMU participants, the authorities announced that they will now pursue EMU participation by 2001. As a first step to that end, Greece joined the ERM in March 1998. This move aimed at sending a strong signal to international financial markets that the country remains fully committed to the nominal convergence effort[16]. However, ERM participation

[16] There is little doubt that this is true. However, there might have been a second motive for the accession of Greece to the ERM, namely that after the more or less forced character of the recent devaluation, the Greek government had to come up with something convincing in order to save face after the devaluation of the drachma. The point is that over the last four years, and especially over the four months which preceded the devaluation, all government officials, including the Prime-Minister, had been stating categorically that the drachma will not be devalued. ERM participation, presented to the Greek public as a step forward for the

came at a cost paid in two forms: First, the accession to the system was accompanied by a 14% devaluation of the drachma vis-à-vis the ECU. Second, Greece had to discontinue the RCP and prepare a new programme, the fourth one in the 1990s, the Updated Revised Convergence Programme (URCP) 1998-2001, aiming at even lower rates of inflation, lower budget deficit and the promotion of the long-overdue structural adjustments promised (but never delivered) by the previous three convergence programmes.

All in all, it would appear that despite the progress achieved, the RCP 1994-99, like the MTAP and the CP 1993-98, fell short of its expectations and did not meet its main target, i.e. the accession of Greece to the EMU in 1999. The reasons behind this failure are not too different from those which led to the invalidation of the previous two programmes. Perhaps more importantly, at a time of increasing urgency regarding the promotion of structural adjustments, the Greek authorities, once again, opted for an over-gradual approach. In few words, the convergence programmes implemented by Greece in the 1990s pursued macroeconomic stabilization mainly based on two pillars whose potential was limited. The first, aiming to lower inflation, was the strong drachma policy. The second, aiming at lower budget deficits, was a fiscal policy placing emphasis on increasing public revenue. With regards to the former, the merits and weaknesses of the strong drachma policy are thoroughly discussed in chapter 4, therefore the discussion will not be repeated here. As far as the latter is concerned, as it will be argued in section 2.5.3 below, although one cannot help but agreeing to the abolition of tax exemptions which are not justified neither from the economic nor from the social point of view, and the fight against tax-evasion, it is not clear at all that fiscal consolidation is pursued in a correct way. Above all, it should be kept in mind that with or without the EMU, Greece is in need of structural reforms on the supply side of its economy and these reforms cannot be achieved just by raising taxes or resorting to "creative accounting" and other "window-dressing tricks" aiming to achieve a short-run reduction in fiscal imbalances and inflation and EMU participation by 2002. The conclusion is that unless the authorities change their strategy and decide to exhibit the necessary political will to achieve the modernization of the public sector, we are very much afraid that the stabilization effort of Greece will continue to be characterized by a lack of credibility and will not guarantee that the Greek economy will be well-prepared to prosper within the highly competitive and policy-restrictive EMU environment.

---

accession of Greece to the EMU, was the only way to reduce the political cost of devaluation. We return to this point in chapter 4 when we discuss the position of Greece in the ERM-II.

2.5. What strategy for Greece ?

2.5.1. Greece at the crossroads

Since Greece has been excluded from the first wave of EMU participants, the best thing the country can now do is to prepare herself for participation at a later stage. Without any doubt, such a preparation is not going to be without difficulties and painful measures as all income groups will be called to contribute to the costs of the adjustment programme. Preparation for full participation in the EMU certainly implies tough policies for the country. To go one step further, even at the early years of a participation, policies taken by the ECB may be considered unpopular by the Greek public, and this last point is something that Greek politicians have failed, so far, to address adequately. However, at the core of the argument for Greece is an assessment of the economic risks of participation and of the political costs of standing alone. The latter are far greater from any short-term economic costs if one considers the fact that Greece is a small country that needs friends as she was never fortunate enough in having the best of neighbours. The danger for the country is obvious. If Greece were to be excluded for a long time from EMU, this might imply that Greece would stand aside from the subsequent economic and political evolution of Europe and this is likely to have far-reaching consequences for the long-term future of the country.

In the rest of this chapter we briefly explain what we believe should be the appropriate strategy for Greece in preparing herself for EMU participation. This strategy should aim at promoting policy reforms and macroeconomic policies that boost the productivity and international competitiveness of the Greek economy; eliminate budget deficits and reduce public debt; lower inflation further; increase production efficiency in public and private sector; reduce market rigidities and distortions; improve public administration and promote a higher education level and professional training; and restore agents' confidence to the announcements of the authorities. These targets can only be achieved by employing bold policy measures which will be at the opposite direction of those taken during the previous decade. Privatization, reduction in employment in the public sector, modest increases in nominal wages, reduction in tax evasion, reduction in the state's intervention in the productive process, elimination of distortionary legislation, abolition of public monopolies and productive allocation of the Package Delors II transfers should be at the top of the agenda. More precisely, our proposed strategy consists effectively of two parts. The first one is the well-known and widely debated structural reforms, while the second one is about the macroeconomic policies to be followed and in particular the fiscal and monetary policies.

2.5.2. Structural reforms

With regard to the first part, namely the long overdue structural adjustments very much needed in making the Greek economy more flexible, we have very little really new to propose except of emphasizing once more the necessity for their immediate implementation. As time is running out for Greece, it is now increasingly acknowledged that these reforms are not really any more a choice for the country but rather a one-way road. On the other hand, it is also true that in areas where measures of structural adjustment have been introduced, an unjustified delay in the full implementation is observed whereas other changes have not been introduced at all. The main reasons behind these delays are the feared political cost of such reforms and the existing inefficiencies of the Greek public administration. Therefore, as long as most political parties and economic institutions recognize that structural reforms in Greece are absolutely necessary, they should promote them with a greater political determination and a less compromising spirit. The EMU issue is relevant in that it may provide an official "rationale" for painful structural reforms which are expected to give rise to social unrest and opposition. Greek governments, by "selling" these policy reforms to the Greek public as part of the country's obligations towards meeting the Maastricht criteria, could succeed better than otherwise. In other words, the prospects for EMU participation can function as a *deus ex machina* mitigating social friction caused by unpopular structural reforms.

Structural reforms in the labour market should be given a priority so that a number of rigidities in the process of wage formation and employment policies are relaxed [17]. On the other hand, the recent reforms in the banking and financial sectors are mostly welcome but these reforms themselves cannot guarantee the existence of an efficient financial system[18]. They should definitely be accompanied by the creation of a credible and effective monitoring system, in order to prevent crises such as those of Bank of Crete in 1989 and, more recently, the Athens Stock Exchange in November 1996; and the development of secondary markets for all sorts of securities. Another salient feature of any genuine attempt towards making the Greek economy more flexible should be the promotion of competition in the markets of goods and services. That would increase production efficiency and would also be a major step towards reducing the existing rate of inflation, which as we shall argue below, is mainly structural. This target can be achieved by means of introducing new, modernizing legislation as well as the implementation of a large scale privatization programme.

The Greek authorities have already applied a number of rescuing programmes for a large number of loss-making, state-owned ailing firms and banks. Most (if not all) of these programmes have failed at a great economic cost and these firms

[17] For a survey of Greek labour market see OECD Survey of Greece, 1996.

[18] For a recent overview and an assessment of the process of financial liberalization in Greece see chapter 3 section 3.3. in the present book, the collection of papers in Provopoulos (1995) and the OECD Survey of Greece, 1995.

continue to accumulate losses and debts. The major benefits of privatization are not expected to come from the proceeds raised by selling these firms but (a) from the reduced wage bill for the public budget and (b) the subsequent substantial transformation of the productive structure of the Greek economy which is expected to lead to efficiency gains. At present, the Greek government, the Bank of Greece and most of the political parties accept the necessity of privatization. This is a mostly welcomed development. However, in spite of the experience from other European countries, Greece seems to be moving rather slowly in this field. Unfortunately, eight years after the initiation of the convergence process, and in spite of the fact that the RCP had placed privatizations at the top of the agenda of macroeconomic policy, very little has been done and in most of the cases, the Greek authorities are still at the stage of announcing their intentions regarding the future of a large number of state-owned firms. During the period 1991-97 there was no well-defined plan with regard to specific measures to be taken in relation to this subject and, as the recent developments in the field of exchange rate developments have clearly shown, this is something which makes little good in terms of promoting the credibility of the currently applied economic policy.

Finally, another step towards improving the infrastructure of the Greek economy, increasing the productivity of the public sector and contributing to the real convergence of the Greek economy is the allocation of a large number of funds best known to Greece as Delors Package I (during the 1980s) and Delors Package II (during the 1990s). With regard to the former, it is generally accepted that a large part of it was wasted in financing government consumption. As far as the latter is concerned, during the period 1994-99, Greece will receive a sum of more than 17 billions ECU, which on an annual basis is translated in 5% of Greek GDP. This is an enormous cash injection, unprecedented in Greek economic history. The majority of the funds will go towards improving the basic infrastructure of the economy (the construction of new airports, motorways, railways, etc.) as well as in improving human capital through training and educational projects. This investment in physical and human capital should have positive long-term effects upon the growth rate of the economy, reducing the wide gap between the Greek economy and the rest of Europe in terms of real convergence. One can only hope that recent Greek governments have learned from their past mistakes[19].

[19] However, Alogoskoufis and Prodromidis (1995) have pointed out a number of serious weaknesses with regard to the allocation of the funds provided by the Delors Package II. In addition, a recent announcement of the European Commission revealed that during the period 1994-97 Greece absorbed only 42% of the funds she has been allocated within the context of the Package. This is a point of great concern which should not be ignored by the Greek authorities.

2.5.3. Fiscal and monetary policies

We now turn to the second part of our proposed strategy concerning fiscal policy where the most serious fiscal problems are the persistent budget deficits and national debt and whose presence continue to jeopardize the whole convergence process. During the 1990s, fiscal consolidation has been mainly attempted through an increase in public revenue, i.e. by increasing direct and indirect taxes and eliminating tax evasion. There is no doubt that there is a strong case for the abolition of tax exemptions which are justified neither from the economic nor from the social point of view and for the continuing fight against tax-evasion[20]. To that end, the recent introduction of the special SDOE *(Service of Detection of Economic Crimes)* force and the announcement of the government that in the future strict fines will be imposed on those who continue to evade taxation, are both to the correct direction. However, it is not clear that a fiscal strategy which is almost entirely directed at an increase in public receipts is to the correct direction. The existence of high levels of public deficit and debt is not a subject of Greek concern only. The fiscal imbalances observed in a number of countries in the late 1970s and the early 1980s encouraged the development of a growing literature referring to the selection of an appropriate fiscal policy to deal with the problems. According to the literature, the selection of such a strategy crucially depends on the form of the causal relationship which exists between government consumption and public receipts[21]. Recent econometric evidence referring to the Greek case (see Arghyrou, 1998), does not reject the hypothesis of a causality pattern running from government consumption to public receipts. This finding is consistent with a state of the world where increases in government consumption are autonomously decided (or forced by pressure groups like the influential trade unions of the public sector) and then the authorities resort to tax increases in order to finance the level of spending on which they have decided. In other words, in terms of macroeconomic policy, higher taxation is not really an option as it is perceived by a number of economists (such as Katseli 1990, Vaitsos 1993); it is mainly a defensive measure to which the

---

[20] The underground economy is currently estimated to represent a figure above 30% of Greek GDP and there are signs that it has increased in the second part of the 1980s. Pavlopoulos (1987) estimated that in 1984 it was equal to 28.6% of GDP whereas Kanellopoulos (1992) finds that in 1988 it was equal to 34.6% of GDP.

[21] Evidence of one-way causality from tax receipts to spending would suggest that tax increases result in higher spending levels and possibly to larger deficits. Therefore, an increase in taxation would have an ambiguous impact on the deficit. Evidence of no significant causal relation would suggest that tax increases do not lead to higher spending or deficit growth, therefore the government can safely proceed to the imposition of new taxation. Evidence of two-way causality would suggest that one could not reject the hypothesis that higher spending levels result from higher revenue levels and would complicate the results for inference purposes. Finally, evidence of one-way causality from government consumption to tax receipts would imply that the dual aim to control the deficit and limit the role of the state in economic life should primarily be pursued by means of reducing public expenditure.

Greek authorities are obliged to resort in order to match the exogenously determined increases in public consumption.

The conclusion is that the fiscal situation of Greece will not improve substantially unless the authorities attack the problem at its root, i.e. proceed to a reduction in government consumption. This necessity is even more imperative in view of the fiscal prospects which have now been created after the signing of the Stability and Growth Pact (see Section 2.2 above). In particular, if Greece is to join the EMU at some stage, she should be able to maintain a small (3% of GDP) budget deficit *indefinitely*. Obviously, this will not be possible only by means of increasing existing taxes and imposing new ones, many of which (according to Greece's own government) are of temporary nature (such as the system of objective taxation criteria). Halikias (1996) broadly shares the above views. He argues that the policy of fiscal consolidation which is currently followed is inefficient and does not guarantee a permanent improvement of the debt problem. The validity of this statement is confirmed by the development of the public debt in the first half of the 1990s. In spite of all stabilization efforts for five consecutive years (1991-96), the latter continued to increase.

In addition to the above, there is a number of further arguments in favour of a reconsideration of the current fiscal policy. Specifically, if Greece is to achieve real convergence to the rest of the EU countries by means of higher growth rates, the primary target of economic policy should be the stabilization of the economy along with the creation of conditions for the attraction of foreign direct investment and for a higher amount of domestic resources to be directed to investment purposes. Increasing corporate taxes is not the best way to achieve this goal. This argument acquires additional importance in the light of recent empirical evidence which shows that successful fiscal consolidation programmes are characterized by government consumption cuts and not by tax increases (see Alesina and Perotti, 1995, 96). The latter policy appears not only to be ineffective in reducing the deficit but also contractionary with regards to GDP growth. Furthermore, in view of the announced intention of the Greek government to reduce the share of external debt in total debt, there are theoretical reasons to believe that public debt stabilization through an increase in public revenue would be a second best solution: Alogoskoufis and Christodoulakis (1991) have shown that stabilization through an increase in public revenues would result in the stabilization of the external debt at a level higher than the one which would be achieved if primary surpluses were pursued through expenditure cuts. Finally, one should not underestimate the practical difficulties associated with an increase in public revenue: Greece is a country characterized by widespread tax evasion (see above) and in spite of all past efforts to reduce it, it seems that so far, the problem has not been tackled in an effective way.

We end this chapter with a brief reference to Greek monetary policy in relation to the effort of Greece to join the EMU. This topic represents the main subject of the present book and it is extensively discussed in its remainder. Therefore, here we restrict ourselves in highlighting some key points of the analysis which can be found in the following chapters. Our first point is that the strong drachma policy, which was initiated in 1988 and assumed an almost fixed-exchange rate regime character in the period 1995-97, contributed to the reduction in inflation which was observed in Greece over the last five years. However, as we argue in chapter 4, in the absence of substantial progress in the fields of structural reforms and fiscal correction, this policy led to a fundamentally overvalued drachma. The impact of this overvaluation was twofold: (a) it led to mounting external imbalances, in the form of a widening current account; and (b) it caused substantial capital inflows (mainly of short and medium term nature) which put pressure on the liquidity of the economy and made Greece vulnerable to speculative attacks. Eventually, as it happened in many countries where the authorities maintained an overvalued exchange rate for too long, Greece decided (or perhaps was forced) to devalue her currency. Our second point is that the participation of the drachma in the ERM does not guarantee exchange rate stability until the accession of Greece to the EMU, especially in view of the recent announcement of the BoG that it will restrict the fluctuations of the drachma within the narrow ±2.5% range around the new central rate (357 drachmas per ECU). The main arguments behind this view are the following: (a) it is not certain that the recent 14% devaluation was enough in order to restore the drachma at its long-run equilibrium, therefore it is not certain that the problems caused by the overvaluation of the drachma have now been eliminated; and (b) there is a substantial probability that the euro will follow an appreciating pattern during the first stages after its introduction. In that case, given the productivity differences which currently exist between Greece and the rest of the EU countries, the close shadowing of the euro may lead to a new serious misalignment of the drachma.

As a result of the above, one can make a case for an alternative monetary strategy to that of participation in the ERM-II. More specifically, as it is argued in chapter 5, such an alternative monetary policy regime could be the *direct targeting of inflation* involving inflation targets higher but gradually converging to the EMU inflation rate. External competitiveness would then be restored by means of the nominal adjustment of the exchange rate (crawling peg). Such a convergence would be less painful in terms of output and employment losses, firstly because of its gradual character and secondly because of the restoration of the competitiveness which would help the "ailing" external sector of the economy, a fact which would contribute to higher growth rates. Within a medium-term convergence programme that aims at removing the existing structural inefficiencies, a direct inflation-targeting regime together with the independence recently granted to the BoG could be more effective than the nominal anchor of the ERM-II in bringing structural inflation down.

Chapter 3

MONETARY DEVELOPMENTS IN GREECE: 1975-97

This chapter reviews the main monetary developments in Greece during the period 1975-97. It also refers to the monetary objectives for the period 1998-99 as they were announced by the Bank of Greece (BoG) after the March 1998 devaluation of the drachma. Over the last ten years or so, the Greek monetary environment has changed significantly. The main differences can be found in the following areas: (1) the objectives pursued by monetary policy and the instruments used in order to meet these objectives; and (2) the institutional framework where (i) changes caused by the process of financial liberalization have created a completely new monetary and financial environment (ii) the Bank of Greece (BoG) has been granted independence in the conduct of monetary policy.

3.1. A brief account of monetary events

The pre-1975 period

Prior to 1975, Greek monetary policy aimed at the achievement of a broad set of policy objectives including: a high growth rate for the economy; a low rate of unemployment; the meeting of the financial needs of the public sector; a low rate of inflation; and a sustainable current account deficit. The main feature of Greek monetary policy before 1975 was the participation of the drachma in the Bretton Woods system of fixed exchange rates. This participation was effected after a 50% devaluation of the drachma in 1953 against the dollar and involved exchange rate pegging of the drachma against the American currency at the level of 30 drachmas per dollar. Prior to 1975 decisions relating to monetary policy were taken by the Currency Committee, a powerful ministerial body whose President was the Minister of Coordination and whose members included the Ministers of Finance, Industry, Commerce and Agriculture and the Governor of the BoG. The Currency Committee was responsible for a number of important decisions including increases in the rate of growth of money supply, interest rates and business credit. The BoG was expected to follow the policy guidelines laid by the Currency

Committee and its Governor was expected to resign when a change of party in office was taking place[1].

In the absence of developed money markets, the instruments used to meet the objectives of monetary policy were, among others, the administratively set interest rates and reserves requirements; the obligation of commercial banks to invest part of their reserves in government securities; and the extensive use of credit controls designed to achieve the channeling of credit into desirable, from the governments' point of view, projects. Finally, the BoG applied strict capital controls in order to maintain exchange rate stability. More specifically, the Greek financial system was heavily regulated with the largest banking groups of the country being under state ownership and obliged to provide the public sector with high proportions of credit at low interest rates. Consumer credit was almost non-existent and in the absence of any developed securities market, the only source of business credit was the state-controlled and oligopolistically structured banking system which consisted of commercial banks and Specialized Credit Institutions (SCIs). With regards to commercial banks, the BoG determined the level of credit creation in line with the decisions of the Currency Committee. This was done by means of manipulating the reserve requirements and other liabilities of the BoG to the commercial banks. With regards to the SCIs, a ceiling for the level of credit was defined at the beginning of each year and the BoG would decide on the allocation of credit by category of loan as well as the terms of the loans, the source of the funds etc. The aim of this heavily regulated system was to satisfy the financial needs of the public sector and the direction of credit to those sectors of the economy where the authorities considered it important to contribute to their development. As a result, a complicated system of administratively fixed and highly differentiated interest rates had been developed [2].

The period 1975-87

In 1974 the Western world experienced a strong recession caused by the first oil shock. In the case of Greece, the shock coincided with the political instability which accompanied the transition from dictatorship to democracy, a fact which

---

1 See Courakis (1981) and Halikias (1978) for a thorough study of the Greek financial system, institutions and monetary policy up to the mid-1970s.

2 This system was introduced in the 1950s. Non-privileged borrowers paid higher interest rates and as banks had an incentive to channel credit there, authorities created a complicated system of reserves and withdrawals in order to eliminate this incentive: in case a bank granted credit to non-privileged borrowers, it had to deposit 20% of the value of the loan to a non-interest bearing account with the BoG. The bank was then allowed to withdraw a part of this deposit in order to provide loans to privileged borrowers at low, subsidized interest rates. As a result, most banks directed credit to privileged borrowers. This situation gave rise to what has been called "round tripping", i.e. privileged borrowers started to lend the funds of their own loans to non-privileged firms in higher interest rates than those they had to pay to the bank.

aggravated the already unfavourable economic climate. In an effort to soften the negative impact of these events and avoid a prolonged recession, the first post-dictatorship government abandoned the official commitment to a fixed exchange rate against the US Dollar. Under governmental instructions, the BoG initiated a crawling peg exchange rate policy against the major foreign currencies with the aim to support the competitiveness of Greek products and thereby allow the economy to overcome the recession.

Compared with the pre-1975 period, the objectives pursued by monetary policy remained more or less unchanged: the Currency Committee and the BoG continued to pursue policies aiming at a high GDP growth rate, a high level of employment and a sustainable current account deficit. They also continued to provide sufficient credit to the public sector. Price stability was also included in the set of targets but, as is evident by inflation developments in those years (see chapter 5), it was not considered as an important one. However, the persisting high inflation rates of the 1974-75 period obliged the authorities to realize that some kind of control over the liquidity of the economy was necessary. As a result, in 1976 the Currency Committee introduced for the first time intermediate targets for the conduct of monetary policy. Specifically, between 1976 and 1982 the BoG set target values for the rate of growth of M0, i.e. currency in circulation[3], and the rate of growth of bank credit. As a result, one could say that after 1974 monetary policy in Greece entered a new phase as the country went from an exchange rate regime to a floating one and exchange rate targets were replaced, at least in theory, by monetary ones[4]. As far as the instruments of monetary policy are concerned, they remained identical to those employed during the pre-1975 period. Authorities continued to set all interest rates administratively and decided alone when, where and on what terms credit should be directed. They also intensified the credit controls imposed on commercial banks and SCIs. In addition, they increased the proportions of the commercial banks' reserves to be invested in government securities and obliged commercial banks to transfer another significant proportion of their reserves to the financing of small-size firms.

In the meantime, the lessons emerging from the first oil-shock and the phenomenon of stagflation which was observed in most of the European countries in the late 1970s resulted in an international understanding of the importance of low inflation and the limitations of the effectiveness of monetary policy in

[3] In Greece, M0 is defined as notes and coins in circulation. M1 is defined as M0 plus private demand deposits. M0 in Greece represents approximately 70-80% of M1.

[4] Monetary targets were set, and continue so up to the present day, according to the desired position in the balance of payments and the BoG projections regarding the rate of growth of real GDP, inflation and interest rates. Having acquired the target value (or target range after 1988) for the rate of growth of the monetary variable used as an intermediate target, the BoG calculates an estimate of the required increase in net domestic credit. Finally, given an assessment for the financial and credit needs of the private sector, the BoG derives a target for the credit expansion to the public sector.

affecting real variables such as output and unemployment. As a result, the central banks of most European countries started to focus on price stability as the primary objective of monetary policy and pursued the creation of an efficient, investment-inducing financial system providing new financial products and financial services. These necessities were also realized in Greece. In view of the obligations which the country undertook with her accession to the EEC in 1981, and also realizing the significant distortions caused by a heavily regulated monetary framework, the authorities proceeded to the creation of the *Harissopoulos Committee* (named after its president) which was given the task of providing a detailed description of the banking system and developing a number of proposals referring to the possibilities of its modernization. In 1981 the Committee published its report which led to a significant institutional change. In July 1982 the newly-elected socialist government dissolved the Currency Committee and distributed its functions between the government and the BoG. The former (and in particular its newly formed Council of Government Policy) undertook the responsibility of setting the objectives for monetary and credit policies whereas the latter was allocated the task of implementing the policies designed by the government. However, the objectives of monetary policy remained unchanged and authorities continued to pursue the same set of, often contradicting, targets. The BoG continued its crawling-peg exchange rate policy and the drachma did not join the Exchange Rate Mechanism (ERM) of the European Monetary System (EMS) created in 1979.

Although the elimination of the Currency Committee empowered the BoG with powers it did not possess in the past, in reality it did not really hinder the government from applying expansionary fiscal and monetary policies. The result was a significant worsening of all macroeconomic indicators which forced the government to take action. In January 1983, the government, under the responsibility of the Minister of National Economy Mr. Arsenis, introduced a stabilization programme whose monetary provisions involved a 15.5% nominal devaluation of the drachma against the US dollar in early January. The devaluation aimed at restoring the declining competitiveness of Greek products and at curbing the rising rate of inflation through the stabilization of the exchange rate at a sustainable level. To that end, it was decided that the BoG should defend the new exchange rate parity against the US Dollar and indeed, during the January-August 1983 period the drachma shadowed the American currency. Also, in an effort to control the liquidity of the economy in a more effective way, in 1983 the BoG introduced the publication of Monetary Programmes and switched from targeting M0 to targeting M3[5]. In spite of the above, the 1983 stabilization programme proved short-lived and it was abandoned by the end of the same year. As a result, within the context of a new five-year Economic Programme introduced in November 1983, under governmental instructions, the BoG continued to provide the public sector with credit facilities and provide credit to small and medium-size

[5] M3 is defined as M1 plus private savings and time deposits, bank bonds and repurchase agreements (repos). Repos were included in the definition of M3 in 1992.

industrial firms, agriculture, export and ailing state-owned enterprises. Credit continued to be allocated through the same system of administratively fixed and highly differentiated interest rates which were kept low in order to hold down the cost of public borrowing and boost the development of the privileged sectors[6].

However, in October 1985 a new current account crisis and the general adverse macroeconomic developments compelled the socialist government to launch a new stabilization programme under the leadership of the newly appointed minister of National Economy Mr. Simitis. In the monetary field, the new programme involved a new devaluation of the drachma by 15%. This time, however, the targets of monetary policy shifted towards price stability. The government announced that domestic credit expansion and the rate of growth of M3 were to be limited and under no circumstances would they exceed the rate of growth of nominal GDP. Furthermore, it was decided that it was high time to take all the necessary steps required to replace the obsolete institutional and operational framework of the financial system. To that end, the government appointed the *Karatzas Committee* (named after its president) with the task of advancing a number of proposals regarding reforms in the financial system. In 1987 the Committee published its influential *Report for the Reform and the Modernization of the Greek Banking System* which, among other things, confirmed the outmoded structure of the financial system, highlighted the distortions for which it was responsible and emphasized the limitations it imposed on monetary policy.

The period 1988-97

The process of financial liberalization which followed the Report of the Karatzas Committee (see section 3.3 below), combined with the macroeconomic imbalances created in the 1980s and the effort of Greece to achieve EMU participation, created a completely new financial environment and a totally different framework for the conduct of monetary policy. As far as the final objective of monetary policy is concerned, after 1987 the BoG gradually abandoned all other policy objectives and started to focus on the pursuit of price stability. With regard to the intermediate targets of monetary policy, the BoG continued to target the rate of growth of broad money supply M3 and started monitoring the movements of M4[7]. However, in 1988 the monetary authority introduced a second intermediate target, namely the rate of nominal depreciation of the drachma against the ECU. More specifically, in 1988 the BoG initiated the *strong drachma* policy which involved a rate of depreciation against the ECU smaller than the inflation differential which existed between Greece and the rest of the EU countries. However, no explicit quantitative exchange rate targets were announced prior to 1995. Nevertheless,

[6] In 1985 the public sector received loans equal to 48.5% of total deposits. The equivalent share for small-size and industrial firms was 10% and 15% respectively.

[7] M4 is defined as M3 plus public securities of maturity up to one year. Official targets for its rate of growth were set only for the period 1995-97.

over the last few years it had become increasingly evident that during the period 1988-97 the BoG had been attaching an increasing weight to the exchange rate target. Gradually, the latter substituted the target referring to the rate of growth of money supply and finally became the primary intermediate target of monetary policy.

Regarding the instruments of monetary policy, most of the traditional ones have now been abolished as all capital, foreign exchange and credit controls have been gradually eliminated. In addition, the obligation of the commercial banks to invest in public bonds and provide loans to small-size firms has also gradually vanished. In the new financial environment created after the deregulation of the banking and financial system, the meeting of the intermediate targets of monetary policy required new means of exercising monetary policy. The BoG responded by introducing new credit facilities and controlling a number of offered and bid interest rates (some traditional, some newly-introduced). One could say that over the past years the BoG has essentially been trying to manage the liquidity of the economy mainly through short-term money market operations in the interbank money market. More specifically, the BoG intervenes on a daily basis in the interbank money market with an aim to control the economy's liquidity by means of influencing the interbank overnight interest rate. In addition, since November 1994 the BoG intervenes on a weekly basis in the one-month interbank market. Within the context of the strong drachma policy, the BoG interventions were usually aimed at absorbing liquidity (accepting funds). The overnight and one-month intervention bid-rates of the BoG are the main determinants of the rates prevailing in the interbank money market (overnight and one-month interbank rates) and at present, they are regarded as the most important instrument used by monetary policy. They are also considered as the most credible indicator regarding the intentions of the BoG and the direction of monetary policy.

Another instrument of monetary policy which has been increasingly employed by the BoG over the last years is the performance of open market operations. These take place by means of auctions in the form of repurchasing agreements (repos) of government securities. This form of intervention, which in contrast to the interventions in the interbank money market influence the liquidity of the system in an indirect way, was established in 1989 but it has been extensively used since mid-1995. At present, there are two types of auctions: the first one takes place every other Wednesday where the BoG conducts an auction in the form of repos whose maturity is a two-week period; the second type takes place every Friday where the BoG conducts an auction in the form of repos whose maturity is a period of one month. This monetary policy instrument has a number of advantages over other instruments (see Filippides, Kyriakopoulos, Moschos, 1995)[8] and it is

[8] First, transactions are reversed at a predetermined date and, as a result, do not affect the liquidity of the system in a permanent way; second, repos constitute a very flexible method of intervention as operations are concluded in a fast way (2-3 hours); third, a high degree of

expected that as the secondary market for bonds and public securities is developed further, its significance will increase.

In addition to the above instruments, in the 1990s the BoG has used three additional credit facilities and their respective interest rates to meet the temporary financial needs of the commercial banks. These are the following. First, the Lombard facility. In June 1993 the BoG allowed credit institutions to borrow funds against a collateral of government securities. The aim of this instrument is to allow credit institutions access to liquidity in periods of unexpected money demand caused by unpredictable circumstances so that a significant increase in interest rates will be averted. The Lombard rate aims to provide a ceiling for interest rates prevailing in the interbank money market (provided that the ability of the BoG to borrow funds on a short-term basis has not been exhausted). However, as there is still a quota for the amount of funds which commercial banks can absorb from this facility, it has not yet operated as such. The Lombard facility was extensively used during the exchange rate upheaval of May-June 1994 but as it is activated on the initiative of commercial banks, it is not considered a flexible instrument of monetary policy. However, its signaling role should not be underestimated.

Second, the discount facility. In June 1993 the BoG reactivated the discount service it used to offer to commercial banks, i.e. it allowed credit institutions to absorb funds by discounting their customers' bills of exchange and promissory notes[9]. In practice however, commercial banks have not made extensive use of the discount facility as the volume of bills and notes presented to banks for discounting by their customers is rather small due to the practical difficulties existing in their monitoring and the high cost involved, in comparison with other methods of financing[10]. Also, the discount facility, like the Lombard one, is activated on the initiative of commercial banks, therefore it is not considered a flexible instrument of monetary policy. As a result, the role of the discount rate is rather signaling.

Third, the overdraft facility. The BoG offers to credit institutions an overdraft facility and charges for the use of this facility an overdraft penalty rate. The overdraft rate is currently the upper limit of the money market rate and, as such, it operates as a counter-motive for excessive credit creation. Other instruments which have been used in the 1990s, mainly with an aim to absorb liquidity, is an increase

---

safety is ensured because transactions are covered by government securities and the amount of financing is restricted by the volume of available securities; fourth, they safeguard the transparency of the system as the rules of the auction are known beforehand; fourth, the BoG is in position to obtain information relating to market expectations about interest rates, not only from the average interest rates but also out of the range of bids.

[9] While the discount facility had existed earlier, it had not been used extensively and the total amount that banks could absorb through it was limited.

[10] It should be noted, however, that promissory bills and bills of exchange are extensively used by private agents as collateral for receiving credit facilities from commercial banks.

in the BoG reserve requirements[11] and an intervention in the spot market of foreign exchange (sterilization) where, in the context of the strong drachma policy, the BoG was typically selling foreign currencies and buying drachmas. Also, on some occasions the BoG has used one-month drachma-dollar swaps in order to inject liquidity. But, overall, when it comes to draining or supplying liquidity, one could say that the most extensively used instrument for monetary policy by the BoG is the intervention in the overnight interbank money market and intervention in the spot market of foreign exchange and, to a lesser extent, the manipulation of the reserve requirements.

We end our discussion of the main monetary events which took place in Greece during the post-1975 period with a brief reference to two important recent developments. First, on December 2, 1997, the Greek government passed in the Parliament a Bill (No. 2548/97) granting independence to the Bank of Greece. The Bill aimed at harmonizing Greek legislation with the provisions of the Maastricht Treaty[12]. Second, on 14 March 1998 the Greek drachma was devalued by 14% against the ECU and joined the ERM. The new central rate against the ECU was set to be 357 drachmas (GDR) per ECU. In theory, according to the existing ERM arrangements, the GDR/ECU spot rate can fluctuate around the central rate within a ±15% band (i.e. it can take values between 303 drachmas per ECU and 410 drachmas per ECU). Finally, in the 1998 monetary programme which was published after the devaluation of March 1998, the BoG announced that it will continue to pursue price stability so that the inflation rate will reach the level of 2% by the end of 1999[13]. The significance of this announcement is that it introduces some elements of an inflation targeting regime in the Greek monetary framework[14]. Another feature of the Monetary Programme is that it does not include any quantitative target for the rate of growth of any monetary or credit aggregate[15]. On the other hand, the BoG announced that the 2% inflation objective in 1999 will be primarily pursued through exchange rate stability. More specifically, according to the provisions of the Programme, the Bank will use all instruments available in order to restrict the average annual fluctuation of the drachma against its current (post-devaluation) central rate against the ECU within the narrow range of ±2.5%. In other words, the intention of the BoG is to restrict

---

[11] Over the period 1985-96 the reserve requirement ratio has taken values between 6 and 11%. In July 1996, in an effort to control liquidity and avoid inflationary pressures, the BoG imposed an 11% reserve requirement on existing non-resident liabilities and increased the commercial banks' reserve requirements from 9% to 11%. Reserve requirement increases had also taken place in August and October 1995.

[12] A full discussion and assessment of this Bill can be found in chapter 6.

[13] See Bank of Greece, Monetary Programme for 1998, presented to the Greek Parliament on 28/4/98.

[14] For further discussion on this issue, see chapter 5.

[15] However, the BoG announced that monetary aggregates will be monitored and their rate of growth is not expected to exceed certain limits. The projected, but not committing ranges are 6%-9% for M3 and 4%-6% for total credit.

the fluctuations of the GDR/ECU spot rate within the range of 348 drachmas per ECU and 366 drachmas per ECU. The BoG has also announced that this target will be primarily pursued by means of increases in short-term interest rates and this practice will not change even if the government applies lax fiscal and incomes policies which are not consistent with the Bank's a low inflation objective[16].

3.2. The process of financial liberalization

The starting point of the process of financial liberalization was the abolition of the administratively set maximum lending rates which led to a gradual liberalization of all interest rates. Interest rate deregulation was completed in May 1993 when the last remaining controls on interest rates of saving deposits were abolished. At the same time (May 1993) the obligation on commercial banks to provide loans to small-size firms and invest in public bonds was eliminated. This was accompanied by the elimination of all sorts of interest rate subsidization. Consumer credit which was almost non-existent up to 1992 was largely liberalized during that year. The lifting of foreign exchange controls which was initiated in 1989[17] was completed in May 1994[18]. Also, in 1992 a forward market for foreign exchange was created.

After 1990 and according to the EU banking directives, Greek banking legislation has become less rigid and, as a result, a considerable number of private and foreign banks and institutions have entered the market[19]. The banking law of August 1992 abolished the distinction between commercial banks and SCIs, allowing each side to undertake activities and offer services which were hitherto exclusively assigned to the other side. This has led to an impressive progress towards eliminating the market segmentation which existed prior to 1992[20]. In 1993 the 3% tax on bank

---

[16] See section 4.4. below for an evaluation of the limits of the participation of the drachma in the Exchange Rate Mechanism.

[17] In 1989 the authorities relaxed some restrictions imposed on commercial banks with regard to the amount of foreign exchange they were allowed to provide to their customers. By July 1992 all restrictions referring to current transactions had been abolished. In 1993 the BoG abolished all restrictions pertaining to long and medium-term capital movements.

[18] The lifting of the remaining foreign exchange restrictions was due by July 1994 but the BoG decided to proceed to it earlier than planned so that the drachma would not be put under pressure from speculators. However, such pressures did develop and the BoG was obliged to increase its overnight intervention rate in order to beat the speculators (see sections 3.4 and 3.5 below).

[19] In 1980 the share of the state-owned banks in total lending and deposits was equal to 92.5% and 87.2% respectively. In 1993 the relative figures were 82.5% and 79%. Also, in 1985 there were three mutual funds whereas in 1994 there were ninety with their assets rising from negligible levels in the late 1980s to 1% of GDP in 1990 and 6% in 1994.

[20] For example, mortgage banks now have the right to open current deposit accounts and the Agricultural Bank of Greece is no longer restricted to agricultural loans. Investment and development banks have acquired the right to accept drachma deposits and grant loans for

loan contracts was eliminated and in 1994 the 8% tax on bank turnover was reduced. In addition, the BoG has initiated a gradual process of eliminating the obligation of the commercial banks to re-deposit their foreign currency deposits with the BoG[21]. In the field of banking supervision, new legislation compatible with EU regulations was introduced and in 1993 the BoG (which is responsible for the supervision of the banking system) introduced new procedures of banking control.

In an effort to facilitate and expand the ability of the BoG to execute money market interventions, in September 1993 the public debt securities held by commercial banks were converted into marketable assets and their trade between the BoG and credit institutions (with or without a repurchase agreement) was permitted. In the secondary market, the bulk of transactions is at present represented by trade in bonds among banks, mutual funds, insurance companies and financial institutions. It is expected however that in the future individual investors will increase their participation because they will be able to hold bond accounts with the banks. Another development, which is also expected to promote the efficiency of the secondary market, is the fact that in 1995 government securities were dematerialized and an electronic book-entry bond trading system operated by the BoG was introduced. Furthermore, in 1994 the BoG introduced the Athibor and Athibid interest rates for the interbank market for transactions of duration of one, two, three and six months. These rates represent the average offered and bid rates of 13 major participants in the money market. The BoG does not participate directly in the daily determination of these two rates which are considered very important for the stability and reliability of the Greek money market and the development of securities market.

Finally, in 1988 a strong effort aiming to modernize the Athens Stock Exchange (ASE) was launched. To that end, in 1992 the Capital Market Committee (CMC) was upgraded and was given responsibility for supervision of the proper operation of the securities market[22]. However, despite the considerable progress which was

---

working capital, issue credit cards and foreign exchange loans. The same Banking Law obliged banks to stop accruing interest on loans that have not been serviced for a period greater than 12 months and obliged them to stop granting new loans in order to repay overdue interest. Finally, it abolished the right of the Finance Minister to vote in the shareholders' meeting of the state-owned commercial banks as a representative of public entities. This has reduced, at least in theory, the control of the government over these banks.

[21] In April 1995 this requirement was reduced to 70% of foreign currency deposits. The released funds are estimated to be between 650 and 700 billion drachmas and were largely used in order to provide loans in foreign currency to small and medium size firms which were not able to borrow from international capital markets.

[22] The CMC is responsible for the licensing and supervision of brokerage firms, mutual funds and portfolio investment companies, the approval of initial public offerings of companies in the ASE including overseeing their operation and the authorization of new financial products.

achieved both in terms of participating companies as well as in the field of legislation and operation, until very recently the ASE was classified as an emerging market as it was (and still remains) a relatively thin market[23]. The fact that the ASE has still a long way to go in order to be comparable with other stock exchanges was clearly shown during the crisis of November 1996[24] and, more recently, the crisis of November 1997 which followed the Hong Kong Stock Exchange crisis and resulted to a substantial reduction in the level of the ASE general index[25]. However, a new situation seems to be emerging since the accession of the drachma in the ERM in March 1998. The first weeks which followed ERM participation saw a substantial increase in the volume of transactions which is mainly attributed to the increased interest of foreign investors in the Greek capital market which has resulted to a dramatic increase in the level of the ASE general index [26]. Although it is still early to draw any conclusions, many financial analysts have claimed that this increase has marked the beginning of a new era for the Greek capital and money markets.

3.3. Money and credit aggregates

This section reviews the historic movements of the main Greek monetary aggregates. To begin with the rate of growth of narrow money supply, for almost the whole of the period under consideration, the rate of growth of M0 (currency in circulation) was almost identical to the one of M1 (currency in circulation plus time deposits) as the former represented approximately 75-80% of the latter. However, as from 1993, and as a result of a significant increase in private sight deposits, M1 has presented much higher growth rates than those of M0 (see Figure 3.1). Both aggregates have displayed quite pronounced fluctuations around their mean but as Table 3.1 suggests, their rate of growth has declined in the 1990s.

---

[23] In January 1997 the ASE had 232 listed companies and an estimated capital of 24 billion US dollars.

[24] In November 1996, as a result of a share-trading scandal, the bourse was shut for three days and authorities hired three international accounting firms to carry out emergency audits of all 65 Greek brokerage houses. The scandal burst when it was revealed that leading Greek brokerage houses, including several controlled by state-owned banks, had manipulated the price of the shares of some companies in an effort to boost their commission income. It followed a dispute over registering shares of construction companies bidding for large public works contracts and the cancellation of a casino license awarded to a consortium of listed Greek companies following allegations of bribes to government officials.

[25] During the first two weeks of November 1997 the General Index of the Athens Stock Exchange lost approximately 20% of its nominal value: from approximately 1750 units in the end of October 1997 it went down to approximately 1350 units in mid-November 1997.

[26] On 29/1/98 the index was at the level of 1380 units whereas on 4/5/98 it was up to 2621 units. This represents a yield of 90% over a period of three months.

As far as the wide money supply is concerned, the rate of growth of M3 (i.e. the monetary aggregate in terms of which the BoG used to set its monetary targets after 1983) used to be consistently higher than the threshold of 20% prior to 1988, reflecting the expansionary economic policies pursued by Greek governments (see Figure 3.2). Such lax policies were particularly pronounced during election years (e.g. 1981, 85, 89). However, the situation has changed significantly since 1989. As from the beginning of the present decade, monetary policy in Greece has become increasingly disciplined, something which has given rise to declining rates of growth for M4 and M3. The latter has now stabilized at a level approximately equal to 10%. To turn now our attention to credit developments, the historical movement of the rate of growth of total bank credit is similar to that of monetary aggregates and very much correlated with the one of M3 (see Table 3.2). More specifically, during the 1975-89 period the total credit growth rate was usually higher than 15% and at times higher than 20% (see Figure 3.2). To a large extent, this growth was driven by the spectacular increase in the rate of growth of bank credit to the public sector whose average value in the 1980s was equal to 32%. The situation has changed significantly after 1989 when the BoG introduced more disciplined monetary policies. At the beginning of the 1990s, the average total credit growth rate has declined by more than 50% and has now stabilized to single-digit levels (8%).

Figure 3.1

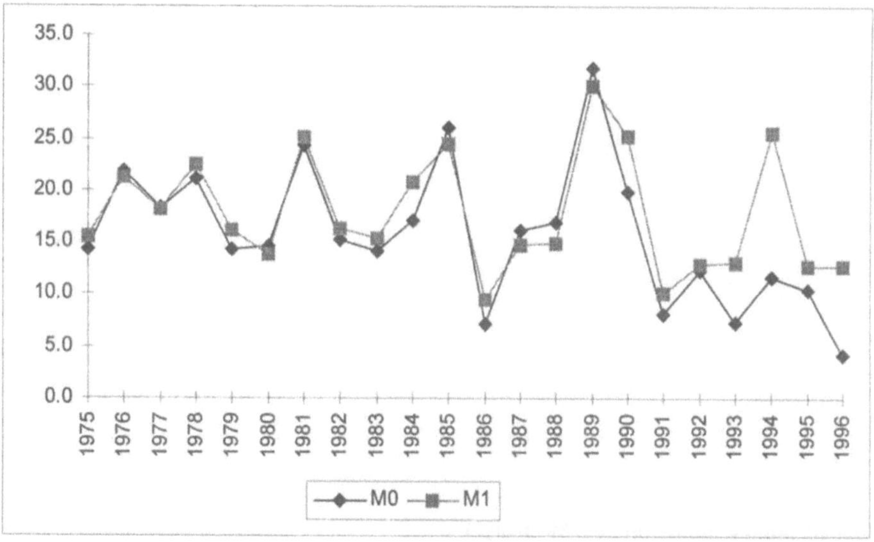

Narrow money supply (annual % change)

Source: Bank of Greece, Monthly Statistical Bulletin, various editions.

Table 3.1

Period	M0	M1	M3	M4	Total Credit	Credit to Private Sec.	Credit to Public Sec.
1975-79	18.0	18.7	24.1	N/A	22.7	23.3	19.7
1980-89	18.3	18.5	25.5	N/A	21.6	19.0	32.5
1990-96	10.5	16.0	12.4	16.3	8.1	13.9	0.5
1975-96	15.8	17.7	21.0	N/A	17.6	18.4	19.4

Money supply and bank credit growth in Greece, average annual % change, 1975-96
Source: Authors' calculations based on data taken from the Bank of Greece, Monthly Statistical Bulletin, various editions.

Figure 3.2

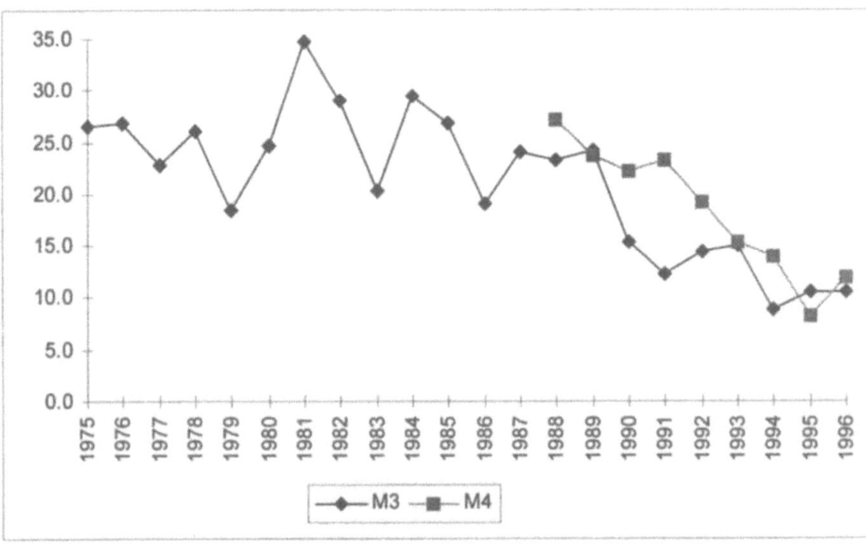

Broad money supply (annual % change)
Source: Bank of Greece, Monthly Statistical Bulletin, various editions

Table 3.2

	M0	M1	M3	Total Credit	Credit to Pr. Sec.	Credit to Pub. Sec.
M0	1.00					
M1	0.83	1.00				
M3	0.67	0.36	1.00			
Total Credit	0.58	0.31	0.89	1.00		
Credit to Private Sector	0.48	0.33	0.53	0.75	1.00	
Credit to Public Sector	0.35	0.04	0.76	0.74	0.33	1.00

Money supply and bank credit growth in Greece, 1975-96, correlation matrix
Source: Authors' calculations based on data taken from the Bank of Greece, Monthly Statistical Bulletin, various editions.

Figure 3.3

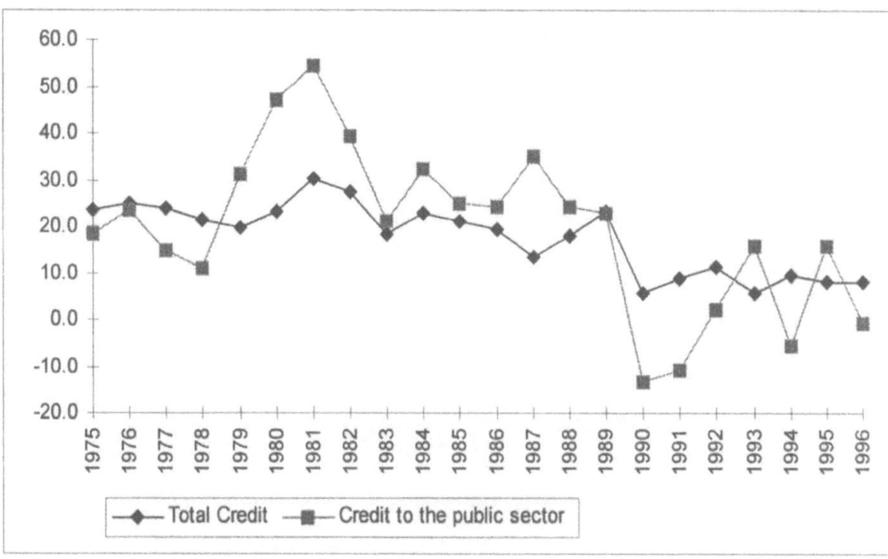

Bank credit (annual % change)
Source: Bank of Greece, Monthly Statistical Bulletin, various editions.

3.4. Interest rates

During the period 1975-86 the then heavily regulated financial system allowed Greek authorities to keep nominal interest rates in relatively low levels by administrative means (see Figure 3.4). Despite some occasional upwards adjustments (especially those which took place in the late 1970s), and although Greek nominal interest rates in the 1980s were well above the level of 10% (see Table 3.3), nominal lending interest rates were frequently kept below inflation. As a result, *ex-post* real deposit rates were approximately equal to zero whereas real lending rates were on many occasions negative (see Figure 3.5).

The situation started changing in 1987 when for the first time, the BoG set a minimum interest rate for short-term bank loans and allowed banks to negotiate interest rates with their clients. The initial stages of financial liberalization were subsequently accompanied by significant interest rate increases which widened the difference which already existed between Greek and European nominal interest rates (see Figure 3.6). As a result, the late 1980s and the early 1990s saw a spectacular rise in Greek real interest rates which eventually took them (for the first time) well above the European ones (see Figure 3.7).

Figure 3.4

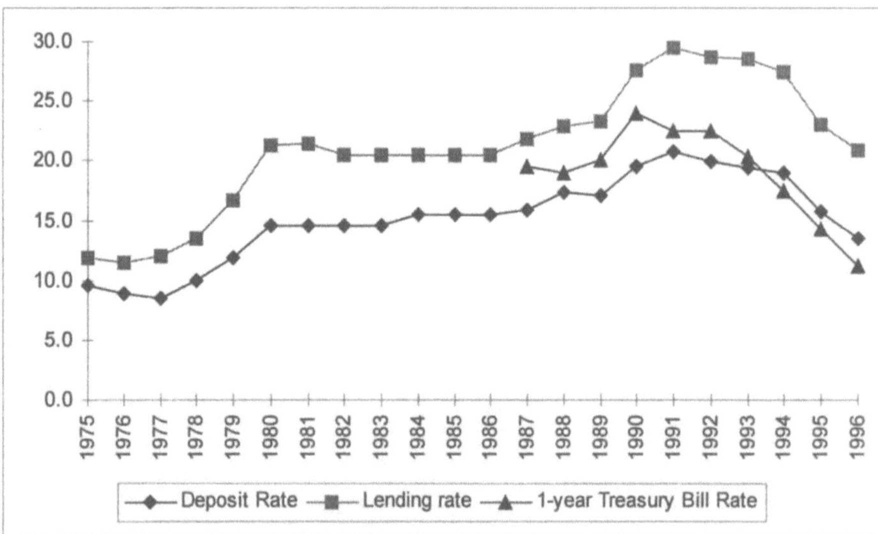

Nominal interest rates in Greece, 1975-96
Source: International Financial Statistics, CD 09-97

During the period 1994-1997 Greece managed to achieve a non-negligible degree of nominal interest rate convergence with the rest of the EU countries. This progress is also reflected in the movements of the lending facilities provided by the Bank of Greece (see Figure 3.8) and the overnight lending rate in the interbank money market (see Figure 3.9). However, in spite of the progress achieved, Greece still has by far the highest interest rates among the EU countries. In fact, as Figure 3.9 suggests, as a result of the November 1997 exchange rate crisis, during the last months of 1997 Greece experienced an increase in the interbank money market, similar to the one which had taken place during the May 1994 exchange rate crisis[27]. The November 1997 crisis also led to an increase in the one-year Treasury Bill rate but did not result to an increase in bank deposit and lending rates.

Figure 3.5

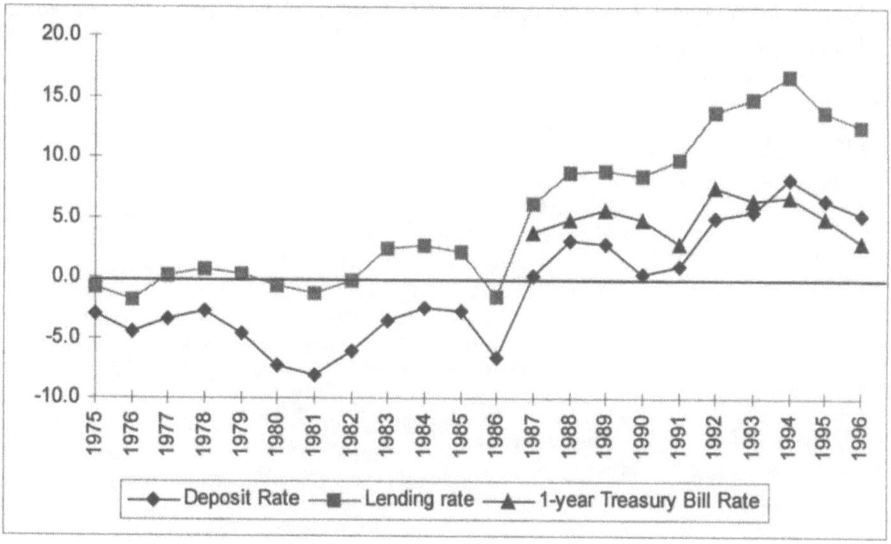

Ex-post* real interest rates in Greece, 1975-96
* Nominal Interest Rates minus CPI inflation
Source: International Financial Statistics, CD 09-97

[27] The increase in the overnight interbank rate which took place in November 1997 was the result of the dramatic increase in the overnight intervention rate of the BoG. We return to this point in chapter 4 when we discuss the limits of the strong drachma policy.

Table 3.3

Period	Deposit Rate	Lending Rate	1-year TB rate	Real Deposit Rate	Real Lending Rate	Real 1-year TB rate
1975-79	9.8	13.1	N/A	-3.7	-0.4	N/A
1980-89	15.5	21.3	N/A	-3.1	2.7	N/A
1990-96	18.2	26.5	18.9	4.5	12.8	5.2
1975-96	15.1	21.1	N/A	-0.8	5.2	N/A

Interest rates in Greece, 1975-97

Source: International Financial Statistics, CD 09-97 and Bank of Greece, Economic Bulletin, various editions.

Figure 3.6

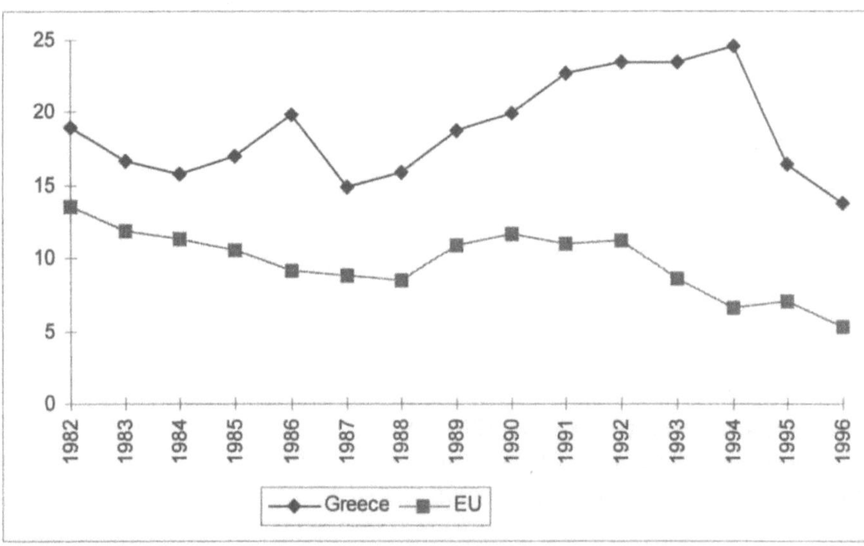

Short-term nominal interest rates in Greece and the EU

Source: European Economy No. 64, Statistical Appendix.

Figure 3.7

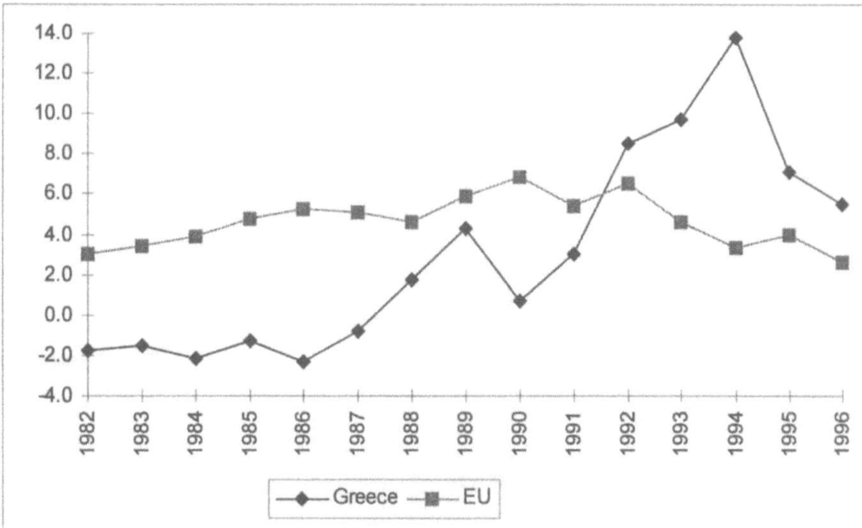

Short-term real interest rates in Greece and the EU
Source: European Economy No. 64, Statistical Appendix.

Figure 3.8

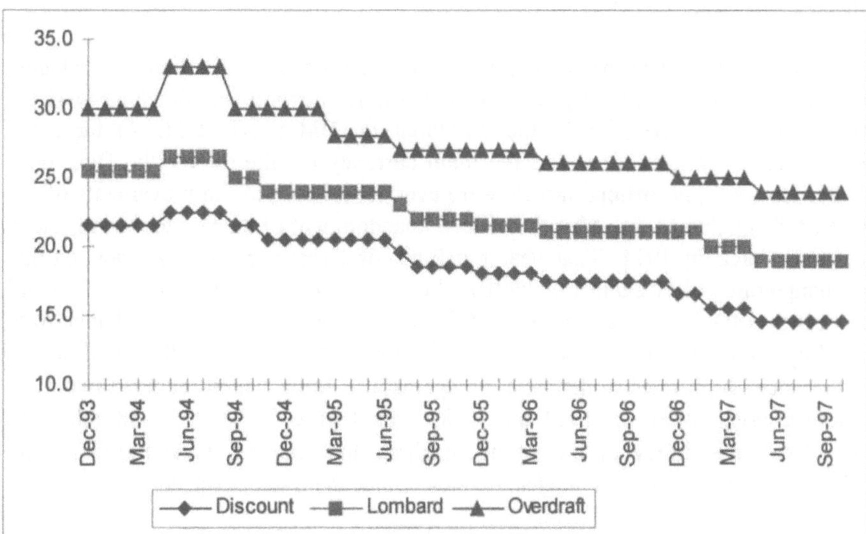

Bank of Greece interest rates
Source: Bank of Greece, Economic Bulletin, various editions

Figure 3.9

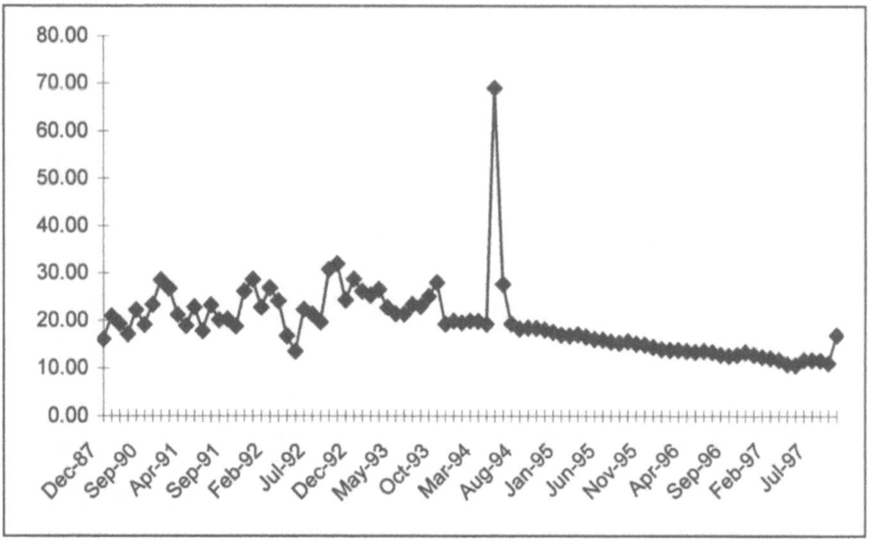

Overnight interbank interest rate
Source: Bank of Greece, Economic Bulletin, various editions.

3.5. Exchange rates

We end this chapter by presenting the main developments in the field of exchange rate movements. Specifically, we review the movements of the drachma *vis-à-vis* three major currencies, namely the US Dollar, the DM and the ECU. As far as the US Dollar is concerned, it was the main currency of interest for the BoG until 1987. However, no official targets were ever set relating to the movements of the GDR/US$ exchange rate after the official abandonment of the peg to the American currency back in 1974. That year the Bank of Greece initiated a crawling-peg exchange rate policy against the dollar which led to a 7% depreciation in 1975 and a further 14% depreciation in 1976[28]. A three-year period of exchange rate stability followed (1977-79). In contrast, during the early 1980s the drachma experienced high rates of depreciation against the dollar which included two 15% discrete devaluations in 1983 and 1985 (see Figure 3.10). In 1988 the BoG introduced the policy of the strong drachma and focused its attention on the GDR/ECU and GDR/DM exchange rates. Since then, the exchange rate of the

[28] In 1974 the average drachma/dollar parity was 30 drachmas per US$; in 1975 it went up to 32.1 drachmas per dollar; and in 1976 it increased further to 36.5 drachmas per dollar.

Figure 3.10

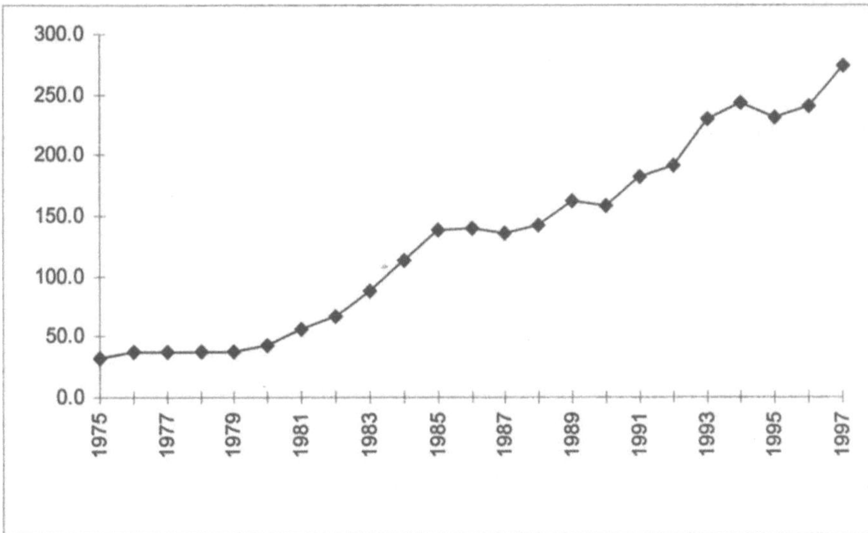

Drachmas per US Dollar
Source: Bank of Greece, Monthly Statistical Bulletin, various editions.

drachma against the US Dollar has become endogenous and it is determined indirectly by the movements of the ECU/$ rate.

Figure 3.11 presents the movements of the drachma against the ECU and the DM. As most of the main European currencies were appreciating against the dollar in the late 1970s, the depreciation of the drachma against the ECU and the DM during that period was more pronounced than what it was against the dollar. The 1980s saw even more pronounced depreciation rates until the introduction of the strong drachma policy in 1988. Since then, the depreciation of the drachma against the ECU and the DM has been declining (see Figure 3.12 and Table 3.4). The drachma stayed out of the wave of depreciations which hit many European countries in 1992-93. In addition, by increasing dramatically its overnight intervention rate in the interbank money market, the BoG managed to avert a drachma devaluation in 1994 after the liberalization of capital movements. Finally, in contrast to the Spanish peseta and the Portuguese escudo, the drachma was not devalued during the European exchange rate crisis of March 1995. All in all, one might say that for some time prior to the March 1998 devaluation, namely over the last three years or so (1995-97), the strong drachma policy had established a near fixed exchange rate regime against the ECU which had even led to a nominal appreciation of the drachma against the DM (and a number of other European currencies) in 1996-97. However, this situation came to an end in March 1998 when the Greek national currency was devalued by 14% against the ECU and joined the ERM.

Figure 3.11

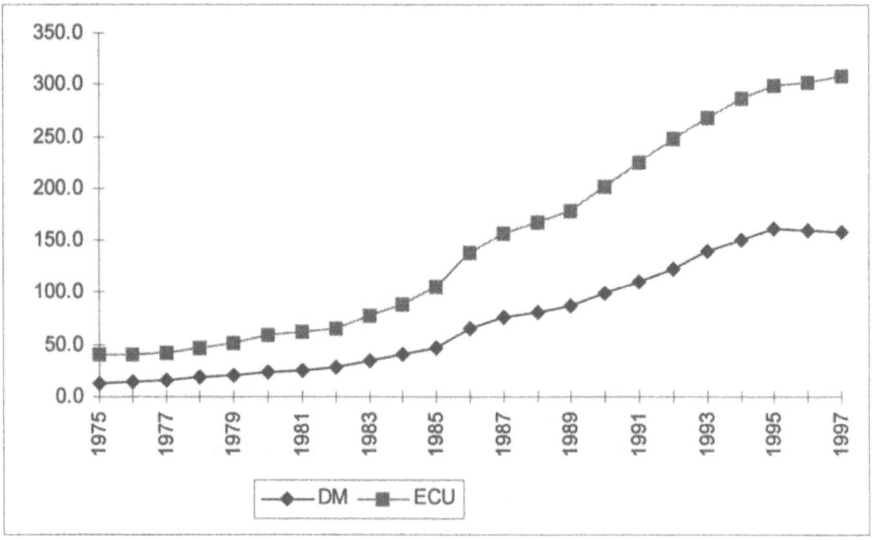

Drachmas per ECU and Drachmas per DM
Source: Bank of Greece, Monthly Statistical Bulletin, various editions.

Table 3.4

Period	US Dollar	ECU	DM
1975-79	4.4	7.3	11.8
1980-89	16.5	13.7	15.9
1990-97	7.0	7.1	7.9

Nominal depreciation of the drachma (average annual % change)
Source: Authors' calculations based on data taken from the Bank of Greece, Monthly Statistical Bulletin, various editions.

Figure 3.12

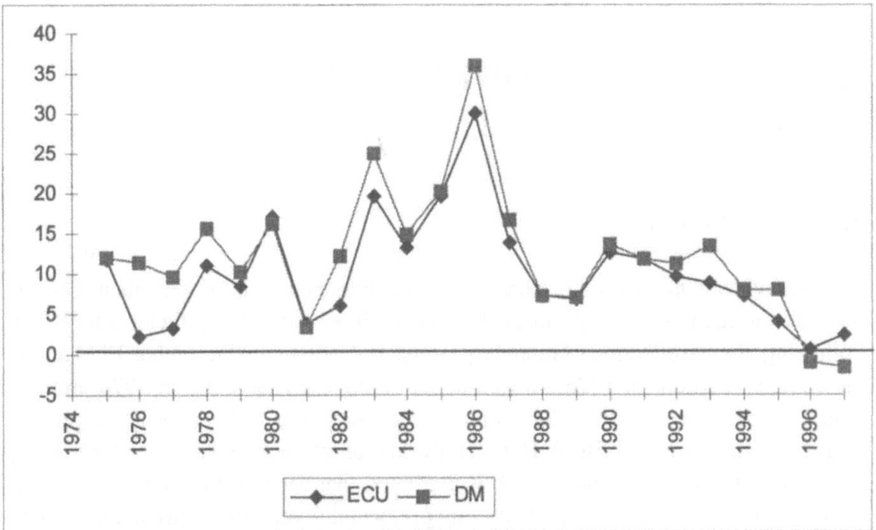

Nominal depreciation of the drachma against the ECU and the DM (annual % change)
Source: Authors' calculations based on data taken from the Bank of Greece, Monthly Statistical Bulletin, various editions.

Chapter 4

RECENT GREEK MONETARY POLICIES

4.1. Introduction

Having reviewed in the previous chapter the main monetary developments in Greece, we are now ready to attempt an evaluation of Greek monetary policies after 1975. Following the introduction of monetary targets in Germany in December 1974 and in the United Kingdom in 1976, Greece adopted monetary targeting in 1976 and this policy regime lasted until 1988. With a few exceptions, all monetary targets set during this period were missed. Here, an evaluation of the monetary targeting policy regime in Greece will be attempted. It is argued that for monetary targets to be an effective policy, a constant (or sufficiently predictable) velocity of circulation and no money financing of government deficits have to be assumed. We draw special attention to a structural feature of the Greek monetary system, the direct financing of the government's deficit from the central bank (a policy that has been effectively banned since 1st January 1994 in accordance with the Maastricht Treaty provisos). This money financing was the main cause of the constant overshooting of monetary targets that resulted in the high inflation rates experienced in Greece throughout this period. Next, an evaluation of the current policy regime will follow, namely, that of nominal exchange rate targeting. The experience from other countries has shown that for a small open economy, exchange rate targeting is quite an effective policy for bringing inflation down (mainly through its effect on imported inflation), but only in the short term. In the long term, such a policy might have serious effects upon the current account of the country. In Greece, there is little disagreement among economists and policy-makers that the *strong drachma* policy has been successful in bringing down the inflation rate to 6% in 1997. However, this has been achieved at the expense of higher and higher external imbalances during the years that this policy has been implemented. Moreover, what is the cause for further concern is that despite the recent welcome drop in Greek inflation, the latter still remains three times higher than the European average inflation rate.

The remainder of the chapter is organized as follows. In the next section, we briefly review the theory of intermediary targets, paying particular attention to the monetary and exchange targeting regimes. In section 4.3. we critically assess the monetary strategies that have been adopted recently in Greece, including the Greek experience with monetary targets, the strong drachma policy and the drachma's recent participation in the Exchange Rate Mechanism (ERM).

4.2. Some preliminaries

The need for intermediate targets arises because the tools, or instruments, of monetary policy (reserve requirements, open market operations, etc.) are not directly related to the final policy goals (price stability, real output growth, etc.). Monetary policy instruments, which are under the control of the monetary authorities, affect directly the so-called *operating targets* which can acquire an aggregate form (e.g. monetary base, non-borrowed reserves). However, even though operating targets are directly influenced by central bank actions, their relationship with the final policy goals might be weak, necessitating the use of an additional group of variables, called *intermediate targets,* which are more closely related to the final policy goals and serve as operational guides to policy. Intermediate targets that fall between the operating targets and ultimate policy goals may take the form of a quantity (e.g. a monetary aggregate like M1 or M2, a credit aggregate and the nominal value of GNP), or of a price (such as an interest rate or the exchange rate).

Intermediate targets should satisfy three criteria: they should be controllable, measurable and have a predictable effect on the final variable they are supposed to influence directly. Controllability is necessary in order for the authorities to be able to get their targets on track in those cases where they have diverged from the desired course. Measurability is needed in order to determine the degree to which the targets of monetary policy are off track. Intermediate targets must also have predictable effects on the variables they are supposed to influence in order for the authorities to determine the type of adjustment in these targets necessary to attain the final goals. Structural breaks like financial innovation and deregulation can lead to variations in the predictability of the effects of monetary policy actions. Hence, the choice of intermediate targets might change over time, particularly when a monetary aggregate is used as an intermediate target.

In practice most countries have used either monetary or exchange rate targets. Germany initiated the use of monetary aggregates as intermediate targets in 1974 against the background of rising inflation. Monetary targets were set annually and, initially, preference was given to central bank money defined as currency in circulation plus banks' required reserves (at constant reserve ratios) on deposits. The setting of the targets was conditional on projected values of inflation rates, output growth and velocity changes. In 1988, the monetary authorities, responding to unexpected shifts in currency demand, replaced the central bank money stock by M3 as the intermediate target.[1] Despite the emphasis laid on monetary aggregates, the Bundesbank has also given at times special consideration to indicators such as the

[1] The size of M3 as a very broad aggregate was not affected by these shifts even though its composition did change. In contrast, the size of central bank money was affected, something that led to its suspension as an intermediate target.

exchange rate. For example, the Bundesbank allowed the targeted aggregate to overrun its target range in 1977-78 in order to control the upward pressure on the DM against the US dollar. The opposite happened in early 1989 in response to a weak DM. In the United Kingdom, a Labour Government adopted monetary targets (M3) in 1976. However, as such a monetary control belt was, at that time, essentially cosmetic. The real job was left to Mrs. Thatcher in 1979 with the Medium-Term Financial Strategy (MTFS). Amongst other things, this strategy consisted of a commitment to a five-year rolling targets for gradually decelerating M3. Mrs. Thatcher deliberately sought to tie the government's hands through the MTFS. As in other countries, the close relationship between M3 and nominal income broke down in early 1980s. The reason for that was the Big Bang of 1979 and the abolition of exchange controls that prompted an inflow of foreign capital and an increase in the borrowing of the domestic private sector. The outcome was the M3's overshooting of its target in 1980, 1981 and the mid- 1980s. In 1986 the authorities announced targets for M0 (monetary base), the narrowest of the monetary aggregates that was thought to be in a stable relationship with economic activity. In March 1987 the use of monetary targets was suspended.

The idea behind the use of monetary aggregates is coming straight from the Quantity Theory of Money, namely that there is a long-run relationship between money supply growth and inflation so that controlling money supply growth is necessary for the control of inflation. This stable relationship between monetary growth and inflation is based upon the assumption of a predictable velocity as it was the case, for example, in the USA until the early 1980s. The choice among alternative monetary aggregates has been based mostly on empirical analysis with respect to the stability and predictability of the relationships of the monetary aggregate with the policy instrument and nominal income. This empirical methodology to identify the "best" monetary aggregate has been criticized in the literature for two reasons (see e.g. Modigliani and Papademos, 1980): first, any observed historical stability of the aggregate/nominal income relationships must depend on the type of monetary policy that is applied during the sample period. Hence, the existence of a stable relationship in the past does not imply that such a relationship should be necessarily observed in the future under a different future monetary strategy; second, the stability and predictability of the monetary aggregate/income relationship should be expected to vary over time as it depends on the structure and stability of the financial markets which vary in time as well.

Turning now to exchange rate targets, one may notice that these can be useful as an anti-inflationary device for countries where inflation arises from expansionary domestic monetary policies, or in the case where it is imported. Exchange rate targeting limits the independence of monetary policy and therefore, it forces governments to pursue conservative inflation policies as their ability to inflate or accommodate inflationary pressures is lost. In addition, as Giavazzi and Pagano (1988) have shown, fixing the exchange to a hard currency country permits the borrowing of counter-inflation reputation as the "tying of the hands" of the policy-makers allows them to establish credible monetary policies with beneficial effects on inflationary expectations. Finally, targeting the exchange rate may also prove a useful policy for countries where inflation is to a large extent imported. Under a strong currency policy, the domestic currency does not depreciate by the full size of the inflation differential between the domestic country and its major trading partners. Such a policy reduces imported inflation at the expense, however, of a loss in competitiveness. Real world examples of exchange rate targeting include the British experience within the context of the Exchange Rate Mechanism (ERM) in Europe. Following the abandonment of monetary targets in 1987, Britain started to shadow closely the DM, something which led to sterling's participation in the ERM in 1990. However, in September 1992, the British currency was forced to exit the ERM; this triggered the collapse of the entire system in less than a year. Since then, the Bank of England has adopted an inflation-targeting policy regime.

4.3. Recent monetary strategies in Greece

4.3.1. The Greek experience with monetary targets

Monetary targets in Greece were introduced for the first time in 1976. Initially, the BoG set point targets for the rate of growth of narrow money supply M0 (i.e. notes and coins in circulation) and the rate of growth of bank credit. The targets were set according to the desired position in the balance of payments and projections regarding the rates of growth of real GDP, inflation and interest rates. In 1983 the BoG abandoned M0 and started targeting the rate of growth of M3. In addition, it switched from point to range targets. This arrangement formed the basis of Greek monetary strategy until 1988, the year that the BoG introduced the strong drachma policy. During the period 1988-94 Greece followed a monetary strategy which can be formally described as monetary targets subject to (increasing) exchange rate constraints. Finally, during the period 1995-97 the BoG focused on the exchange rate target[2].

[2] Here we have to mention that the BoG continued to announce annual range targets for the rate of growth of credit and M3 until 1997. However, the 1998 Monetary Programme did not set any target for these variables.

Figure 4.1

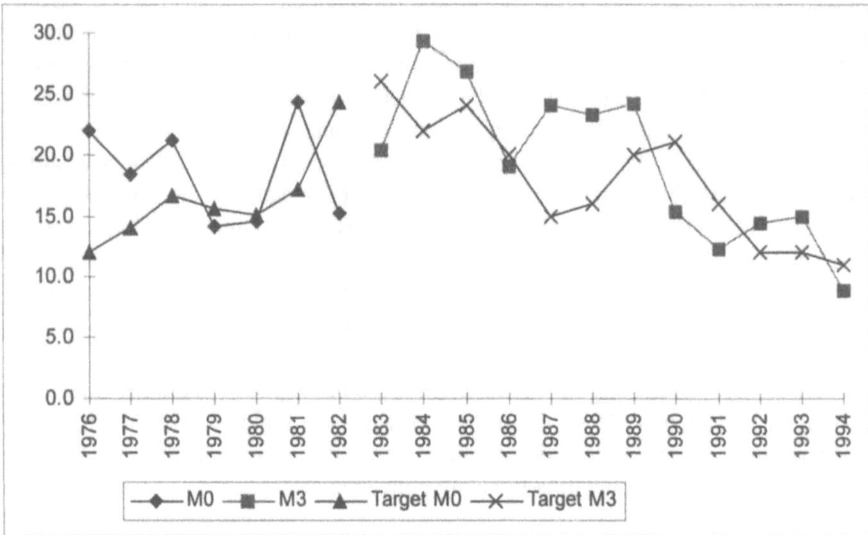

Rate of growth of money supply: targets and outcomes, 1976-94
Target values for M3 represent the upper limit of the target zone.
Source: Bank of Greece, Monthly Statistical Bulletin, various editions.

Speaking in general terms, one might say that the Greek experience with monetary targets has been rather disappointing. The overwhelming majority of the money and credit growth targets were missed and, perhaps more importantly, during the period of their implementation (i.e. 1976-94) Greece experienced quite high inflation rates[3]. More specifically, between 1976 and 1982, i.e. the period that the authorities targeted the rate of growth of M0, the BoG met the target only on two out of seven occasions and average CPI inflation was equal to 17.1% (the EU15 average being 11.2%). On the other hand, during the period 1983-94, the BoG met its target only on five out of twelve occasions and average CPI remained at 16.6% (the EU15 average being 5.1%). All in all, during the 1976-94 period, monetary targets were met only on eight out of nineteen occasions (see Figure 4.1). A similar

[3] Inflation developments in Greece during the period 1975-97 are examined in chapter 5, section 5.3.

Figure 4.2

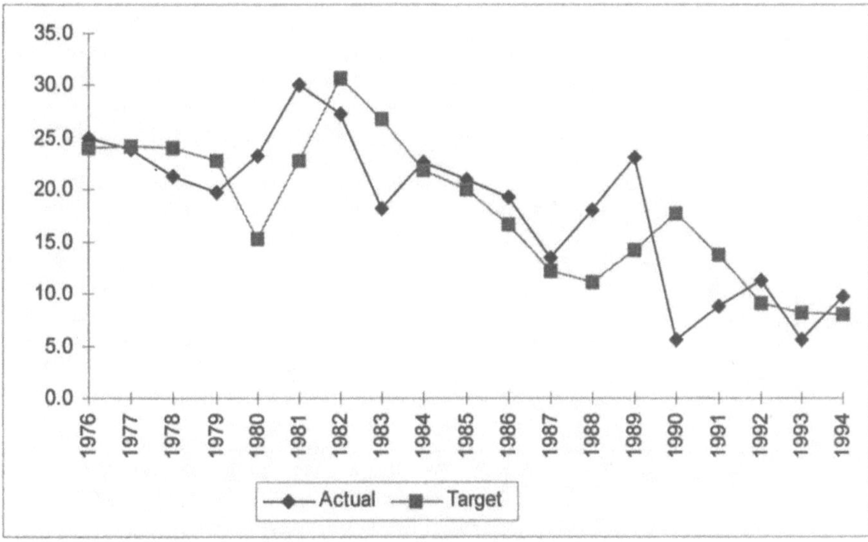

Rate of growth of bank credit: targets and outcomes, 1976-94
Source: Bank of Greece, Monthly Statistical Bulletin, various editions.

case is observed in the case of the percentage change of total banking credit (see Figure 4.2). Finally, the actual level of inflation took values above its projection in all but four cases (see chapter 5).

The question which naturally arises is why the Greek record with money supply targeting turned out to be so unimpressive. The first answer which can be provided has to do with the fiscal policy followed in the post-1975 period. More specifically, in the face of fiscal expansion which was discussed in chapter 2, the BoG, which at the time enjoyed no independence from the government, was actually obliged to provide the latter with direct excess deficit financing, mainly in the form of increased credit to the public sector. As a result, during the period 1979-89, and even in years when monetary restraint had been announced (i.e. 1982-83 and 1986-87), the percentage change of credit to public sector was consistently well above the threshold of 20%. The latter increased its share in total bank credit almost threefold (from 12% in 1979 to 30% in 1989, see Figure 4.3). In relation to the above, another factor explaining the missing of the monetary targets refers to the effect of the political budget cycle over the economy. One might observe that years of general elections (1981, 85, 89, 93) were characterized by money supply and credit growth rates well beyond the targets set (see Figures

Figure 4.3

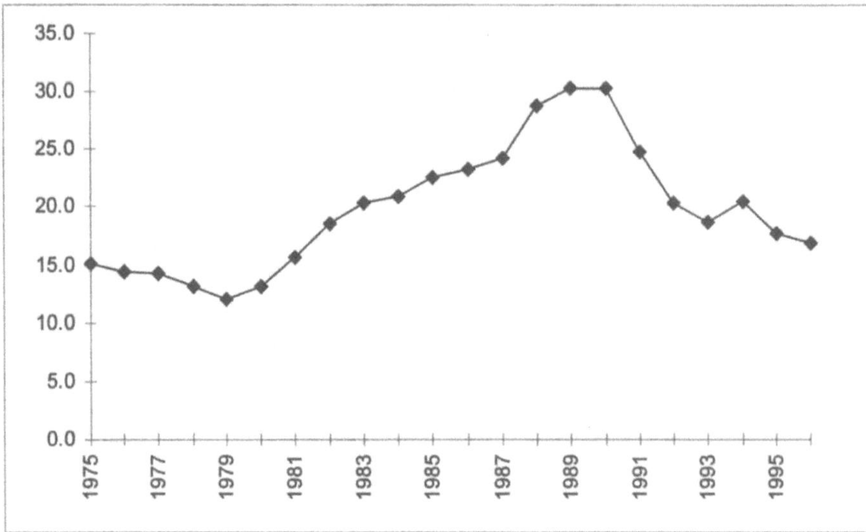

Credit to the public sector as % of total bank credit
Source: Bank of Greece, Monthly Statistical Bulletin, various editions.

4.1 and 4.2).

The second reason behind the failure of the BoG to meet its monetary targets refers to the instability of the income velocity of money. As we have seen earlier in this chapter, the quantity theory of money, i.e. the basic theory behind a monetary targeting regime, implies that the successful conduct of monetary policy by such a regime presupposes that the percentage change of money velocity is either constant (or stationary) or largely predictable. However, Figures 4.4 and 4.5 reveal that velocity[4] in Greece is not stationary. On the other hand, it would appear that the condition referring to the predictability of velocity is not valid either. Figure 4.6 suggests that during the period 1976-82, i.e. the years that the BoG targeted the rate of growth of M0, the percentage change of velocity fluctuated around its mean in a non-systematic way. A similar phenomenon is observed for the period 1983-

[4] In Figures 4.4 and 4.5, the value of velocity is estimated by means of dividing the value of nominal GDP by the level of M0, M1 and M3 respectively.

94 when Greece targeted the rate of growth of M3.

Space limitations do not allow a detailed discussion of the reasons behind the above mentioned instability of money velocity in Greece and the year-to-year fluctuations of its growth rate. Therefore, here we restrict ourselves in highlighting some key points. A standard argument in the literature explaining the instability of the narrow money supply velocity is that the use of monetary aggregates such as M0 leads to a mispecification of the equation describing the quantity theory of money. In relation to this, another argument is that nominal GDP is not the appropriate variable for the estimation of velocity because it does not capture wealth effects in the money demand function caused by changes in expectations regarding the future incomes stream. As far as the velocity of M3 is concerned, in addition to the above, one might also suggest that the high inflation conditions which prevailed in Greece after 1975 may have had a negative impact on agents' demand for money, a fact which may be partly responsible for the decline of M3 velocity between 1975 and 1987. The improvement in inflation expectations which

Figure 4.4

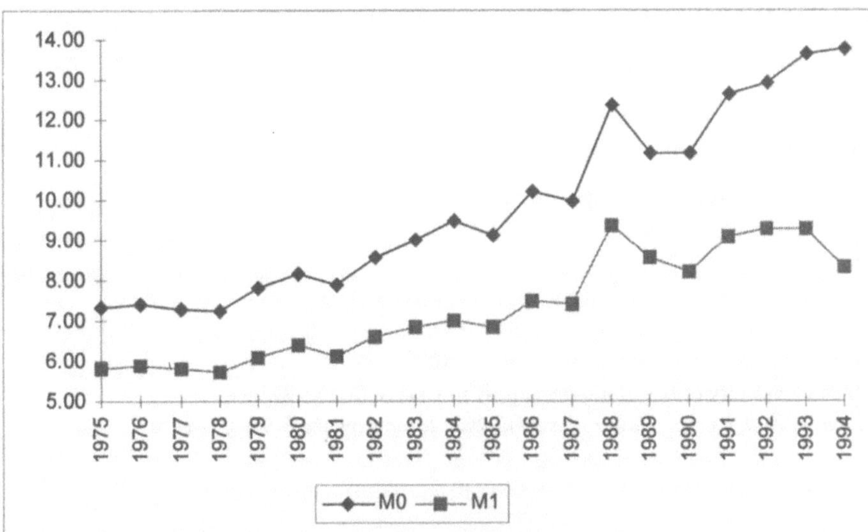

Income velocity of narrow money supply in Greece, 1975-94

Source: Authors' calculations based on data taken from the Bank of Greece, Monthly Statistical Bulletin, various editions.

took place in the 1990s may have reversed this trend [5]. Furthermore, it can also be argued that the long and variable lags present in the conduct of monetary policy imply that the high growth rates of money supply and credit increase which were taking place during those years were not accompanied by similar increases in GDP, thus leading to a reduction in velocity. In addition, the instability of velocity in Greece after 1988 and the unpredictability of its rate of growth is most probably related to the regime shift caused by the process of financial liberalization introduced in 1987, the introduction of government bonds and the increase in nominal and real interest rates which took place between 1988 and 1994. Moreover, the fact that financial liberalization did not take place in a "big-bang" fashion but in a gradual way, which meant continuous changes over a prolonged

Figure 4.5

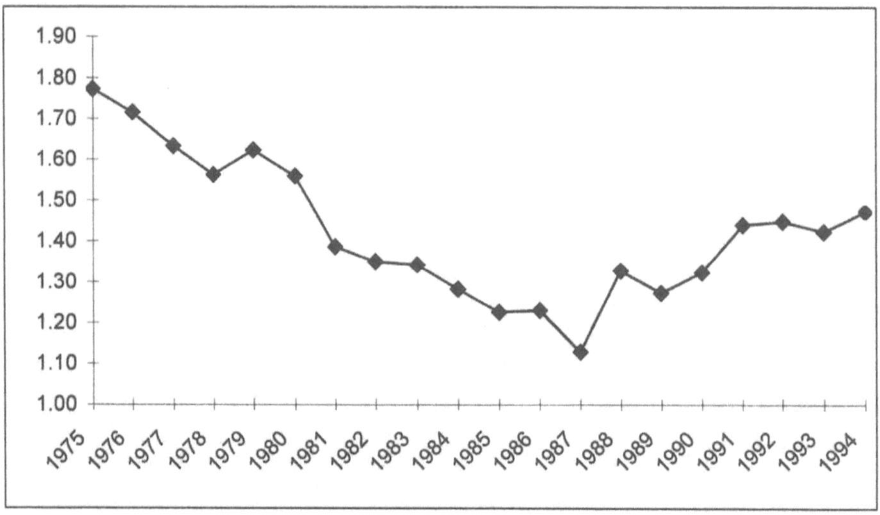

Income velocity of broad money supply in Greece (M3), 1975-94
Source: Authors' calculations based on data taken from the Bank of Greece

[5] Here we have to make a special reference to year 1988 when the definition of nominal GDP was revised to include more items. The revision implied an increase in the value of nominal GDP approximately equal to 15%-20%. The dramatic increase in velocity observed in 1988 is definitely related to this revision.

Figure 4.6

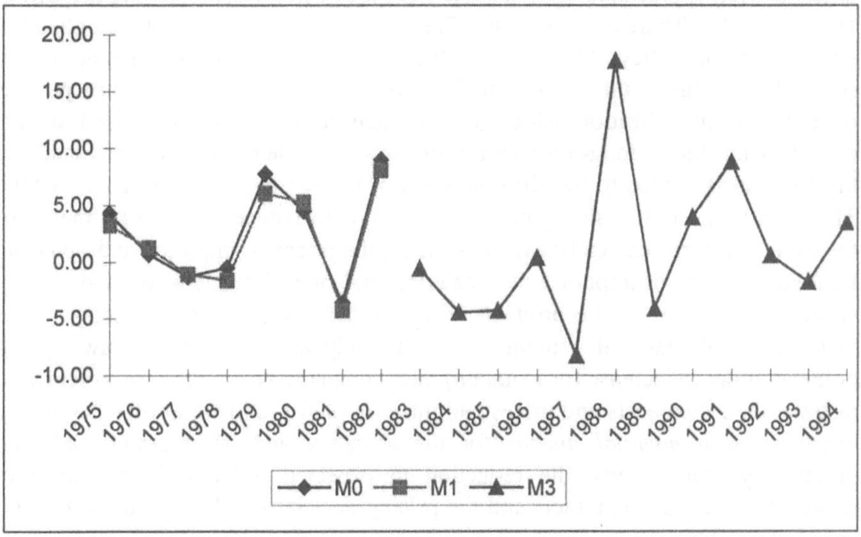

Annual percentage change of income velocity of money, 1975-94
Source: Authors' calculations based on data taken from the Bank of Greece,

period of time, makes the assessment of its impact on velocity even more difficult. However, as far as the increase in M3 velocity which took place after 1988 is concerned, one might suggest that financial innovation and the introduction of government bonds offering investors attractive rates of return led to a substantial shift of savings from time deposits to government securities and other forms of investment which are not included in M3. This fact, combined with the more tight monetary conditions imposed by the BoG in the 1990s, has contributed to a rate of growth of M3 lower than the one of nominal GDP, thus leading to an increase in M3 velocity.

4.3.2. The *strong drachma* policy

(i) The case for a "strong drachma" policy

The strong drachma policy was introduced in 1988 and involved a rate of nominal depreciation of the drachma against the ECU smaller than the existing inflation differential between Greece and the EU average. The rate of nominal depreciation against the ECU had been declining all along the 1988-97 period and in fact, over the period 1995-97 the strong drachma policy had effectively created an almost fixed exchange rate regime against the ECU. Actually, over the last three years the drachma even appreciated against some European currencies, including the DM in 1996 and 1997. There are a number of reasons which led to the BoG adopting the strong drachma policy. The first was the failure of the BoG to meet its money supply targets during the 1976-87 period (see above). The second was the process of financial liberalization which was introduced in 1987 and raised doubts regarding the future long-run stability of the money demand function. Finally, a third reason is related to the firm intention of Greece to participate in the EMU. The main purpose of a strong currency policy is to reduce inflation by means of the following three channels: (a) by reducing the prices of imported and domestic final goods made of imported raw materials and other intermediate goods (b) by reducing the prices of the products of the traded sector of the economy: firms exposed to international competition cannot rely any more on a crawling-peg policy in order to increase (or maintain) their competitiveness: they are expected to restraint their own costs and prices and increase their production efficiency (c) by operating as a *nominal anchor* for the economy and, as a result, reducing inflationary expectations: the reduction in expected inflation is subsequently reflected in the wage contracts and the pricing decisions of firms and, ultimately, in actual inflation.

(ii) Some positive results

The introduction of the strong drachma policy back in 1988 was not accompanied by the best possible economic circumstances. The year 1988-89 was a period of particularly strong fiscal expansion which aggravated the already huge and mounting imbalances of the Greek economy and led to a substantial increase in inflation in 1990-91. As a result, during the early days of its implementation, private agents were rather sceptical about the sustainability of the new policy and fears were expressed that it would not be possible to avoid a new, major devaluation of the drachma, similar to the ones of 1983 and 1985. However, in spite of all the difficulties, these fears were not confirmed. In contrast, the BoG managed to beat speculators by not devaluing the currency on four occasions of exchange rate crisis[6]. These achievements, combined with the stabilization attempt undertaken in the 1990s, succeeded in convincing the private sector that the BoG was indeed determined to defend the parity of the drachma, a fact which

6 Namely, the two EMS crises of 1992-93, the crisis of May 1994, and the European monetary upheaval of 1995. The BoG also managed to beat speculators during the crisis of November 1997 but, as we will argue below, the implications of that crisis were more serious compared to the previous ones.

Figure 4.7

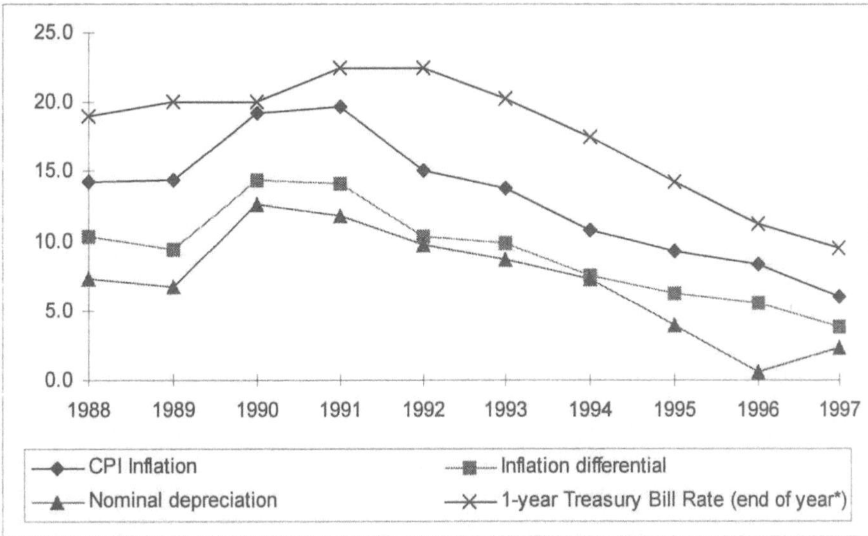

Annual CPI inflation, inflation differential against the EU and nominal depreciation against the ECU

* the 1997 figure refers to September

Source: European Economy No 64, Statistical Appendix and Bank of Greece, Economic Bulletin, various editions

increased the credibility of the national currency and allowed the monetary authority to continue on the same path by further reducing the rate of crawling peg. Figures 4.7 and 4.8 suggest that during the last five years, the results of the application of the strong drachma policy became obvious as the average CPI inflation rate went down to 6% in 1997 compared[7] with 19.7% in 1991.

(iii) The limits of the strong drachma policy

The recent reduction in inflation represents, of course, a most welcome development. However, such an improvement has come at a cost and this is an issue which, until recently, had not been adequately addressed in Greece. The

[7] For further discussion on the effects of the strong drachma policy on inflation, see also chapter 5 section 5.3.2.

Figure 4.8

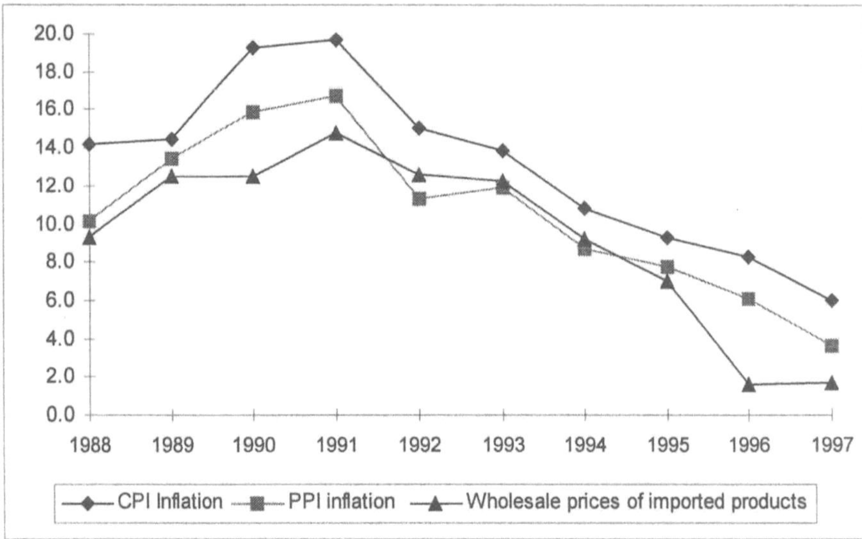

Domestic and imported inflation
Source: Bank of Greece, Economic Bulletin, Statistical Appendix, various editions.

point is that by its very nature, a strong currency policy has certain limits which in the case of Greece had become increasingly evident and were indicating that eventually, it would not be possible to avoid a devaluation of the drachma.

The first limitation of a strong currency policy is that in the absence of a tight fiscal and incomes policy it creates competitiveness problems which are reflected in an increasing current account deficit. For a small open economy like Greece, the current account constraint is of particular importance. For this reason, it is necessary to analyze this point in some detail. A standard textbook approach to the determination of exchange rates is the Purchasing Power Parity (PPP) theory. The PPP theory states that in the *long-run,* nominal exchange rates move in such a way as to maintain the real exchange rate constant. In other words, their long-run movements reflect differences in inflation rates. From that point of view, a high inflation country should have a depreciating (in nominal terms) national currency[8].

[8] However, it is by no means the case that the adjustment of exchange rates to price

Recent empirical evidence (see Arghyrou, 1999c) suggests that in the case of Greece, the long-run PPP hypothesis is valid. The implication of this is the following: (a) As the real exchange rate is a measure of relative prices and, as such, an indicator of international competitiveness[9], the recent reduction in Greek inflation (caused by the application of the strong drachma policy) has come at the cost of a competitiveness loss. The recent developments in the field of the current account indicate that this loss has put pressure on the external sector of the economy; and (b) as long as the currently applied strong currency policy had driven the drachma off its long-run equilibrium, the probability of a forced devaluation could not be ruled out. Such an eventuality was even more probable in the light of the recent developments in the fields of fiscal and incomes policy as well as the latest movements of the current account. The point is that during the adjustment period (i.e. the time needed in order to eliminate the inflation differential against the EU average) the existence of an overvalued currency implies that the maintenance of competitiveness of Greek products could be achieved by means of the following two ways: either through a reduction in the profit margins of domestic firms, something which has obvious limits; or through a reduction in the rate of change of the nominal unit labour costs in the traded sector of the economy, i.e. through a restraint in nominal wage increases or/ and the realization of productivity gains. This option is clearly preferable in comparison to the previous one, as it maintains a high profitability level, but presupposes a certain degree of flexibility in the labour market and an adequate fiscal and incomes policy.

Table 4.1 presents the movements of the real exchange rate over the last ten years. When domestic and foreign price levels are approximated by CPI inflation rates, it seems that the drachma had appreciated all along the post-1988 period with the appreciation being more pronounced in 1988-89 and 1995-97. When nominal unit labour costs are employed, it appears that the drachma had depreciated during the 1991-93 period but appreciated significantly thereafter. Furthermore, the 1988-89 and 1995-97 competitiveness losses indicated by the movements of nominal unit labour costs exceed by far those indicated by the alternative definition for the two price levels. The above mentioned reduction in competitiveness influenced both the profitability level and the external sector of the economy. Tables 4.1 and 4.2 suggest that over the last five years (1993-97), in the absence of a restrictive incomes policy, Greek firms attempted to retain the market shares by means of reducing their profit margins. This stands in contrast to the period 1990-93 when restrained increases in nominal wages gave rise to an increase in profitability.

---

variations takes place instantly. In the *short-run*, spot exchange rates can deviate substantially from the rates implied by the PPP condition.

[9] As such, it is even more appropriate in the case of Greece, a country whose exporting products do not possess a high degree of monopolistic power (as they belong to the traditional, low-technology sectors of the economy) and compete with products of other similar countries on a more or less perfect competition basis.

Table 4.1

Year	Nominal depreciation against ECU (1)	Inflation differential* (2)	NULC Growth differential* (3)	Real Appreciation (-) Depreciation (+) (4) =(1) - (2)	Real Appreciation (-) Depreciation(+) (5) = (1) - (3)
1988	7.2	10.3	12.4	-3.1	-5.2
1989	6.7	9.5	14.7	-2.8	-8.0
1990	12.6	14.4	14.1	-1.8	-1.5
1991	11.8	14.1	2.3	-2.3	9.6
1992	9.7	10.3	6.9	-0.6	2.8
1993	8.7	9.6	8.5	-0.9	0.2
1994	7.2	7.6	12.2	-0.4	-5.0
1995	4.0	6.3	8.7	-2.3	-4.7
1996	0.5	5.7	8.0	-5.2	-7.5
1997	2.3	3.8	6.1	-1.5	-3.8

NULC stands for Nominal Unit Labour Cost
* against EU15 average

Real appreciation (-) / depreciation (+) of the drachma against the ECU (annual % change)

Data source: European Economy No. 64, Statistical Appendix.

Productivity gains, which were made possible by the discontinuation of the operation of a number of inefficient marginal firms and the reduction in personnel to which the remaining firms proceeded, also helped. But over the last five years (1993-97), a rather loose incomes policy highlighted the limitations of strong drachma policy as it has led both to a profitability reduction and increasing difficulties in the external sector of the economy, giving rise to a widening current account deficit (see Table 4.2). This deterioration has come as a result of a near-stagnation of exports and significant increases in imports of goods[10]. Of course, these developments are not determined exclusively by the strong drachma policy. For example, the European recession in the early 1990s and the only modest recovery which followed during the 1994-96 period must have played a role. However, it is straightforward that in the absence of labour cost restraint, the strong drachma policy increased the relative price of Greek products and services against foreign competitive products.

All in all, the implications of the present policy mix (high increases in labour cost and strong drachma policy) are quite serious. In addition to creating problems in

Table 4.2

Year	CPI inflation*	Wage inflation*	% change in NULC*	Profitability (1961-73=100)	Current account (% in GDP)
1988	14.2	18.6	15.2	52.9	-1.8
1989	14.4	24.0	19.9	48.8	-4.3
1990	19.2	23.1	24.6	49.9	-4.7
1991	19.7	14.3	9.1	57.5	-3.8
1992	15.0	10.7	11.7	62.0	-3.2
1993	13.7	8.1	8.7	66.5	-1.7
1994	10.8	12.2	11.9	66.4	-1.0
1995	9.3	12.5	11.3	65.4	-2.7
1996	8.3	11.7	10.1	65.6	-3.5
1997	6.0	9.4	7.3	66.5	-3.7

* annual percentage change
NULC stands for Nominal Unit Labour Cost

Inflation, labour cost, profitability and current account, 1988-97
Data source: European Economy No 64, Statistical Appendix.

[10] It is quite striking that while the 1988 figure for exports of goods was 5613.6 million US Dollars, in 1995 the same figure was just 5774.2 (in market values). As far as imports are concerned, the 1995 figure (22854 million US$) is nearly twice as much when compared with the 1988 figure (12556 million).

Figure 4.9

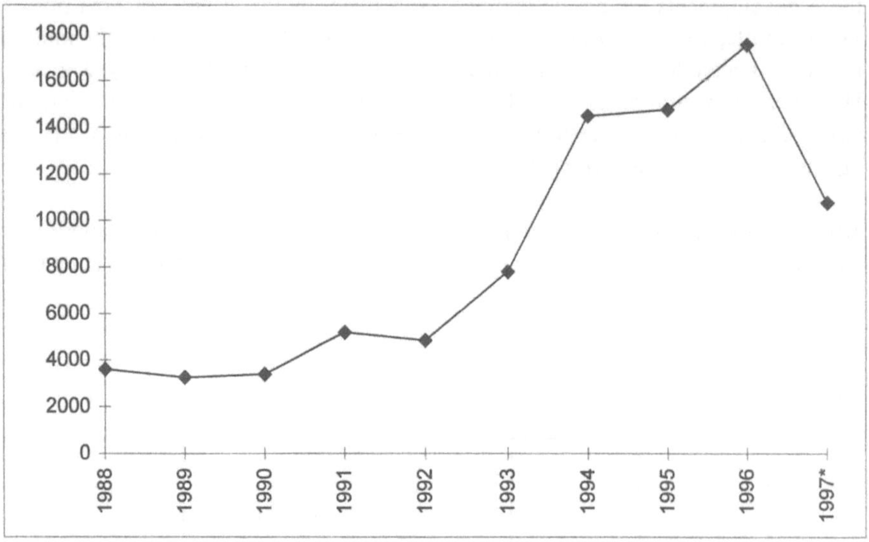

Foreign exchange reserves minus gold (end of year, millions of US Dollars)
* October 1997
Source: IMF International Financial Statistics, CD 09-97

the external sector of the economy, the policy mix had a strong anti-development character because by squeezing the profit margins of the firms operating in the traded sector of the economy, it discouraged private investment and increased the scope for further development of the already big share of the black economy. The conclusion is that, as the scope for further productivity and efficiency gains must now be rather limited, in the sense that during a period of nine years (1988-97), Greek firms must have nearly exhausted their limits for improvements of this kind. The viability of a number of Greek firms given the continuation of the strong drachma policy was, at least, questionable.

A second limitation of the strong drachma policy refers to the increasing *liquidity problems* which it had been creating. As the implications of excess liquidity for inflation are quite serious, it is necessary to discuss this point in some detail. The strong drachma policy implied that the domestic nominal interest rate should be higher than the sum of the average foreign interest rate and the expected rate of the nominal drachma depreciation. The difference reflects a risk premium which private agents demand in order to invest in drachma denominated assets. This premium reflects the risk of an unexpected drachma devaluation and the risk of a public debt default. The remarkable determination which the BoG displayed in defending the drachma and the resulting exchange rate stability which prevailed during the period 1995-1997 seem to have convinced agents (at least until recently) that the above risks were small. This resulted in capital inflows of unprecedented levels (see Figure 4.9) which were primarily due to: (a) foreign portfolio investment, mainly of short and medium-term nature, attracted by the real interest rate differential existing between Greece and the rest of the world; (b) increasing borrowing of Greek (private and public) firms in foreign currency[11]. The problem with the above mentioned capital inflows is that they tend to increase the money supply (M3 and M4) and, as a result, they jeopardize the anti-inflationary stance of monetary policy.

Under these circumstances, the BoG had three options: First, to create conditions which would allow a reduction in interest rates. Second, to follow a less tight exchange rate policy. Third, to intervene in the money market (by means of manipulating the interbank bank interest rate and through open-market operations) and the foreign exchange market. Up to March 1998, the BoG had been mainly employing the third solution. It is only fair to say that in this effort the Bank has been successful but has faced increasing difficulties[12] (see Brissimis and Gibson, 1997). The problem is that the monetary authority had been pursuing two parallel targets (a stable exchange rate and limited liquidity) using one policy instrument (interest rate) only. Of course, it is true that since 1993, when the secondary market for public bonds was created, the BoG has also been employing open market operations in the form of repurchasing agreements but the main instrument of controlling liquidity has been the manipulation of the interbank interest rate. Since the end of 1990 the BoG has been pursuing a gradual reduction in its intervention interest rates which is reflected in the movement of the interbank interest rate and the BoG rates (see Figure 4.10). However, it has been very cautious in doing that because a big reduction could have negative consequences in the form of undermining the very basis on which the strong drachma policy is based and increasing liquidity by means of a higher demand for drachma denominated loans. Therefore, on the one hand the BoG would like to see its intervention rates decline (in order to control capital inflows and support the external sector of the economy), but on the other hand it would like this reduction not happen too fast (in order to avoid exchange rate pressures and a domestically driven increase in liquidity). In the 1990s, this cautious, well-balanced attitude of

[11] In January 1997 the foreign exchange reserves of the Bank of Greece stood at 19600 million US Dollars compared with 4800 million in December 1992 and 7800 million in December 1993.

[12] Brissimis and Gibson (1997) have estimated that over the period 1991-95 the BoG managed to sterilize 65% of total capital inflows.

Figure 4.10

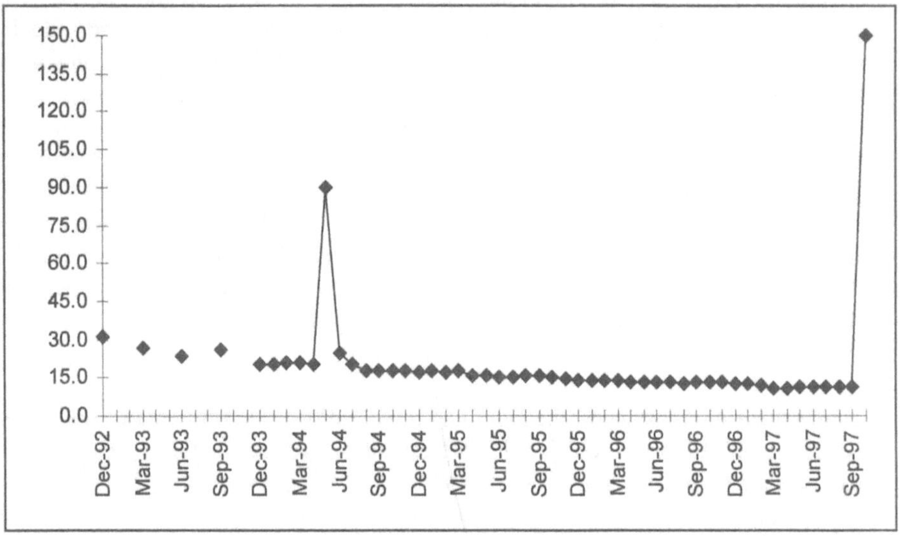

Intervention rate of the Bank of Greece in the interbank money market (monthly average)
Source: Bank of Greece, Economic Bulletin, various editions

the BoG has been disturbed by three factors: the occasional European exchange rate upheavals, the process of financial liberalization and the fiscal situation of the country.

With regard to the first factor, the four exchange rate crises which have taken place in autumn 1992, autumn 1993, May 1994 and March 1995 obliged the BoG to increase its intervention rates significantly, especially during the 1994 crisis. However, these increases were of temporary nature only and did not have any major impact in the market lending and borrowing rates. As far as the process of financial liberalization is concerned, this has put pressure on the liquidity of the economy by means of consumption credit and the development of new financial products. With regard to the third factor, the point is that the Treasury would like to see interest rates on public bonds declining as soon as possible in order to lighten the burden of interest payments on public debt. This created conflicts between monetary and fiscal policy, especially over the last three years (1994-97) when there have been some incidents of rather premature reductions in the interest rates of Treasury Bills. The importance of these premature reductions was clearly shown during the recent crisis of November 1997 (see below). As long as these reductions lead to a positive difference between the inter-bank and the Treasury Bill interest rates, they contribute to inflationary pressures by means of an increase in liquidity through an increase in M3; and an increase in consumption. In addition, liquidity problems were aggravated by the increasing borrowing of public firms in foreign currency. Such borrowing is equivalent to direct financing from the BoG, it was in direct conflict with the anti-inflationary stance of monetary policy and put pressure on the prospects of the public debt and in particular external debt, whose cost of servicing has now reached an unprecedented point by historical standards.

To sum up, the strong drachma policy contributed to a significant increase in liquidity with quite serious implications. The enormous capital inflows put pressure upon the BoG to reduce its interest rates but, on the other hand, a non-cautious reduction would deprive the policy of strong drachma its *raison d'être* and would jeopardize the anti-inflationary stance of exchange rate policy.

(iv) Credibility and sustainability problems leading to the March 1998 devaluation

The main message emerging from our discussion so far is that in spite of the fact that the strong drachma policy has indeed worked in lowering inflation, its limitations along with the rather limited progress achieved in the fields of fiscal consolidation and structural adjustments undermined its future credibility and sustainability and finally led to its discontinuation in March 1998. The truth of the matter is that as basic macroeconomic theory itself suggests, within the framework of a near-fixed exchange rate regime and in the presence of a continuing inflation differential with the rest of the countries of the system, the continuation of an overvalued currency policy for a long period of time, if not accompanied by other corrective measures, has negative effects on the real side of the economy. Such an economic situation cannot be sustained in the long-run. A strong currency policy can have long-lasting beneficial effects only if it is used as a "grace period" period for the realization of structural adjustments in the markets of goods, labour and money as well as a substantial improvement in the fiscal front. In the case of Greece however, over the last ten years very little has been done to that end and the burden of macroeconomic adjustment has been mainly carried by the exchange rate policy. On the other hand, it should always be remembered that in an environment of high capital mobility, the short-run portfolio investment attracted by the existing interest rate differential can fly out of the country at any moment. A negative domestic economic or political event, an international crisis, an increase in foreign interest rates could all create such conditions that a forced devaluation would be inevitable. This is a scenario which has already taken place in the case of many European currencies during the EMS crisis of 1992-93, in the case of Spain, Portugal and Mexico in 1995 and, more recently, during the South-East Asia crisis in 1997. In addition, the starting point of the crisis in Mexico, a country whose pre-crisis policy mix presented a number of interesting similarities with the policy mix applied by Greece before March 1998[13], was a political crisis and such events in Greece are not really rare. Only during the twenty months which preceded the crisis of November 1997 a number of upsets of this sort took place[14], confirming how quickly capital can fly out of the country[15].

---

[13] In the early 1990s the Mexican government, facing a large stock of public debt and a high inflation level, introduced a stabilization plan which included the following three features: (a) a strong-peso policy (b) a fiscal correction effort including a number of privatizations (c) a number of trade liberalization measures. This policy resulted to a primary public budget surplus but also to an overvalued peso which gave rise to an increasing deficit in the current account which was largely financed by an impressive amount of capital inflows in the form of short and medium-term maturity bonds payable in pesos but denominated in dollars in order to reduce the exchange rate risk associated with this form of investment. In December 1994 a political crisis in Mexico and an increase in the USA interest rates led to a sudden mass outflow of capital which obliged the Mexican government to devalue its currency and led to a real danger of public default. The International Monetary Fund and the USA government, anxious about the position of USA commercial banks (which had invested huge amounts of dollars in Mexico) rushed to the rescue of the Mexican government by lending an amount equal to 40 billion US Dollars. As a result, the Mexican government managed to pay its creditors (who left as they came, i.e. with dollars in hand and not with pesos) but at the end Mexico was left with an almost total elimination of its foreign reserves, a significant devaluation of the peso and a higher inflation rate thereafter.

[14] These events include (i) the leadership crisis in the ruling party (PASOK) in December 1995 when the late Prime Minister Andreas Papandreou got seriously ill and as a result he resigned (ii) the governmental crisis of spring 1996 when the forthcoming Congress of PASOK created uncertainty about the future course of economic policy (iii) the extreme tension in the relations between Greece and Turkey in January 1996 which almost led to a war between the two countries and (iv) the extreme tension in Cyprus in August 1996 which momentarily created the suspicion that the formation of a new major crisis between Greece and Turkey was well under way.

[15] At the beginning of the second leadership PASOK crisis the foreign exchange reserves of the BoG were equal to 16.5 billion US$. The party Congress was then set for the 28th of June 1996 and the odds were that the "orthodox" PASOK wing (considered as the advocates of a tax-and-spend policy) would prevail over the "modernization" wing led by the Prime Minister Mr. Kostas Simitis who is thought to be an advocate of a more disciplined economic policy. As a result, in March 1996 the reserves fell to 15.2 billion, in April to 15.1 billion, and in May to 11.9 billion. However, the "modernization" wing emerged victorious from the Congress and the reserves started increasing again thereafter.

Figure 4.11

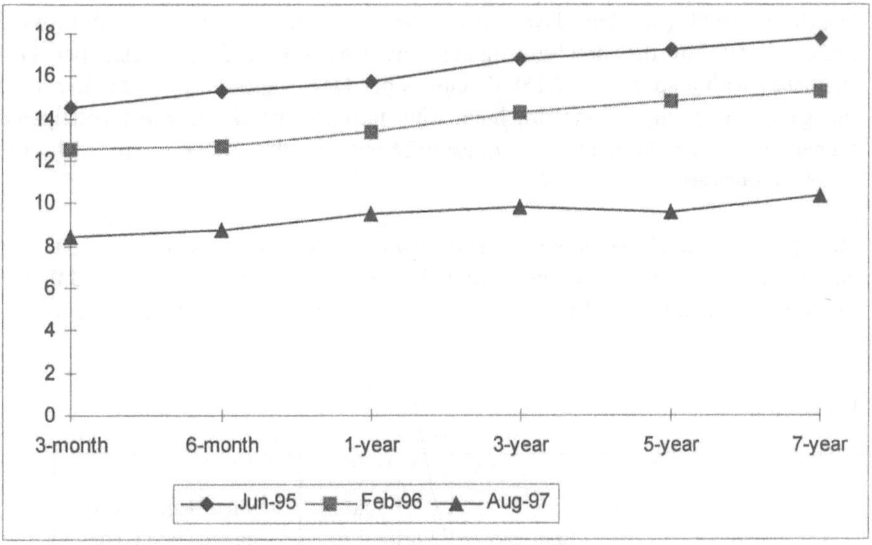

The yield curve in Greece, June 1994-August 1997
Source: Bank of Greece, Economic Bulletin No. 10, Statistical Appendix

The experience from these countries provided, in principle, some useful lessons regarding the policy of strong drachma and its sustainability. It was quite clear that one could not exclude the possibility that history might repeat itself in the case of Greece, especially in view of the rather loose (under the circumstances) stance of fiscal policy, the widening current account deficit, the high stock of public debt, the prospect of the accession of the drachma to the ERM (see below) and the unwillingness of the Greek government to issue long-term public bonds (i.e. bonds of maturity longer than a ten-year period) bearing interest rate similar to the EU average. By issuing such bonds the government would send a strong signal that the hard core of inflation has been put under control and will continue to be so in the future. Their absence was simply a signal to the opposite direction

Finally, the signals emerging from the shape of the yield curve in Greece before the October 1997 crisis were, if not discouraging, at least confusing. As Figure 4.11 reveals, during the period June 1994-August 1997 (i.e. a period when the drachma was effectively pegged to the DM), the slope of the yield curve remained positive. To the extend that forward interest rates reflect agents' expectations regarding the future movements of inflation, this might be interpreted as a sign that the markets were not convinced that a further reduction in inflation would take place. In other words, the shape of the yield curve can be seen as an indication that agents had concluded that the strong drachma policy had reached its limits and they were demanding a high risk premium in order to hold drachma-denominated government securities. Further support to this view is provided by Table 4.3. On March 4, 1998 (i.e. ten days before the devaluation) the one-year forward exchange rate of the drachma against the DM was 175 drachmas per DM compared with a spot rate of 158 drachmas per DM, suggesting an 11% expected change in the parity of the drachma. This implies that the markets anticipated exchange rate developments in a quite different way than those predicted by the Greek authorities.

The upshot of the above is that over the last three years or so, it was obvious that the future sustainability of the strong drachma policy was doubtful and that it would be difficult to avoid a devaluation of the Greek national currency. This is a

Table 4.3

	Spot rate	1-year Forward rate	Implied % of expected appreciation (-) or depreciation(+)
Austria (Sch)	7.06	7.05	-0.1
Belgium (BFr)	20.69	20.66	-0.2
Denmark (DKr)	3.82	3.83	0.1
Finland (FM)	3.04	3.03	-0.4
France (FFr)	3.36	3.36	0.0
Greece (GDr)	***158.5***	***175.9***	***11.0***
Ireland (IP)	0.40	0.41	0.9
Italy (L)	987.60	996.78	0.9
Luxembourg (LFr)	20.69	20.66	-0.2
Netherlands (FI)	1.13	1.13	-0.5
Portugal (Es)	102.72	102.94	0.2
Spain (Pes)	85.06	85.27	0.2
Sweden (SKr)	4.42	4.46	0.9
United Kingdom (GBP)	0.34	0.35	3.5

Spot and forward rates of EU currencies against the DM, March 4, 1998
Source: Financial Times, 4 March 1998

view which had been expressed explicitly in due course, i.e. well before the events of March 1998 (see Mourmouras 1997c and Mourmouras and Arghyrou, 1997) but was also inferred by some statements of the Governor of the BoG. A careful reading of the latter clearly reveals that the monetary authority was aware of the limitations of the strong drachma policy and was convinced that, in the absence of substantial progress in the fields of fiscal and structural adjustment, it would be difficult to sustain it. Clearly, under such circumstances the maintenance of the pre-devaluation exchange rate parity would most probably necessitate further increases in interest rates which would harm the economy further by means of increasing interest payments on public debt and surpressing investment expenditure without guaranteeing that a forced devaluation would be avoided in the event of a new exchange rate upheaval.

The validity of the views expressed above were largely confirmed during the exchange rate crisis of November 1997 which followed the Hong-Kong Stock Exchange crisis as the drachma was the only currency in the EU which was put under so strong pressure. Once again, the BoG defended the Greek national currency successfully by means of intervening in the spot foreign exchange market and increasing dramatically the Bank's intervention rate in the interbank money market. The latter reached the level of 150% in October 1997 compared to an 11.3% in September 1997 (see Figure 4.10). However, this victory was a pyrrhic one. On November 7, 1997, i.e. at the end of the crisis, the foreign exchange reserves of the Bank were down to approximately 10.5 billion US dollars compared to 19.5 billion US dollars on 30/1/97 (see Figure 4.9). In addition, the Treasury was obliged to increase the interest rates on government securities by almost two percentage points (from 9.5% in September 1997 to 11.3% in October 1997), something which implies that in 1998 interest payments on public debt would be significantly higher than previously anticipated.

All in all, the November 1997 crisis clearly showed that the markets had lost confidence in the drachma. The realization of this fact prompted (or perhaps obliged) the Greek authorities to proceed to a devaluation and ERM accession in March 1998. Both choices do not seem to have been part of the authorities' immediate intentions. This view is based on a number of government official statements which took place before and after the November 1997 crisis[16] but also

[16] In October 1997, during the first days of the crisis, the Prime Minister stated that "the stability of the drachma remains a reference point for the economic policy of the government and will continue to determine the government's actions". On 24th February 1998, he added that "the government will insist on defending the parity of the drachma and will not succumb to any pressures which might develop in the following months". On 9 January 1998 the Minister of National Economy Mr. Papantoniou went a step further by stating that "the stability of the drachma represents the cornerstone of the government's economic policy. The government is determined to take all necessary measures in order to support the current parity of the drachma". He repeated the statement on 3 March 1998 when he stated that "the government wants drachma stability and will continue to support

on the argument that if the authorities had indeed decided to proceed to a devaluation of the drachma long ago, there was no reason to defend the national currency in such a determined way as they did in November 1997. If that was the case indeed, there is little doubt that the BoG would have let the drachma to float during the crisis. The reason is that the cost of defending the national currency at that particular point in time, expressed by higher interest payments on public debt and a partial loss of the policy credibility (caused by the discontinuation of the strong drachma policy after so many official statements expressing the authorities' commitment to it) seems to be much higher compared to the benefits resulting from four additional months of exchange rate stability.

Having said that, one has to admit that the timing of the March 1998 devaluation was well chosen (see also Mourmouras 1997c, Mourmouras and Arghyrou 1997). Obviously, no government pre-announces its intention to devalue its national currency. However, there are good reasons to believe that as the date of the establishment of the EMU would get closer, the drachma would be put under new pressure which could result in a forced devaluation. This view is based on the argument made by Begg *et al*, (1991) who suggested that the announcement of the establishment of the EMU on a specific date defines a finite time-horizon to the game played between the government and the private sector. National central banks would have an incentive to inflate in the last year prior to the EMU in order to extinguish part of the national debt. The reason is that because the national currencies would cease to exist in the subsequent year, central banks are not afraid of the expectations' reaction of the private sector. Thus, they would most probably go ahead with a devaluation. Rational agents understand this devaluation incentive and as the 1999 or 2002 deadline defines a clear time-horizon, they would (i) incorporate the anticipated devaluation in their future contracts (something which might partly or fully offset the competitive gains of the planned devaluation) and (ii) proceed to a

effectively the current parity of the drachma". Finally, on 25 February 1998 the deputy Minister of National Economy Mr. Dris stated that "the government will maintain the current parity of the drachma against the ECU both now and between 1999 and 2001, i.e. the date when Greece will join the EMU" (*To Vima,* 15/3/98). A further argument in favour of the view that the devaluation of the drachma was not part of the authorities' intentions is the fact that only ten days before its realization (i.e. on 4/3/1998) the Greek Deputy Minister of Finance Mr. N. Christodoulakis signed on behalf of Greece a 1.25 billion US$ external loan. As far as ERM participation is concerned, in December 1997 the Minister of National Economy Mr. Y. Papantoniou had stated that "Greece does not intend to join the ERM in the near future". He added that the strong drachma would remain the basic pillar of Greek macroeconomic policy and declared that the authorities will continue to defend its parity "by all means, including increases in interest rates".

speculative attack in due course which could produce the forced devaluation[17].

4.3.3. The future of the drachma and the ERM-II

(i) Some preliminary comments

Turning now to monetary policy in connection with the prospects for Greece after 1999, it has now been announced officially that Greece will join the ERM-II and will continue to pursue exchange rate stability around the newly established (post-devaluation) ERM central rate against the ECU. The obvious rationale behind the future participation in the ERM-II is that if Greece's ultimate objective is to become a full member of the EMU, it has to display a pro-European face and joining the ERM-II is a good opportunity to achieve this target. In addition, there is also the standard argument that the shadowing of the euro is a commitment to continued low inflation. This might sound good, but there are a number of problems at both the theoretical and the practical level with any participation in the ERM-II.

Before coming to these problems, a small digression on the experience of EU currencies within the present ERM may be due. Actually, the record of the ERM as a fixed exchange rate regime in Europe has not been too impressive. In the early 1980s, the ERM was characterized by numerous and substantial realignments of the French Franc and the Italian lira against the DM. More recently, the exchange rate stability of the late 1980s was followed by a number of devaluations in the early 1990s which finally led to the collapse of the system in August 1993. Furthermore, the adoption of wide bands of fluctuation (±15%) was not enough to avert exchange rate turbulence and currency devaluations in 1995 involving the Spanish peseta and the Portuguese escudo. Having such an experience, one might suggest that any new ERM arrangement (especially one with relatively narrow bands) could suffer from all the drawbacks characterizing a near fixed exchange rate regime, namely that there are limits regarding the efficiency of such a regime in a world of increased international capital movements, fiscal imbalances and asymmetric real shocks. It is, of course, true that some of the soft European currencies did survive within the present ERM between 1989 and 1992 but what people often tend to forget is the fact that this has been achieved under two special conditions: capital controls and compulsory central bank intervention. Neither of the two conditions is any longer met today, making any proposal for the participation of countries with fiscal imbalances in a new ERM at least questionable. Further support to this argument is provided by the numerous episodes of forced devaluations which took place in the 1990s, involving currencies of non-ERM countries which were pegged either to the DM or the US dollar without

[17] According to the same argument, the narrower the allowed band of exchange rate fluctuation prior to the establishment of the EMU, the earlier the date of the speculative attack would be.

being supported by the necessary macroeconomic fundamentals (e.g. the Mexican devaluation in 1994, the Czech devaluation in 1996, the South-East Asia devaluations in 1997 and the Brazilian devaluation in 1998)

(ii) ERM-II participation: back to the future ?

The objective of the March 1998 devaluation was to restore the drachma's long-run equilibrium value and ensure that the participation of the Greek national currency in the ERM would be achieved with a sustainable exchange rate. The assessment of the Greek authorities (as it emerges from various statements of Greek officials) is that this objective has now been achieved and that the drachma will join the euro on 1st January 2001 with a conversion rate identical to the present (post-devaluation) central rate against the ECU, i.e. 357 drachmas per ECU. However, given the prolonged character of the strong drachma policy, it is very difficult to suggest with certainty that the recent 14% devaluation, was enough to restore long-run equilibrium conditions regarding the position of the Greek national currency vis-à-vis the ECU. In contrast, what is clear is the following:

(a) There were economic (and political) constraints regarding the order of the devaluation. A realignment of an order higher than 14% could have serious inflation implications and a strong inflation shock could derail the whole process of nominal convergence.

(b) Greek nominal and real interest rates still remain the highest among the EU countries. As there is little doubt that the recent devaluation has reduced substantially the *short-run* exchange rate risk associated with the movements of the drachma (in the sense that a decision on the part of the Greek authorities to proceed voluntarily to a second drachma devaluation immediately after the first one seems highly unlikely), this makes drachma-denominated bonds quite attractive to international investors.

(c) Even if the recently announced package of measures aiming to accelerate the process of structural reforms is fully implemented without any delay, its effect on core inflation, productivity and competitiveness will most probably appear with a reasonable time lag as structural adjustments do not take place instantly;

(d) Greek inflation remains three times higher than the EU average, and may even increase temporarily due to the impact of the recent devaluation on the prices of imports. This fact, combined with (c) above, implies that as far as the foreseeable future is concerned, Greek and European price levels will continue to diverge. This, in turn, implies that if the BoG sticks to its recent commitment to pursue exchange rate stability against the new central rate against the ECU (i.e. restrict exchange rate fluctuation within a ±2.5% range), the relative price of the output of the Greek traded sector vis-à-vis foreign products will continue to increase, therefore any competitiveness gains emerging from the devaluation will be reduced. This, in relation with the possibility of a J-curve effect, suggests that the current account constraint may continue to exercise pressure on the external sector of the economy.

(e) Last, but not least, there is little doubt that the accession of Greece to the ERM has increased the degree of international exposure of the drachma. This implies that the probability of speculative attacks against the Greek national currency will be higher compared to the past, especially if the drachma enters the ERM-II with an overvalued central rate against the euro. In other words, experience has shown that in an environment of high capital mobility, investors appear to be extremely sensitive to movements of the fundamentals of the economies which participate in formal exchange rate arrangements and they stand ready to "punish" countries which appear unwilling to improve their macroeconomic imbalances.

The emerging conclusion is that if the March 1998 devaluation did not restore drachma at its long-run equilibrium (and given the prolonged character of the strong drachma policy this is likely to be the case), the problems caused by the overvaluation of the drachma have not been eliminated and the dangers discussed earlier in this chapter are still present. In this context, a crude, but still valid way to assess the present situation would be to compare the level of the recent devaluation with the cumulative drachma overvaluation caused by the strong currency policy. The latter can be approximated by the sum of the figures in columns (4) and (5) in Table 4.1. Both columns suggest a drachma overvaluation exceeding the threshold of 20% (21% and 23% respectively). In other words, the participation of the drachma in the ERM-II may not be immune to exchange rate turbulence. Here, the experience from the rest of the countries of the *Club-Med*, i.e. Italy, Portugal and Spain, might be illustrating. All three countries experienced *forced* devaluations *within* the ERM in 1992-93. Furthermore, both Spain and Portugal, despite three discreet devaluations in 1992-93 (of a cumulative order of 19% and 12% respectively) had to proceed to a further 7% (forced) devaluation two years later, i.e. in 1995. In the light of such an experience, we cannot see how one could exclude completely the possibility that history might repeat itself in the case of Greece, a country where, after all, despite the progress achieved in the 1990s, fiscal imbalances are more pronounced and structural adjustments in the 1990s have been pursued with the speed of a turtle.

(iii) A strong euro ?

A second factor which casts doubts on a smooth participation of the drachma in the

ERM-II has to do with the possibility that the euro will be appreciating during the early stages of its introduction. Of course, it is not yet clear whether the euro will be as strong as the DM or a softer currency. There are certain arguments for both scenarios. The arguments behind the latter view (a euro softer than the DM) include the following: (i) It will take some time for the euro to establish itself in international financial markets, especially with all the uncertainties regarding the political context in which it will operate. (ii) In the same spirit, because of the surrounding uncertainty of anything "newly born", risk averse investors may prefer the safe and tested old dollar from the new euro. (iii) As some of the countries in the first wave of EMU participants have historically displayed a higher degree of tolerance against inflation than Germany did, monetary policy of the ECB could well represent an average of these preferences (see Kenen 1995, pp. 178-79). As a result, the euro as a currency that will be created from the amalgamation of the strong DM with less stable currencies, could be a *priori* a currency less strong than the DM.

On the other hand, there are some plausible arguments which can make a case for a strong euro. These arguments include the following: (i) The ECB will be anxious to establish quickly its anti-inflationary credentials with a tight monetary policy in order to be able to meet its explicit mandate to preserve conditions of low inflation within the EMU. Moreover, the loss of monetary policy for European governments may lead to expansionary "fine tuning" national fiscal policies. The combination of these two (tight monetary and loose fiscal policies) could lead to an increase in euro interest rates (as it happened in the case of the US Dollar in the early 1980s) and finally to an overvalued euro. (ii) The creation of a homogeneous single economic area including more than 300 million consumers, combined with a low inflation rate (less than 2-3%), may be attractive to foreign investors leading to a surge in the demand for euros. In addition, the EU as a whole has had over the years significant current account surpluses which may further put some upward pressure to the euro. (iii) Finally, some analysts suggest that the euro should become soon an important international reserve and vehicle currency[18]. Given the major importance of the EU as a whole in the world's economy[19], the immediate

---

[18] According to Fred Bergsten (Director of the Washington-based Institute for International Economics) after 1999 between 30% and 40% of the world's financial assets will be denominated in euros, between 40% and 50% in dollars and the rest in yen and a few other currencies (see the Economist, 29 March 1997). This would mean a shift of between 500 billion and 1 trillion dollars into euros, primarily out of dollars. Bergsten's opinion is further reinforced by the fact that despite the dollar's major importance in international financial markets, its role has been declining over the last years. In 1973 it constituted 76% of official international reserves whereas its current share is 65%.

[19] In 1995 figures, the EU's share of world output was 30%, followed by USA (27%) and

implication of such a big portfolio shift would be a significant increase in the demand for euros which would result in an appreciation of the euro above its long-run equilibrium value. If this scenario (a strong euro) is finally confirmed, the drachma, through its official link to the euro will be shadowing an appreciating currency (as it did during in 1983 when it was shadowing the then appreciating US Dollar with the well know consequences). In that case, the problems discussed above would be even more pronounced. Given the existing macroeconomic imbalances, the combination of ERM-II participation and a strong euro would imply further increase in Greek interest rates, further overvaluation of the drachma (with all the resulting negative fiscal and growth implications) and, probably, a forced exit from the system in the event of a serious speculative attack, as it happened in the case of the pound sterling in 1992.

(iv) Wide versus narrow bands

A final, important matter that needs careful consideration is the adoption of a wide band of fluctuation (±15%) against a narrow one (±2.5%). The adoption of a wide band, has really to do with two issues: First, with the degree of flexibility for divergent monetary policies: A wide band (±15%) would allow the drachma to crawl, if necessary, at the rate of the inflation differential against the EMU average, thus supporting the international competitiveness of the economy and domestic activity in a period of fiscal discipline. Second, with the raising of the riskiness of speculation which would make speculative attacks less probable. This is so because speculative gains are possible in case speculators manage to create a major jump of the spot market exchange rate by forcing the monetary authority to proceed to a realignment of the central parity of the currency under consideration. A wide band of fluctuation might be more suitable in preventing pressures of this kind. This might be so for the following reasons:

First, a wide band will allow the competitiveness problems of the Greek economy to be less pronounced in comparison to those which would appear if a narrow-band was selected. As a result, the expectations regarding a future devaluation and the subsequent pressures on the drachma will be less strong.

If, however, such expectations are finally formed and pressures against the drachma do appear in the future, a wide band will allow the BoG to proceed to a realignment in due course which will involve a new central exchange rate falling *within* the old upper and lower limits. This implies that a major jump of the market spot exchange rate (on which speculators count in order to make money) will be less likely to happen. In contrast, the adoption of a narrow band makes such a jump more likely for two reasons: First, the narrower the band of allowed

---

Japan (15%). In 1995 figures again, the EU's share of world trade (excluding intra-EU trade) was 20%, followed by USA (18%) and Japan (11%).

fluctuation, the bigger is the probability that the new central rate will not fall within the old limits. Second, given a positive inflation differential between Greece and the rest of Europe, a narrow band would create bigger competitiveness problems than the wide one.

If the possibility of a major jump of the market exchange rate exists anyway, a wide band discourages a speculative attack because it increases the probability of significant capital loses for speculators. Let us suppose that the drachma enters the ERM-II with an overvalued parity against the euro and as a result of competitiveness problems it experiences pressure and approaches the upper limit of the band. Speculators, in anticipation of a devaluation of the drachma, would sell drachmas and buy euros. There are then two possibilities. One is that the devaluation which speculators anticipate does not take place and the drachma recovers by moving towards the lower limit of the band (i.e. it starts appreciating against the euro). For those speculators who would have sold drachma and bought euros, this would imply a capital loss[20]. However, if the band is a narrow one, this loss would be smaller as there is a certain limit (the lower limit of the band) with regard to the potential recovery of the drachma. From that point of view, speculating against the drachma represents a sort of one-way bet: Speculators cannot loose much but they can gain a lot if they force the BoG to a major devaluation. In contrast, if the band is a wide one, an impressive drachma recovery might imply significant capital losses for speculators.

The other possibility is that the significant devaluation which speculators expect does indeed take place. In this case, the magnitude of capital gains made by speculators would depend on the subsequent movement of the exchange rate within the *new* band. On some occasions, the following interesting phenomenon has been observed (see Kenen, 1995, p.173): as speculators receive their gains immediately after the devaluation, the demand for the devalued currency increases and its market exchange rate starts moving towards the lower limit of the new band (i.e. it starts appreciating). Such a development implies a reduction in the speculators' capitals gains. If the band is a narrow one, this reduction cannot exceed a certain level. If however the band is a wide one, the reduction in capital

[20] Another cost for speculators, which always exists (i.e. irrespective of whether a major devaluation takes place or not), is the interest payments foregone by the selling of drachmas and the buying of euro: it is reasonable to assume that after 1999 nominal (and real) Greek interest rates will continue to be higher than the European ones, therefore any transaction which involves switching drachmas to euros would imply a cost in terms of foregone interest payments. However, as speculative transactions are of very short-term nature, the importance of these costs is expected to be limited.

gains might represent a significant percentage of the initial gains and, in the limit, the former can fully offset the latter.

As far as Greece is concerned, it is most probably the case that the drachma participation in the ERM-II will involve a relatively wide formal band of allowed fluctuation. This might be the present ±15% band of the existing ERM. However, as far as the *effective* band is concerned, the BoG has already announced that exchange rate movements against the ECU will be restricted to a ±2.5% range around the present central rate[21]. In our view, under certain circumstances (e.g. in the absence of swift progress in the fields of fiscal consolidation and structural adjustments or in the event of a new international exchange rate crisis), the adoption of a narrow effective band could create problems similar to those created by the strong drachma policy. Under such circumstances, international financial markets and especially speculators, who are expected to follow the developments of the Greek economy very closely, may sooner or later start having doubts about the sustainability of the parity of the drachma, and they may form expectations about a new realignment of the drachma's central rate. This, in turn, could provide incentives for a new speculative attack against the drachma. All in all, given the policy mix which was followed during the 1991-97 period and the productivity gap which continues to exist between Greece and most of the EU countries, it is far from certain that participation of the drachma in the ERM-II will stand the test of time.

[21] See Bank of Greece, Monetary Programme for 1998.

Chapter 5

FROM INTERMEDIATE TARGETS TO FORMAL INFLATION TARGETS IN GREECE

5.1. Introduction

Having examined in detail the Greek experience with exchange rate targeting and the serious limitations associated with the continuation of this two-stage approach to monetary policy, we are now ready to develop a new, alternative proposal regarding the future course of Greek monetary policy on the road to EMU participation. More specifically, in this chapter we argue in favour of abandoning altogether intermediate monetary targets in favour of the adoption of formal, direct inflation targets. Direct inflation-targeting should not be seen as merely just a policy rule; rather, it should be seen as a full monetary policy framework whose ultimate objective is the achievement and maintenance of price stability. In other words, inflation targeting is not an anti-inflationary policy in the sense this latter term is used in the theory and practice of stabilization policies; it is rather a unified monetary policy regime defined in terms of targets, instruments and policy indicators. Its main attraction is that it addresses the time-inconsistency problem inherent in monetary policy without presenting some of the problems associated with the implementation of intermediate monetary targets.

Recently, a number of countries in Europe and elsewhere have adopted inflation targets along with the introduction of various forms of independence for their national central banks. Speaking in terms of inflation performance, the experience from these countries which have adopted inflation targets is rather impressive. Furthermore, some of them (i.e. Finland, Sweden and the United Kingdom) have managed to meet the inflation criterion set by the Maastricht Treaty, showing that an exchange rate arrangement like the ERM is not a one-way road for the meeting of the requirement. In this chapter we argue that inflation targets could also help Greece in its effort to reduce and maintain a low inflation rate without causing problems similar to those caused by the strong drachma policy. The remainder of the chapter is organized as follows: section 5.2 refers to some theory on inflation targets and the existing international evidence from those countries in which they have been adopted. Section 5.3 is dedicated to an overview of inflation developments in Greece during the period 1975-97; and an examination of the main characteristics of Greek inflation today. Finally, section 5.4 presents the arguments in favour of an inflation-targeting regime in Greece and outlines what we believe should be the main characteristics of such a regime in the case of Greece.

5.2. Inflation-targeting: theory and international evidence

5.2.1. Some theory

Inflation-targeting can be defined as a monetary policy framework "under which the overriding policy objective is the maintenance of price stability; and policy decisions are guided by expected future inflation relative to a formally announced inflation target" (Green 1996, p. 2). Typically, inflation-targeting regimes have three characteristics:

First, an explicit, formal inflation target which specifies the targeted index, the level of the target, the tolerance interval, the time frame, and circumstances under which the inflation target would be modified or disregarded altogether[1].

Second, the lack of any intermediate target for the rate of growth of money supply or the exchange rate[2].

Third, a more open and transparent monetary framework achieved by means of various channels of communication between the central bank and the public (e.g. an Inflation Report, publication of minutes of meetings etc.) through which the monetary authority announces its policy decisions and presents to private agents its independent assessment and forecasts regarding the past and future movements of inflation. Such mechanisms encourage public discussion on monetary policy; increase public monitoring of inflation performance; and help private agents predict how the monetary authorities will react to developments in the economy (see King, 1997)[3]. From a theoretical point of view, the adoption of formal inflation targets is widely perceived as the latest approach in the search for a

[1] All these aspects of inflation-targeting are discussed later in this chapter in the context of our discussion on Greece.
[2] However, Leiderman and Svensson (1995, p. 1) argue that "in principle, there is nothing that prevents the use of an intermediate target consistent with the inflation target, as long as it is clear that the inflation target has priority if a conflict arises. Whether an intermediate target is used is then only a practical issue, depending for instance upon the stability of the relation between the intermediate target and the inflation target". However, this view is not shared by all economists. For example, Freedman (1994), argues that in a world of full capital mobility a central bank cannot adhere both to exchange rates and inflation targets. One target has to be subjugated to the other.
[3]We return to the significance of these arrangements later in this chapter.

solution to the time-inconsistency problem inherent in monetary policy which has been extensively discussed in the "rules versus discretion" economic literature[4], pioneered in the seminal papers by Kydland and Prescot (1977) and Barro and Gordon (1983).

The prototype model of inflation-targeting is attributed to Svensson (1997a) who has shown that by adopting an inflation target lower than the socially desired level of inflation, the central bank can reduce average inflation to a value lower than the one which would have prevailed in a discretionary monetary policy regime. In addition, Svensson has shown that there exists a specific value for the inflation target which, if adopted by the central bank, delivers average inflation equal to the socially desired level of inflation. Furthermore, this reduction does not result in an increase in output volatility as in the prototype model of Rogoff (1985). However, the credibility problem associated with monetary policy is not entirely solved. The main disadvantage of Svensson's specification is that in his model the inflation target is systematically missed. The question which then arises is how credible is a monetary strategy which leads to a systematic overshooting of its target[5]. Furthermore, there are a number of other problems associated with inflation-targeting (see Svensson, 1997b). Inflation targets may be difficult to implement because central banks do not have full control over the current level of inflation. The latter is predominantly a function of past decisions, therefore central banks can only target future inflation. But then, inflation-targeting becomes inherently difficult due to the existence of long and variable lags associated with the impact of monetary instruments on the actual rate of inflation and the impact of other, non-monetary shocks, on inflation. Furthermore, the imperfect control over inflation implies difficulties in terms of monitoring the inflation performance of the monetary regime.

To begin with the first issue raised above, an answer to the systematic overshooting problem might be a combination of the results provided by the models of Svensson and Rogoff. More specifically, the introduction of inflation targets can be accompanied by the delegation of monetary policy to an independent central bank. De Grauwe (1996b) has shown that within the above framework, the problem of systematic overshooting of the inflation target existing in the model by Svensson is not eliminated but becomes less pronounced. In De Grauwe's model, the delegation of monetary policy to an independent monetary authority together with the adoption of formal inflation targets results in an average rate of inflation which is lower than the average rate of inflation prevailing in the model of Svensson. The average rate of inflation remains higher than the adopted inflation target but the difference between the two variables is less than

---

[4] For further discussion on this point, see chapter 6.

[5] The results derived by Svensson imply that the question is trivial in those societies which are completely inflation averse. However, the credibility problem remains in those countries where output stabilization does matter.

the one existing in the model by Svensson. Hence, a reduction in the value of the systematic overshooting of the target is achieved. The lower the weight attached to output stabilization in the central bank's objective function, the higher the reduction in the systematic overshooting. Furthermore, as far as the practical implementation of inflation targets is concerned, the literature offers a number of further insights regarding the specification of inflation targets (e.g. the adoption of target ranges rather than target values)[6]. However, the cost of increased credibility implied by the arrangement described above is the reduction in the degrees of freedom available to authorities to cope with output shocks[7].

The problems of implementation and monitoring effectively raise the issue of a trade-off between the high degree of transparency offered by an inflation-targeting regime and the high degree of controllability of the target variables offered by a regime of intermediate monetary targets (see Cukierman, 1994a,b). The point is that in contemporary economies agents need a "pre-commitment technology", signaling the intentions of authorities regarding the future course of monetary policy, revealing to market participants the systematic factors guiding the use of policy instruments and reducing the uncertainty associated with the future effect of current economic decisions (see Crockett, 1994). The question which then arises is which of these two alternative monetary frameworks serves the purpose in the best possible way.

In this context, it has been suggested that one major advantage of formal inflation targets is that such targets constitute a superior signaling mechanism because, combined with the communication mechanisms existing in inflation-targeting regimes (e.g. Inflation Reports etc.), they increase the degree of *transparency* of monetary policy as all interested parties are in a position to see what the central bank is trying to do, how it pursues its targets and the rationale behind the use of the preferred practices. This in turn, provides the monetary authority with a superior structure of incentives to deliver price stability by means of increasing the degree of *accountability* of the central bank to the society in general, an element which appears to be of great importance in view of the recent introduction of legislation establishing the independence of the central bank in many countries[8] (see also Bowen 1995 and chapter 6). From that point of view, inflation targets are a nominal anchor superior to

---

[6] See section 5.4 below.

[7] Green (1996) suggests that an alternative solution to the credibility problem would be to announce both inflation and output targets, provided that they are consistent. He suggests the interesting view that those countries which have adopted inflation targets implicitly set output targets. The reason is that the inflation reports published by these countries include the prospects for output relative to its potential, i.e. the output gap. Therefore, "by making known its views on inflation pressures in this context, the central bank signals an implicit output target".

[8] According to Fischer (1995, p. 202), "accountability is needed for two reasons: first, to set incentives for the central bank to meet its goals and explain its actions; and second, to provide democratic oversight of a powerful political institution".

any intermediate monetary target and can promote the anti-inflation credibility of monetary policy in a more effective way because they are unambiguous and better understood by the public[9]. On the other hand, the limited control which the central bank has over the current rate of inflation might imply that the usefulness of inflation targets as a pre-commitment mechanism might be weakened. As the monetary authority has no full control over the targeted variable, agents may have difficulties in extracting the appropriate signals by means of observing the current inflation rate. Therefore, one might argue that intermediate targets, whose movements are more easy to control, may be more effective as a signaling mechanism aiming to stabilize inflationary expectations and reducing uncertainty[10].

Both arguments presented above are based on a sound foundation. However, a question whose importance seems to have been underestimated by some authors is that of the importance of the controllability/transparency trade-off in practice. As Cukierman (1994a, p. 1443) argues, "as a matter of principle, the ultimate choice of a target should take into consideration the impact of those elements (i.e. transparency and precision) on the formation of inflationary expectations and credibility". Thinking along these lines, one might suggest that controllability of intermediate targets *itself* does not offer any major advantage. Controllability is an advantage only if the movements of intermediate targets affect the expected rate of inflation and the final objective variable, i.e. the future actual rate of inflation. To take an extreme example, controllability itself would be an element of dubious character if the intermediate variable chosen were unrelated to these two variables. Of course, there is little doubt that both the rate of growth of money supply and the level of the exchange rate (which are the two variables most commonly used as intermediate targets) are related to the *future* level of inflation. But having said that, one can argue that in many countries where an intermediate target approach to monetary policy has been implemented, the relationship which links the movements of intermediate variables with actual and *expected* inflation might have been subject to a structural break caused either by the velocity instability problem discussed in chapter 4 or by the collapse of the exchange rate pegging arrangements which took place during the EMS crisis in 1992-93 (see De Grauwe, 1996b). In other words, policy announcements regarding the future movement of intermediate targets may not be in position to influence the inflationary expectations of agents. Therefore, as far as the controllability/transparency trade-off is concerned, it would appear that the importance of controllability has declined in recent years. The case of Greece is a typical example supporting this

[9] The standard argument here is that the concept of inflation is much more familiar to the "man in the street" compared to the rate of growth of money supply or the rate of nominal depreciation of the domestic currency against the major foreign currencies.

[10] Fisher (1995, p. 203) has summarized this view in the following words: "obviously, it would be best for the central bank to target a policy variable directly under its control that also closely controls an ultimate target variable, such as the inflation rate and output".

view. Despite the fact that over the last three years (1995-97) announced exchange rate targets were actually met, the credibility gains emerging from this success were not enough to avert a forced devaluation of the drachma in March 1998. Furthermore, the high degree of controllability of the exchange rate has resulted in only limited progress in reducing inflationary expectations (see section 5.3 below).

Svensson (1997b) goes one step further and puts the existence of the controllability/transparency trade-off into question. More specifically, he shows that "inflation-targeting implies inflation *forecast* targeting: the central bank's inflation forecast becomes an explicit intermediate target. Making this explicit simplifies both implementation and monitoring of monetary policy. The central bank's inflation forecast is indeed an ideal intermediate target: it is by definition the current variable that is most correlated with the goal (i.e. actual future inflation), it is more controllable than the goal and it can be made more observable than the goal. It can also be made very transparent and may therefore facilitate the central bank's communication with the public, and the public's understanding of monetary policy" (Svensson 1997b, p. 1114)[11].

The upshot of the above is that the increased transparency of an inflation-targeting regime, along with the superior structure of incentives it provides to the central bank to achieve price stability, seems more attractive compared to the advantages emerging from policy announcements regarding the future movements of intermediate targets. Experience has shown that under certain circumstances, the latter may be reduced to the status of what is defined in game theory as *cheap talk*, with limited effect on inflationary expectations[12]. From that point of view, inflation targets would represent a more effective formal commitment on the part of the authorities that monetary policy would remain disciplined. To put it in the words of

[11] A counter-argument to that made by Svensson is that inflation-forecasts targeting may also suffer from credibility problems because agents know that specific-value forecasts are unlikely to be met. However, according to King (1995) that would not be a valid criticism. The point is that inflation forecasts do not involve point estimates but probability distributions of future inflation which take into consideration the risks and uncertainties involved in monetary policy. In King's words (p.6), "the fact that we cannot foresee the future with perfect certainty is no reason to ignore it".

[12] Commenting on Freedman's (1994) paper, Driffill (pp. 45-46) points out the following: "cheap talk is a signal sent from one player in a game (typically one who has some private information) to the other player(s), before the players take the actions which affect their payoffs. The cheap talk itself does not affect any payoffs and it does not restrict the subsequent choices of actions made by the players. The talk is cheap because the messages cost nothing to spend. This distinguishes it from costly signaling mechanisms which are useful because the costs of sending signals gives players incentives to send true and often revealing signals in situations when, in the absence of the cost of sending the signal, all players would like to send the same signals. In these cases, the (costly) signal sent by a player can serve to communicate information about that player's type, and provide useful information to other players in the game which affect the actions they take. If inflation targets were a signal in this sense, they might affect the inflation expectations of the private sector".

Freedman (1994 p.19), "by providing a formal commitment regarding the downward path for inflation over the medium-term, specific (and credible) inflation targets can help agents see beyond the temporary shocks to the levels of prices to the existing underlying downward trend of inflation and to take this element into account in their economic decision making".

Another advantage of inflation targets often quoted in the literature is that such a regime can be more effective for stabilization purposes in the event of demand shocks than a rigid rule restricting the movements of an intermediate monetary target. This would imply less volatility in the economy's performance, i.e. less pronounced output fluctuations. The underlying argument here is that the adoption of inflation targets establishes a "constrained discretion" monetary framework (see Bernanke and Mishkin, 1997). The implication of this is that if demand pressures develop to an extent incompatible with the inflation target, monetary conditions can tighten and a boom situation can be avoided. In a similar fashion, weak demand conditions will offer no inflationary pressures and would allow the central bank to ease monetary policy somewhat without running significant inflation risk. Finally, another argument in favour of the introduction of direct inflation targets is the fact that they provide the monetary authority with additional degrees of freedom in the conduct of monetary policy. More specifically, their introduction allows the central bank to use all available information in its fight against inflation by choosing the instrument which is judged to be the most effective at any period of time and not merely to concentrate on an intermediate monetary target such as the exchange rate which, as experience from other countries has shown, can let the monetary authorities down any time (see Bank of England, 1996).

5.2.2. Inflation targets and the EMU Outs

According to the existing arrangements, the EMU Outs are expected to join the ERM-II in 1999, or some time in the near future[13]. However, as it was argued in chapters 1 and 4, such a participation might not suit the economic fundamentals of these countries in the best feasible way. Our discussion there highlighted the danger that ERM-II participation might lead to currency overvaluation and credibility problems which could lead to a collapse of the peg to the euro. An alternative monetary strategy for the EMU Outs could be the adoption of formal inflation targets. Such a choice would have a number of advantages compared to ERM-II participation (see also Arghyrou and Mourmouras, 1998). Dewatripont *et al* (1995) and Persson and Tabelini (1996) share this view. The latter argue that the ERM-II will be a "very risky strategy as a unilateral peg to the euro by the outside countries alone is not likely to resist speculative attacks (p.3)"... "Hence,

[13] This is certainly true for Greece and Denmark. The position of the United Kingdom and Sweden is not yet clear. However, there is speculation that these countries may join the ERM-II in due course.

considerable exchange rate risk would remain, even in the absence of observed fluctuations of the nominal exchange rate (p.21)"... "Moreover, the burden of defending the exchange rate would fall entirely on the outsiders[14] who would have to destabilize their economies not only to resist speculative attacks but also in the face of shocks originating from the inside countries" (p.3). The reason is that shocks of various forms within the EMU (e.g. a velocity shock or a supply shock) would spill over on the Outs' inflation and output through the targeting of the exchange rate against the euro. Furthermore, the ERM-II arrangement would not prevent idiosyncratic shocks hitting countries outside the EMU, a fact which could well imply real exchange rate volatility for the Outs. Under such circumstances, any attempt at output stabilization could give rise to a competitive depreciation bias in the monetary policy of the Outs which, in turn, may invite political retaliation on the part of the Ins, making monetary cohabitation in Europe even more difficult.

According to Persson and Tabelini, these problems could be mitigated if the Outs adopt an inflation-targeting regime, irrespective of the monetary strategy to be adopted by the European Central Bank (ECB)[15]. Such a choice would have a number of advantages. First, it would diminish the incentive to engage in competitive devaluations. Second, as the meeting of the inflation targets would imply an automatic response to currency depreciation (in the sense that authorities would be bound to react in order to prevent exchange rate fluctuations giving rise to higher prices) an inflation-targeting regime would tend to reduce exchange rate volatility and inflation. These, in turn, would imply lower real exchange rate volatility.

De Grauwe (1996b) considers two "countries", the EMU and an EMU Out (e.g. Greece) whose aim is to join the EMU. Assuming that average inflation in Greece is higher than average inflation in the EMU and that the desired level of inflation in both countries is equal to zero, De Grauwe derives the result that if Greece selects a monetary strategy involving exchange rate pegging to the euro, the drachma would experience an average annual real appreciation against the euro equal to the difference between the inflation bias existing in Greece and the one existing in the EMU. This annual appreciation is defined by De Grauwe as the credibility gap of the pegging arrangement. De Grauwe (p. 16) argues that, "as long as the exchange rate peg is maintained, the real appreciation of the currency of the Outs country continues through each period, producing an *increasing* overvaluation of that currency. The longer the exchange rate is maintained, the larger the degree of overvaluation becomes. This is bound to invite speculative crises when agents anticipate that the fixed exchange rate cannot be sustained".

---

[14] According to Persson and Tabelini (1996), a symmetric peg would be unfeasible. The credibility of the ECB would suffer too much and Germany would never accept it.

[15] In fact, Persson and Tabelini (1996) argue in favour of inflation targets both for the ECB and the central banks of the Outs.

Based on this result, De Grauwe makes a case for the adoption of inflation targets by the EMU-Out country, in which case the inflation target should be equal to the average rate of inflation in the EMU minus the inflation bias of the EMU-Out country. Furthermore, De Grauwe argues that this choice must be accompanied by the appointment of a mildly conservative central banker in the EMU Out country who places on output stabilization an identical weight with the one existing in the EMU. Otherwise, the inflation target will suffer from the credibility problems mentioned in section 5.2.2 above (i.e., average inflation in the Outs countries will systematically overshoot the target set). The appointment of such a "Europeanized" central banker does not eliminate but reduces the systematic error of the inflation-targeting regime in the EMU-Out country. According to De Grauwe, such a strategy would be more credible than the pegging alternative and could have more success in enforcing inflation convergence in Europe.

5.2.3. International evidence

In the 1990s, a number of countries in Europe and elsewhere adopted an inflation-targeting regime. This choice reflected either a failure to achieve a low rate of inflation using money supply targets (e.g. Canada) or the collapse of a strategy involving exchange rate pegging (e.g. the United Kingdom). This section presents a brief review of the institutional arrangements and inflation performance of five countries which adopted the inflation-targeting approach. More specifically, we examine the cases of New Zealand, Canada, the United Kingdom, Sweden and Finland[16].

New Zealand

Inflation targets were first introduced in New Zealand along with the Reserve Bank of New Zealand (RBNZ) Act which was passed by the Parliament in 1989. The latter established price stability as the only objective of the RBNZ and was part of an effort to improve macroeconomic performance in New Zealand after many years of low growth and high inflation. According to the Act, the inflation targets are jointly decided by the Governor of the RBNZ and the Minister of Finance in the form of Policy Target Agreements (PTAs). However, the government has the right to override the PTAs and announce objectives other than price stability for a period of from two to twelve months[17]. The Bank is solely responsible for the selection of the means which will lead to the achievement of the PTAs and the

[16] Other countries which have adopted some form of inflation targets include Australia (see Stevens and Debelle, 1995) and Israel (see Ben-Bassat, 1995). Spain has also announced inflation objectives without, however, abandoning altogether the exchange rate intermediate target (see Ortega and Bonilla, 1995). Space limitations oblige us to abstain from further reference to these cases.

[17] Under such a scenario, the override has to be approved by the Parliament.

Governor can be dismissed if the PTAs are not met (see Mayes and Chapple, 1995). The first two PTAs (announced in March 1990 and December 1992) defined a CPI inflation range between 0%-2% as the eventual target of monetary policy but as the inflation rate in 1989 was equal to 5.7%, ranges of a higher order were adopted as inflation targets for the transition period towards price stability. The present PTA has adopted the 0%-2% range as the target range. However, temporary deviations from the target caused by natural disasters, increasing indirect taxes, interest rate increases and large shocks in the terms of trade are to be tolerated.

In terms of monetary policy operation, the RBNZ acts when the inflation forecast for a period of two to six quarters ahead exceeds the 2% ceiling[18]. In that case, monetary conditions are tightened so that the exchange rate appreciates until the forecast of inflation falls again within the desired range. However, it should be made clear that the exchange rate is used only as an instrument, not as an intermediate target for monetary policy. In other words, the RBNZ does not intervene in the foreign exchange market in order to support the value of its currency. The introduction of inflation targets in New Zealand was followed by a clear inflation progress. All inflation targets set by the first two PTAs were met and by 1994 inflation had declined to 1.7% per annum. However, in 1995 CPI inflation recorded an increase (3.8%) before declining again in 1996 (2.3%).

Canada

On 26 February 1991 the Bank of Canada and the Canadian government jointly announced CPI inflation-reduction targets (excluding food and energy prices and changes in indirect taxes), setting out an explicit time-plan for the achievement of price stability. However, there was no change in the statute of the Bank of Canada. The joint plan was that inflation would fall in the range of 2%-4% by the end of 1992; 1.5%-3% in mid-1994; and 1%-3% by the end of 1995. The operation of the inflation-targeting regime in Canada involves the use of an econometric model in order to calculate the time path of a monetary conditions index (which comprises changes in exchange rates and interest rates) required to achieve an inflation path close to the midpoint of the target range. When the Bank judges that the value of the index has to be increased, it adjusts the level of liquidity in the monetary system producing an appropriate rise in interest rates (see McCallum, 1996). The experience to date is quite encouraging. All inflation targets set by the Bank of Canada were met and by 1996 inflation had declined to 1.6% from 5.6% back in 1991.

[18] The main indicator used to derive the forecast for the future rate of inflation is an exchange rate index. This is a weighted average of the exchange rate of New Zealand's national currency against New Zealand's main trading partners with the weights being equal to the participation of each partner in New Zealand's external trade. Short-term interest rates are a secondary indicator used for the derivation of the inflation forecasts.

United Kingdom

Inflation targets in the United Kingdom were introduced in October 1992, immediately after the forced exit of the pound sterling from the ERM. The main provisions of the monetary framework introduced by the conservative government and recently revised by the Labour government which emerged from the May 1997 elections are the following. The Chancellor of the Exchequer sets an explicit inflation target as the overriding objective of monetary policy. Without prejudice to this target, the Bank of England (BoE) is expected to set monetary policy in a manner compatible with the general economic policies pursued by the government. According to the 1997 arrangements, the BoE is left free to choose the instruments of monetary policy (i.e. to set interest rates independently) with the aim of delivering the inflation targets set by the government. Changes in interest rates are decided by the Bank's Monetary Policy Committee (MPC) which includes nine voting members. The Chancellor of the Exchequer is entitled to override the decisions of the MPC *in extremis* but under such a scenario he must explain openly the reasons for his decision.

The inflation target is expressed in terms of the rate of growth of the retail price index excluding mortgage interest payments (RPIX). The first target set by the conservative government was a range target in the order of 1% to 4% for the period 1993-97, aiming at a long-term inflation less than or equal to 2%. The current target (set in May 1997 by the Labour government) is a point target of 2.5% for an unspecified period. According to the new (1997) monetary arrangements, the target is not expected to be hit exactly year-by-year. However, it is expected that average inflation will be equal to 2.5% over a reasonably long-period of time. Furthermore, if during the course of one year RPIX inflation records a value outside a range defined as 1.5% to 3.5%, the Governor of the BoE is expected to write an Open Letter to the Chancellor of the Exchequer explaining the reasons for the deviation and the assessment of the MPC regarding the expected duration of the deviation. The Open Letter should be sent yearly as long as the inflation rate remains outside the 1.5% to 3.5% range. However, this band is explicitly defined *not* to be a target range. It only defines the points at which the Open Letter mechanism is triggered (see Bean, 1998).

Other important elements of the new monetary regime in the UK include the quarterly publication of an Inflation Report which presents the Bank's independent assessment regarding the prospects of inflation and a probability distribution of future inflation assuming no change in interest rates; and the publication of the minutes of the monthly meeting between the Governor of the BoE and the Chancellor (see also Bank of England, 1996)[19]. So far, the British experience with

[19] The importance of both arrangements is discussed later in this chapter.

inflation targets is quite impressive. During the first four years of its implementation the new regime has coincided with very favourable inflation developments. During the period 1993-97 RPIX inflation has mainly taken values in the lower part of the specified 1% to 4% range (see Bowen, 1995) whereas headline CPI inflation has been consistently lower than 4%.

Sweden

Inflation targets were introduced in Sweden on 15 January 1993, following the collapse of the peg of the Swedish krona against the ECU in November 1992, against the background of political uncertainty caused by the September 1994 elections, and the result of the referendum regarding the participation of Sweden in the EU (see Svensson, 1995). Despite existing proposals for the replacement of the existing statute of the Riksbank and its replacement with new institutional arrangements defining price stability as the overriding objective of price stability, this was not achieved. However, at the time of its announcement, the target was endorsed by the liberal-conservative coalition. It was also accepted by the social democrat government which took office in September 1994.

The inflation target announced by the Riksbank in 1993 involved a CPI inflation rate equal to 2% for 1995 and later years (excluding increases in indirect taxes and subsidies) with a tolerance interval of ±1 percentage point per year. The main operational instrument used by the Riksbank for the meeting of the target is a 2-week repo rate which is increased in case inflation forecasts exceed the 3% ceiling. The decision to increase the repo rate lies with the governing board of the Riksbank. The latter includes seven members who are appointed by the Parliament (four of whom are appointed by the parliament's ruling party or coalition) and the governor, who is appointed by the seven members for a term of five years. However, here it should be noted that the governor is not the chairman of the governing board. This position is assumed by one of the seven members. Furthermore, the vote of the chairman carries a double weight in the event of a tie vote. These arrangements have given rise to concern that the decisions of the Riksbank could be subject to political interventions (see McCallum, 1996). Nevertheless, during the period 1994-96 the Riksbank managed to keep CPI inflation within the range specified by the target.

Finland

Finland introduced inflation targets in February 1993 following the collapse of the peg of the markka to the ECU in September 1992. At the time of this collapse CPI inflation in Finland was already equal to 2.1%, therefore the inflation target set by the Bank of Finland was "to stabilize the rate of inflation permanently at the level of 2% by 1995", i.e. a point rather than a range target. The target refers to CPI inflation excluding increases in housing capital costs, indirect taxes, mortgage

Table 5.1

	1980-89	1990	1991	1992	1993	1994	1995	1996	1997
Canada	6.5	4.8	5.6*	1.5	1.8	0.2	2.2	1.6	1.4
Finland	7.3	6.0	5.6	4.1*	4.2	1.4	0.2	1.2	0.9
New Zealand	11.9	6.1*	2.6	1.0	1.3	1.7	3.8	2.3	0.8
Sweden	7.9	9.9	10.3	2.2*	5.7	3.0	2.4	1.2	1.6
UK	7.4	5.5	7.5	5.0*	3.4	2.5	2.6	2.8	2.3
EU15 average	5.3	4.9	5.6	4.6	3.8	3.3	3.0	2.7	2.2
Industrial countries	5.8	5.0	4.5	3.3	2.9	2.3	2.4	2.3	2.0

CPI Inflation in inflation-targeting countries (annual % change)
* denotes the year when inflation targets were introduced
Source: International Financial Statistics

payments and government subsidies[20]. Although the government immediately endorsed the target set by the Bank of Finland, it would appear that the new policy regime initially received a cool welcome by the markets. Furthermore, no changes in the statute of the Bank of Finland took place. Inflation expectations were that time quite high and "a seemingly low and strict inflation target was considered to be a severe brake on economic activity. Viewed from this angle, it was no surprise that inflation expectations as indicated by household and business surveys were not affected in any significant way" (see Brunila and Lahdenpera, 1995, p. 130). However, despite high inflationary expectations, actual inflation did not increase after the floating of the markka. In fact, as nominal wage restraint, productivity gains and fiscal moderation offset the inflationary impact of the devaluation, CPI inflation recorded a decline in 1993. This development, together with the endorsement of the inflation target by the new government which emerged in April 1995, provided a higher degree of confidence regarding the future prospects of

[20] This reflects the situation after a revision of the index which took place in June 1994.

Figure 5.1

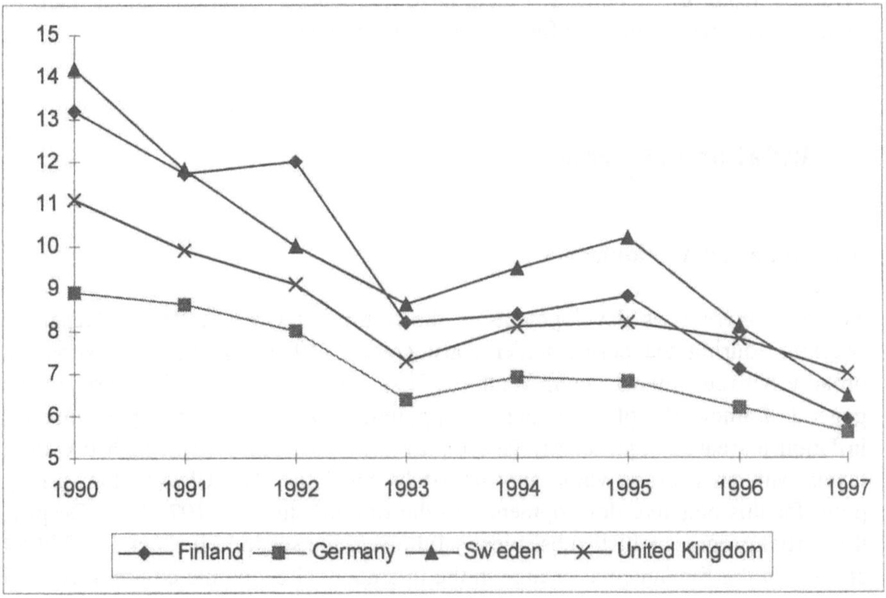

Long-term interest rates in EU inflation-targeting countries: convergence with Germany
Source: European Economy No 64, Statistical Appendix

the target. Subsequent developments confirmed the optimistic projections.

A summary of the evidence

The main message emerging from the above discussion is that in those countries where inflation targets have been introduced, inflation targets have been largely met and actual inflation has declined to the extent that it has taken values below the EU15 average and the average of the 25 countries which are classified by the IMF as industrial (see Table 5.1). Furthermore, in those EU countries which have adopted inflation targets, the credibility of monetary policy as it is implied by the convergence of long-term interest rates to the German low level seems to have improved over the last years (see Figure 5.1). This is certainly true for Finland and Sweden after 1995 (i.e. after the end of the period of political uncertainty in that country) whereas in the case of the United Kingdom the evidence is less conclusive. Nevertheless, all three countries were judged to have met the long-term interest rate criterion set by the Maastricht Treaty. Reductions in long-term interest rates have also taken place in New Zealand and Canada. All in all, the existing evidence from the countries which have introduced inflation targets can be regarded as a promising start for the new policy regime.

5.3. Inflation in Greece

5.3.1. Inflation developments

This section reviews developments in the history of Greek inflation. Generally speaking, during the period under consideration (1975-97) one can distinguish broadly between two different regimes. First, the period 1975-92 where, in the general framework of a rather disappointing macroeconomic performance, inflation increased significantly (see Figure 5.2) and stabilized at high two-digit levels with an average value approximately equal to 17%. Clearly, the turning point for this negative development was the first oil-shock in 1973-74[21]. Despite, the partial progress which subsequently followed, the second oil shock in 1979-80 confirmed the fundamental change in the international economic environment and pushed Greek (and European) inflation further up. However, in contrast to the improvement which subsequently took place in the other EU countries (see Table 5.2) in the 1980s, Greece failed to return to conditions of price stability and inflation remained at two digit levels[22]. Second, the period between 1993 and 1997 where, in the context of the stabilization/convergence programmes which had been implemented by Greek governments, together with the strong drachma policy which was introduced in 1988, inflation declined substantially. As a result, it has now returned to single digit levels. However, it still remains well above the EU average (see Figure 5.3)

One important difference between the years which preceded and followed 1993 refers to the announcement of *implicit* inflation objectives set by Greek governments. These were announcements for the path of price levels as both the Convergence Programme (CP) 1993-98 and the Revised Convergence Programme (RCP) 1994-99 have set quantitative targets for the rate of growth of consumer prices. However, despite the undeniable inflation progress which has been achieved since 1993, it is also true that with the exception of 1994, all these targets set by the government have been missed (see Table 5.3). In fact, one may notice

[21] The pre-1973 period saw the Greek economy achieving price stability, with an average annual rate of inflation less than 3%. During that period, Greek inflation performance was in line with that of the rest of the Western European countries.

[22] This was mainly due to the monetary accommodation of expansionary fiscal policies and the introduction of a wage-indexation scheme (ATA) that led to high and persistent inflation rates during the 1980s.

Figure 5.2

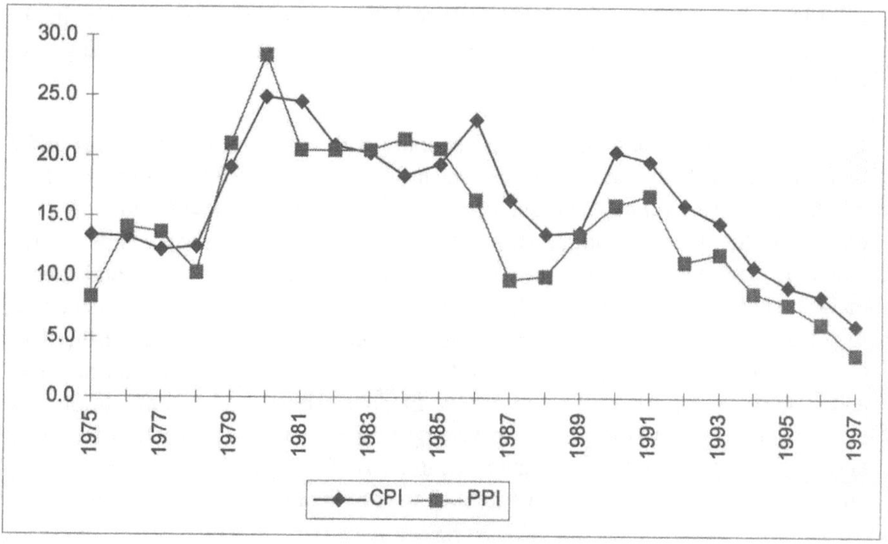

Inflation in Greece (average annual % change in CPI and PPI)
Source: Bank of Greece, Monthly Statistical Bulletin, various editions.

that over the last five years the deviation from the target has been rather substantial and has even followed an increasing pattern during the last three years[23]. As a result, despite the prolonged character of the stabilization effort, inflation remains three times higher than the EU average and in 1997 Greece was the only country of the Union which failed the Maastricht criterion with reference to price stability.

5.3.2. The main characteristics of Greek inflation

The main points of the previous section give rise to the following two questions: First, why, in the context of a number of stabilization programmes, all the (implicit) inflation targets set by successive Greek government have been missed? Second, despite the undeniable inflation progress which has been achieved in the 1990s, why does Greek inflation remain three times higher than the EU average ? In order to answer the above questions, one has to consider the main characteristics of Greek inflation within the context of the last ten years, namely

[23] Of course, even before 1993 the BoG used to announce inflation projections as an integral part of the annual Monetary Programmes. However, one might suggest that these loose inflation objectives were merely of a cosmetic nature as, at the end of the day, they were the outcome of the expected money financing of budget deficits.

during the application of the strong drachma policy. Such an examination would reveal that this policy, as a means of fighting inflation, has a certain degree of usefulness but, on the other hand, it also has certain limitations which, in the absence of a set of other necessary policies, render it a rather unconvincing anti-inflationary policy as far the future is concerned.

In the case of Greece, a small open economy with structural inefficiencies and a bad inflation record, one may argue that inflation is influenced, to a great extent, by the standard cyclical demand pressures in the goods market and cost-push effects in the labour market, structural weaknesses in the supply side of the economy (reflecting out-of-date institutional features in the goods and labour markets) and a widely-spread inflationary psychology embedded into the decisions of private agents, firms, and government. In other words, one may notice that CPI changes are influenced by imported inflation and the level of aggregate demand, and distortions in the goods and labour markets which hinder competition and allow firms to follow high mark-up pricing policies thereby preventing the price system from adjusting to real demand conditions. These distortions are created by factors such as price controls, restrictions in entering and leaving the markets of

Figure 5.3

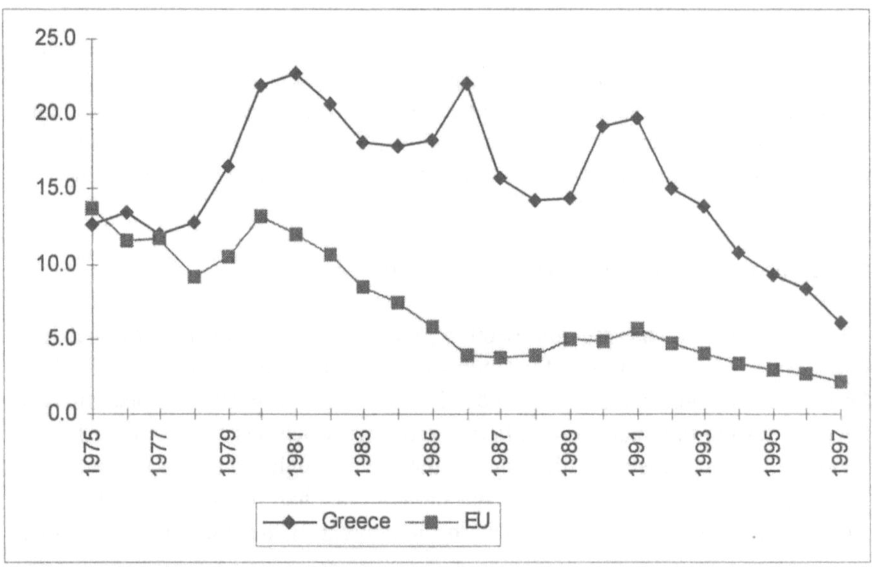

CPI inflation in Greece and the EU

Source: European Economy No 64, Statistical Appendix.

Table 5.2

Period	CPI	GDP deflator	PPI	CPI EU15	CPI USA	CPI Japan
1960-73	3.5	4.5	4.3	4.7	3.1	6.2
1975-92	17.1	17.2	16.3	8.1	5.7	3.9
1993-97	9.6	9.5	7.6	3.0	2.3	0.6

Average inflation in Greece and Western countries
Source: Bank of Greece, Monthly Statistical Bulletin, various editions and European Economy No 64, Statistical Appendix

certain goods and services, (state monopolies, "closed-shop" markets[24], rigid labour legislation, etc.), and are reflected in variables such as wage inflation, high - administratively set- prices of state monopolies etc.

Furthermore, one might argue that inflation in Greece is influenced by deeply-rooted high inflation expectations (something which is reflected in high wage demands) which, in turn, are affected by past inflation performance (i.e. the backward-looking part of inflationary expectations), labour and goods' markets distortions like those described above, the fiscal situation of the country, and perhaps more importantly, the degree of credibility (as it is perceived by agents) of an economic policy aimed at reducing inflation (i.e. the forward-looking part of inflationary expectations).

In the light of the above, it appears that the implicit inflation targets which have been set by the government have been all missed because the strong drachma policy, by its very nature, could not possibly address all the above components of

[24] A typical example of such a closed-shop market is the one of air flights to the Greek islands. At present, the national (state-owned) air-carrier of Greece, Olympic Airways, has the exclusive right of scheduling and conducting flights to these islands. As a result, the price of a return ticket from Athens to Rhodes is approximately equal to a return ticket from Athens to London! Other examples of closed markets include electricity supply, water supply, postal services, train services and other public utilities. The lack of competitive conditions in these markets is reflected both in the high prices which the state-controlled monopolies charge for the provision of the services and by the relatively low quality of the services provided. Furthermore, despite their dominant position in the markets, most of the state-owned utility companies present huge operating losses which are subsequently covered by the budget deficit.

Table 5.3

Year	Projection	Outcome	Deviation (Outcome-Projection)
1976	10	13.4	3.3
1977	9.5	11.9	2.7
1978	10	12.8	2.5
1979	11	16.5	8.0
1980	15	21.9	9.9
1981	N/A	22.7	N/A
1982	12.5	20.7	8.4
1983	20	18.1	0.2
1984	18	17.9	0.4
1985	19.5	18.3	-0.2
1986	16	22.1	7.0
1987	10	15.7	6.4
1988	12.0	14.2	1.5
1989	13	14.4	0.7
1990	15	19.2	5.4
1991	17	19.7	2.5
1992	11.9	15.0	3.9
1993	12.6	13.8	1.8
1994	10.8	10.8	0.1
1995	7.9	9.3	1.4
1996	6.1	8.3	2.3
1997	3.9	6.0	2.1

Inflation projections and outcomes
Source for outcomes: European Economy No 64, Statistical Appendix.
Source for projections: 1976-93 Garganas (1994); 1994-97 Bank of Greece, Economic Bulletin No 4, November 1994, p. 15.

inflation. More specifically, the strong drachma policy has been able to reduce a significant part of inflation, primarily by means of reducing imported prices, by reducing the profit margins of the firms which are exposed to international competition and by affecting the volume of aggregate demand pressure through its effect on domestically produced traded goods. However, one of the predominant

Figure 5.4

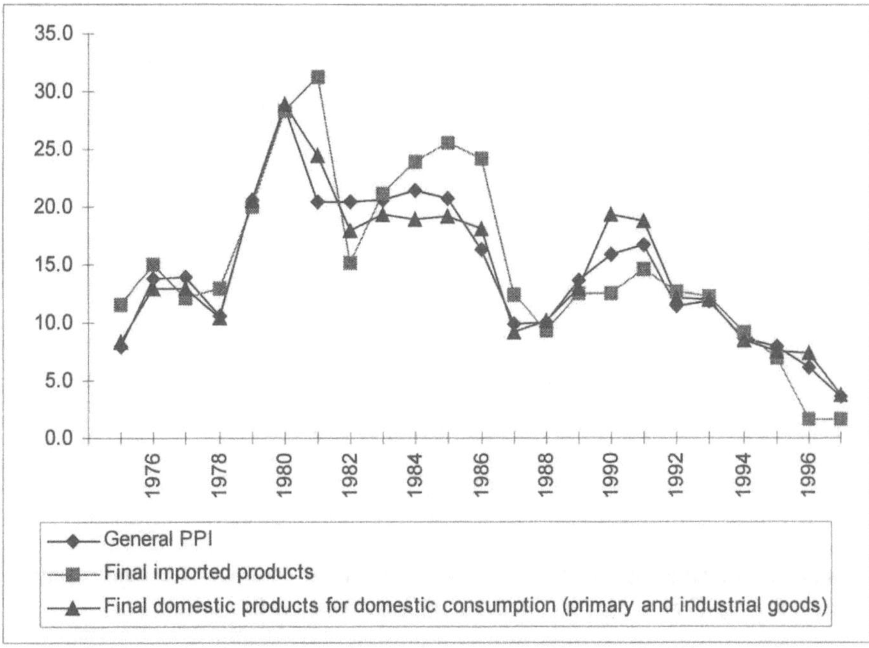

Domestic and imported inflation (average annual % change)
Source: Bank of Greece, Monthly Statistical Bulletin, various editions.

characteristics of Greek inflation today is of structural nature and, as a result, a number of adjustment reforms are necessary to take place in order to eliminate the existing distortions in the goods market (especially those of the non-traded goods sector of the economy) and labour market or even to improve the fiscal situation of the country. As a result, the strong drachma effect on actual inflation may be significant but it is of limited potential. In addition, there are now clear indications that this potential has almost been exhausted. In other words, in the 1990s the burden of anti-inflationary policy has been left with the exchange rate policy, something which has resulted in a relatively lax fiscal policy and very limited progress in the field of structural adjustments. However, for further inflation progress to take place, both fiscal consolidation and structural reforms have to be promoted in a more active way than in the context of the strong drachma.

Figure 5.4 presents the average annual rate of growth of producer prices in the goods market of the economy. One may notice that prior to 1988, imported inflation was typically higher than inflation in domestic products and the general price index. That situation obviously changed after 1988. Since 1991

Figure 5.5

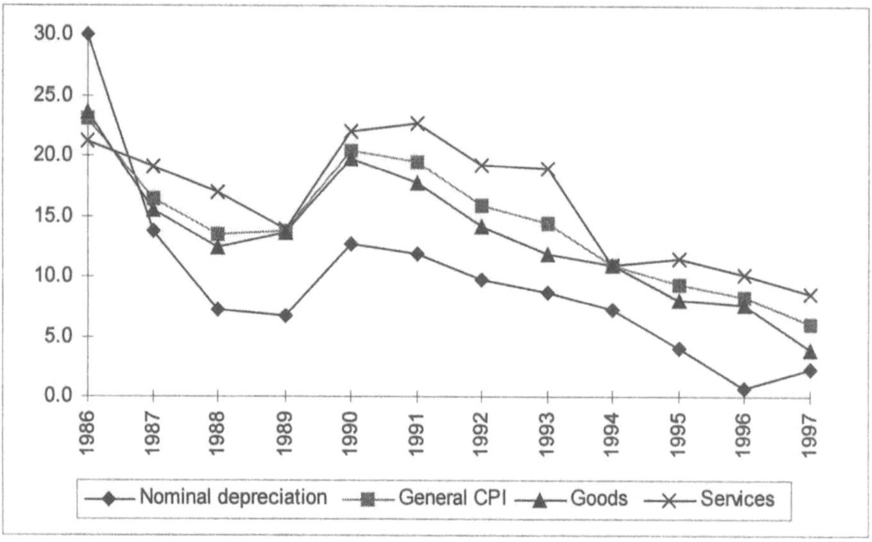

Nominal depreciation against the ECU and CPI inflation (average % annual change)
Source: Bank of Greece, Monthly Statistical Bulletin, various editions.

inflation has declined for all three categories of commodities (imported, domestic and general). However, it is also clear that the close shadowing of the ECU which has taken place over the last three years (1994-97) has resulted in a near elimination of imported inflation. Therefore, one might argue that the remaining rate of inflation, which is significantly higher than the European average, is due to structural weaknesses and to the forward-looking component of inflationary expectations. Further evidence for this view is provided when one examines developments in the field of consumer price indices. Figure 5.5 presents the post-1988 movements of the nominal exchange rate against the ECU and inflation in the fields of goods (imported and domestic) and services. Two points are worth mentioning: first, the increasingly stronger shadowing of the ECU during the period 1994-96 has coincided with a downwards rigidity in CPI inflation; second, inflation in the services sector (which largely represents inflation developments in the non-traded sector of the economy) has been consistently higher than that in the goods sector (which includes all imported goods). These developments are more evident in Tables 5.4 and 5.5 which present inflation developments in a number of indices which belong to the traded sector and non-trade sectors of the economy respectively. Table 5.4 reveals that in the 1990s inflation in the traded sector of the economy (and especially in durables and household supplies which represent the bulk of Greek imports) has consistently been below the level of general CPI

Table 5.4

Year	General CPI	Durables and household supplies	Clothing and footwear	Food
1988	13.5	9.3	18.1	11.1
1989	13.7	10.7	14.6	19.2
1990	20.4	15.3	17.2	21.1
1991	19.5	17.8	16.5	19.3
1992	15.9	12.3	14.0	14.1
1993	14.4	8.8	11.0	12.7
1994	10.9	8.9	10.1	12.9
1995	9.3	8.4	9.9	9.2
1996	8.3	6.2	9.3	8.1
1997	6.0	6.0	6.9	4.1

Inflation in the traded sector (annual % change)
Source: Bank of Greece, Monthly Statistical Bulletin, various editions.

inflation. In contrast, Table 5.5 shows that in the 1990s, inflation in those sub-indices which largely reflect developments in the non-traded sector of the economy, has either been in line with or higher than the rate of growth of general CPI. A possible exception to this rule is the sub-index which refers to transport and communication. However, this is a sector where state monopolies are concentrated, therefore inflation developments do not necessarily reflect cost developments. In contrast, it has been the case that on some occasions, Greek governments have deliberately delayed necessary price adjustments in these monopolies in an effort to keep general CPI inflation at levels consistent with those predicted by the RCP.

Another important reason which might explain the failure of the authorities to meet the implicit inflation targets set by the RCP refers to developments in the field of labour costs which are an important part of production costs and, by implication, of inflation. Figure 5.6 reveals that in contrast to the period 1991-93, when a disciplined incomes policy was implemented and increases in nominal wages were significantly lower than CPI inflation, during the period 1994-97 wage inflation developments were not favourable. Two important points emerge from this observation: First, in the absence of a disciplined incomes policy, the strong

Table 5.5

Year	General CPI	Housing	Health & personal care	Education & recreation	Transport and communi-cation	Other goods and services
1988	13.5	13.4	17.9	15.9	8.3	15.7
1989	13.7	10.0	13.1	13.3	6.8	12.6
1990	20.4	23.7	17.6	16.2	26.3	17.7
1991	19.5	26.4	18.6	18.6	19.4	18.4
1992	15.9	17.3	14.1	17.6	20.3	16.0
1993	14.4	15.8	20.3	14.5	18.8	15.0
1994	10.9	10.5	10.6	12.0	5.6	12.0
1995	9.3	9.7	9.1	14.8	6.2	10.3
1996	8.3	9.6	9.0	9.3	8.1	8.3
1997	6.0	2.7	4.3	8.0	5.3	8.3

Inflation in the non-traded sector (annual % change)
Source: Bank of Greece, Monthly Statistical Bulletin, various editions.

drachma policy has little (if any) impact on nominal wage inflation. Second, the rigidities existing in the current labour legislation do not allow wage adjustment in the labour market to adjust to real labour demand conditions (which are reflected in the field of an increasing unemployment rate) and combined with limited productivity gains, do not contribute to a substantial reduction in unit labour cost inflation.

All in all, the conclusion from the above is that the strong drachma policy has indeed contributed to a reduction in inflation primarily in the traded sector of the economy, by means of reducing imported inflation and firms' profit margins, and also by reducing the backwards-looking inflationary expectations. However, it is now quite clear that the strong drachma policy has certain limitations in terms of inflation progress. This is so because imported inflation has now been almost eliminated and the remaining rate of inflation is mainly structural and cannot be affected by a strong currency policy. A reduction in structural inflation presupposes a reduction in the rate of growth of prices in the non-traded sector of the economy as well as a reduction in the forward-looking component of inflationary expectations. For these components of inflation to be affected, Greek governments should implement policies which will break the inflationary psychology which has been established in the economy over the last twenty years. Such policies include the following:

First, an active promotion of further fiscal consolidation, with emphasis on a reduction in public consumption (see chapter 2) and hence the level of aggregate demand.

Second, an active promotion of competition in the market of all goods and services and in particular those which belong to the non-traded sector of the economy. To that direction, the liberalization of the remaining "closed" markets and the full or partial privatization of a number of loss-making state monopolies would be of the greatest importance.

Third, an organized effort to achieve the modernization of the labour market. Reforms aiming to reduce wage inflation and increase productivity gains, should also be accompanied by an appropriate incomes policy, consistent with the implicit inflation targets pursued by the authorities.

Figure 5.6

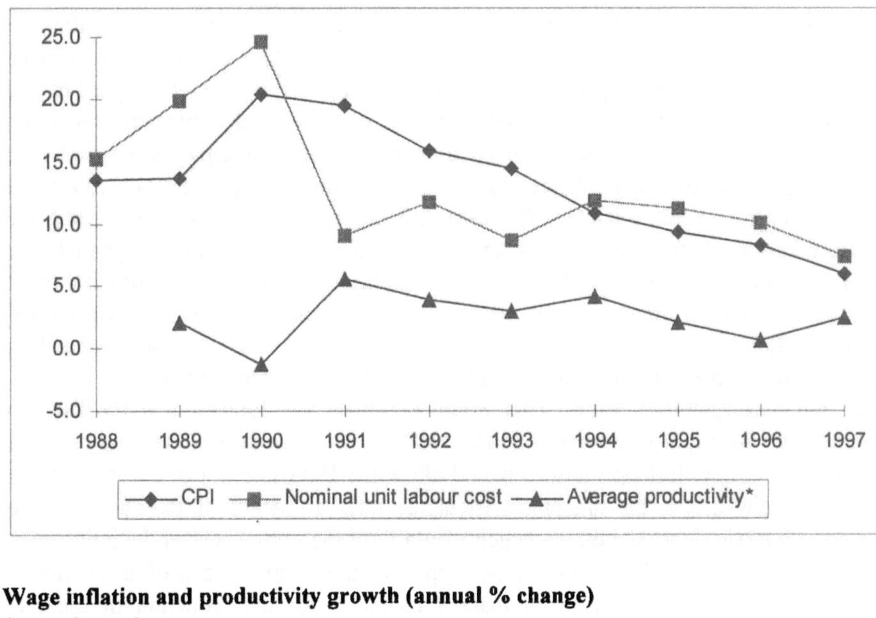

Wage inflation and productivity growth (annual % change)
** in industrial sector*
Data Source: Bank of Greece, Report of the Governor for 1996, p. 109 and Bank of Greece, Economic Bulletin No 10, p. 35.

Fourth, further promotion of the anti-inflationary credibility of macroeconomic policy. This is a point of particular importance, as our analysis in chapter 4 has highlighted the fact that apart from the difficulties in the field of inflation progress, the strong drachma policy faces more general limitations which create doubts regarding its future credibility and sustainability, especially after the recent accession of the drachma to the ERM.

In the rest of this chapter we will outline the main ingredients of what we believe could be a convincing alternative monetary strategy for Greece on the road to EMU. More specifically, such an alternative monetary policy regime could be the *direct targeting of inflation* (which may or may not be identical to the inflation rate prevailing in the EMU) together with granting *economic and political independence* to the BoG[25].

5.4. Main features and operation of an inflation-targeting regime in Greece

5.4.1. Why an inflation-targeting regime for Greece ?

The first reason behind our proposal for the introduction of a direct inflation-targeting regime in Greece is that such a regime has certain theoretical advantages compared with a monetary strategy based on exchange targets. As was argued earlier in this chapter, the latter has certain limits as its prolonged implementation often leads to currency overvaluation, speculative attacks and a collapse of the exchange rate pegging. Furthermore, as the introduction of inflation targets establishes a more open and transparent monetary framework, it can reduce uncertainty regarding the future course of monetary policy and provide the monetary authority with better incentives to deliver price stability through increased accountability. From that point of view, inflation targets can be seen as a more credible nominal anchor for the stabilization of inflationary expectations. In the context of an inflation-targeting regime in Greece, the drachma should be left without any intervention from the BoG to find its equilibrium value. This would eliminate the obligation of the BoG to defend an overvalued currency, and as such, it would enhance the credibility of monetary policy. Inflation targets would allow the BoG to readjust occasionally, if the necessity arises, the drachma's exchange rate, by means of foreign exchange market interventions, something which would limit the output cost of the adjustment process towards EMU participation by supporting the external sector of the economy. It would also ensure a more permanent character for the reduction of the risk

[25]As a matter of fact, on December 2 1997, the Greek government passed a Bill in the Parliament (No 2548/97) granting independence to the Bank of Greece. This is a mostly welcome development in the conduct of monetary policy.

premium associated with drachma-denominated portfolio investment caused by the March 1998 devaluation. Furthermore, inflation targets would provide the BoG with additional degrees of freedoms in the conduct of monetary policy for purposes of stabilization in the event of unforeseen economic circumstances such as a demand shock.

A second argument for the introduction of a direct inflation-targeting regime in Greece refers to its expected impact on fiscal policy. As we have seen in chapter 2, in the 1990s the stabilization of the Greek economy has been mainly based on the exchange rate anchor. This course has resulted in a rather lax fiscal policy (placing little emphasis on reducing public consumption) which cannot guarantee a substantial improvement in the current fiscal imbalances. The introduction of formal inflation targets would result in a more disciplined fiscal policy and hence a lower level of aggregate demand because it would establish a non-cooperative game between the government and the central bank. This argument runs as follows. Suppose that an inflation target is set and the government subsequently follows a fiscal policy inconsistent with this target. Under such circumstances, the BoG will have to take all necessary steps to meet the inflation target and these steps would almost certainly include an increase in short-term interest rates. This would be costly for the government in the following two respects: It would increase the cost of servicing the public debt and it could result in an economic slowdown for which the public would most probably hold the government responsible. As both developments would certainly be quite costly for the government, the result of the game would most probably be a more disciplined fiscal policy with the level of the interest rate being the "enforcement mechanism". In other words, the adoption of an inflation-targeting regime is expected to "tie" the government's hands by preventing it from applying inconsistent fiscal policies.

In practice, a similar non-cooperative game between the government and the central bank is also emerging when an exchange rate pegging policy is introduced. The question which then arises is why inflation targets should be expected to impose a higher degree of discipline on Greek fiscal authorities than exchange rate targets. The answer has to do with the fact that under an exchange rate pegging regime, the interest rate is not the only instrument available to the central bank to meet the exchange rate target. The latter can also resort to direct intervention in the foreign exchange market. The implications of this option are two-fold. First, the government does not have the same degree of motivation to apply disciplined fiscal policies since there is a serious possibility that, after all, the central bank may not raise interest rates or not raise them to the extend that would be necessary to maintain the peg in the absence of the intervention option. This is particularly true in cases where the government has the ability to exercise informal pressures on an otherwise institutionally independent central bank. Second, and most important, the intervention option undermines the incentive structure of the central bank to "punish" the government in case the latter follows a lax fiscal policy. One should not forget that the central bank is not an organization detached by society: it operates within the same political/economic environment with the government and can receive criticism (either by the government or the electorate) when it resorts to measures reducing the citizens' welfare. It is rather plausible to assume that if two options are available to the central bank to pursue an exchange rate target, one unpopular with the government and the electorate (raising interest rates) and one neutral (intervention), the bank will be biased towards the first option as long as it is able to meet its monetary objective (exchange rate stability) and its professional reputation as an efficient institution able to meet the monetary targets set is not question. However, the situation may be different under an inflation targeting regime where the professional competency of the central banker will be judged by the inflation performance it delivers. Under such circumstances, the central bank may be less tolerant of fiscal policies which are inconsistent with the inflation target set and threaten its professional reputation, hence be more willing to raise interest rates in response to such policies. In brief, inflation targets produce a superior incentive structure for both the government and the central bank to follow policies consistent with price stability. In the case of Greece, where in the 1990s heavy intervention in the foreign exchange market was common practice, inflation targets may be more efficient in terms of establishing the non-cooperative game earlier mentioned.

A third argument in favour of inflation targets in Greece is related to its superiority in terms of affecting the volume of total aggregate demand. As is well known, controlling the level (and composition) of aggregate demand is perhaps the most effective way of controlling inflation. In principal, under an exchange rate pegging regime the central bank loses control over interest rates, hence it loses its ability to affect aggregate demand by means of this instrument[26]. For example, a country facing an economic boom calling for increases in its interest rates to control inflation will not be able to take action since an increase in domestic interest rates would cause an appreciation of the national currency. In contrast, in an inflation-targeting regime, where the main policy instrument is the short-term interest rate, the central bank can have an effective control over the level of aggregate demand through the interest-rate effects on the volume of both traded and non-traded goods and services (which in the case of Greece, a semi-industrialized economy, is quite large). Hence, by adopting

[26] In a fixed exchange rate regime, there is only one degree of freedom available in the filed of monetary policy. This represents a major disadvantage as there is no straightforward answer as to how this degree will be used. A hegemonic solution may be adopted, in which case one country conducts independent monetary policy and the rest of the countries of the system adjust their interest rates to the one selected by the reference country. Alternatively, a symmetric solution can be adopted, in which case the countries participating in the system jointly decide on the level of the (common) interest rate. However, the latter solution is often unattainable, in which case the system becomes hegemonic *de facto* (see De Grauwe 1994,b). For the case of Greece, it is plausible to assume that the unilateral shadowing of the euro after 1999 is equivalent to operating within a hegemonic regime as it is difficult to assert that the ECB will be influenced in any significant way by the BoG in setting the interest rate for the euro area.

inflation targets, the BoG would be able to increase short-term interest rates in due course in order to reduce inflationary pressures.

Of course, one might suggest that in practice, exchange rate management is often achieved by means of changes in interest rates (for example, exchange rate pressure is often accompanied by increases in interest rates). In that case, exchange rate control is equivalent to aggregate demand control. That would certainly be a valid argument. However, it would not always be applicable due to the intervention option earlier mentioned. If the central bank pursues its exchange rate target mainly by means of intervening in the foreign exchange rate market rather than through changes in the interest rates, exchange rate management does not imply total aggregate demand management. Under such a scenario, the central bank's policies mainly affect aggregate demand through their effects on the volume of demand for traded goods but leave the volume of demand for the non-traded goods largely unaffected. In the case of Greece, where foreign exchange market intervention has been quite common in the 1990s, it is plausible to argue that the introduction of inflation targets will contribute to a reduction in inflation through better control on the demand volume of the non-traded sector of the economy, an area in which inflation has displayed significant downwards rigidity (see section 5.3.2 above)

Finally, a fourth argument in favour of direct inflation targets has to do with the widely endorsed opinion that such a monetary policy regime is more likely to succeed in maintaining price stability and reducing inflation variability if introduced after the stabilization of the economy has taken place, rather than in conditions of two-digit inflation rates (see Brunila and Lahdenpera 1995, De Grauwe, 1996b). Certainly, Greece now meets this requirement as inflation has fallen from 20% in 1990 to approximately 6% in 1997. Furthermore, economic conditions as a whole now look favourable for the introduction of the new policy regime: Domestic labour demand is not particularly strong as unemployment in Greece has now been stabilized around 10%. Furthermore, inflation in the main trading partners of Greece (i.e. the EU) is quite low (2%) and it is projected to stay so in the foreseeable future. From that point of view, the adoption of formal inflation targets would "cash-in" on the inflation gains achieved in the 1990s, providing, at the same time, the necessary momentum to break the currently observed downward rigidity of inflation.

5.4.2. Implementation and operation of inflation targets in Greece

An inflation-targeting regime does not represent only a policy rule but rather a full monetary policy framework. As such, it should be characterized by a clear final objective, defined to be the maintenance of price stability; an unambiguous policy target; and a number of policy indicators and instruments through which the BoG would gather information to assess the situation at any point in time. A condition *sine qua non* for inflation targets to function as an effective nominal anchor for the Greek economy is for these targets to be regarded by the public as operationally and politically credible[27]. In the absence of these prerequisites, the adoption of inflation targets may fail to produce inflation progress and may even lead to increased output variability[28].

5.4.2.1. *Implementation of inflation targets*

The first issue related to the operational credibility (feasibility) condition of inflation targets refers to the definition of price stability they aim to deliver. A number of economists (e.g. Hoskins 1991, Freedman 1991) have suggested that the thoroughly debated literature on the costs of inflation makes a case for a zero inflation target. However, it is now increasingly acknowledged that a virtually zero inflation target might not be optimal and, as a result, there is a good case for the BoG to set a low, positive-value inflation target. First, there is evidence suggesting that official statistics may overestimate the actual rate of inflation[29], hence a zero inflation target may actually lead an economy into deflation. Second, on the realistic assumption of downward rigidity in nominal wages, reductions in real wages (often desirable for labour market adjustments), can only take place through an increase in prices. Hence, a zero inflation target may hinder relative wage and price adjustments which in turn would hinder economic efficiency, increase distortions in the labour market and lead to an increase in the natural rate of unemployment (see Fischer 1995). Third, a zero rate of inflation implies the existence of a zero downward limit for real *ex-post (ex-ante)* interest rates, namely minus the observed (expected) rate of inflation. It has been suggested (see Yates,

[27] Andersson and Berg (1995, p. 214) define operational credibility as the ability of the central bank to fulfill the announced target of monetary policy. Operational credibility, which is directly linked to the feasibility of the targets set, is influenced by the conduct of monetary policy but also by fiscal and structural policy. On the other hand, political credibility reflects the investor's assessment about the probability of a policy regime shift, i.e. an abandonment of the direct inflation-targeting approach. According to the authors, political credibility depends on the political support for the price-stability target, the degree of central bank independence, the record of anti-inflationary policy and, to a lesser extent, on the conduct of monetary policy. Furthermore, political credibility is negatively correlated with a large and increasing public debt.

[28] Under certain circumstances (e.g. in the event of an adverse supply shock) inflation targets which lack credibility may result in a worse economic performance in the form of a higher output variability. The reason is that under such circumstances, the meeting of the inflation targets would necessitate a tighter monetary policy compared to the one which would have been implemented otherwise.

[29] This overestimation, which in the case of the USA is thought to be in the range of 0.5 to 2.0 percentage points (see Moulton 1996, Shapiro and Wilcox 1996), is mainly due to a substitution bias in the fixed-weight index, "new goods" bias and failure to account adequately for quality improvements. Commodity substitution bias refers to the situation where consumers substitute commodities whose prices are increasing more rapidly with commodities whose prices present lower rates of increase. In a similar fashion, new goods bias describes the situation where consumers substitute commodities whose prices are increasing more rapidly with commodities which may be new and not included in the index.

1995) that there may be circumstances where a negative real interest rate may be desirable, not least for short-run output stabilization purposes. By imposing a zero limit on this rate, the authorities would deprive monetary policy of its "constrained discretion" in coping with unexpected economic circumstances.

The second issue to be addressed is whether the inflation target in Greece should be specified in terms of the price level or its rate of growth. The main disadvantage of setting a target for the inflation is that under such a scenario, large unanticipated shocks will be treated as bygones and will never be offset. This would increase uncertainty regarding future economic conditions through an increase in the variance of the probability distribution of price level forecasts because ensuring stationarity for the inflation rate only would leave a unit root in the price level (see Bernanke and Mishkin, 1997). On the other hand, a price level target could import significant volatility into monetary policy in the short run which could imply an increase in output volatility (which, however, might be mitigated by allowing the central bank to set level targets drifting upwards in a pre-determined way); and increased instrument instability which could increase speculation regarding the future course of monetary policy as, due to the well known lags associated with the effects of monetary policy, one-time shocks would affect the central bank's policy over a considerable and uncertain length of time. Although both sets of arguments seem plausible and well-founded, Mayes and Chapple (1995) argues that experience comes down in favour of an inflation rather than a price level target since the inflation rate *per se* is a more familiar concept to the general public than the level of a selected price index. Furthermore, setting a target for the rate of growth of the price level allows some room for manoeuvre in the short run while still adhering to the general principal of price stability. Finally, and perhaps more importantly, as Andersson and Berg (1995) argue, a price level target is much more ambitious than an inflation target. The reason is that a period with higher-than-targeted inflation must be followed by a period with lower inflation, which could imply zero inflation or even deflation. All in all, existing international practices and feasibility considerations argue that it would be preferable for the BoG to adopt a target for the rate of growth of prices rather than the price level itself.

A third issue concerns the selection of the index whose rate of growth will be targeted by the BoG. The choice of an appropriate targeted index involves balancing three key characteristics: comprehensiveness, visibility and accuracy (see Laidler and Robson, 1993). A comprehensive price index is one which comprises all fields of economic activity, namely consumer goods and services, investment and government expenditure, exports, accumulated inventories and payments to production factors (i.e. wages, profits, rent and interest payments). From that point of view, the GDP deflator is superior to other indices. However, the GDP deflator presents a number of important visibility and accuracy disadvantages. First, estimates regarding the movements of some of its components (e.g. those which refer to public services or imputed items like the rent of owner-occupied accommodation) usually entail a considerable degree of bias. Second, estimates regarding its movements are published with a considerable time lag and they are often revised. In contrast, both the CPI and the RPI are published monthly and are not revised regularly. When it comes to a choice between these two, Archer (1995 p.248) argues that because the most important costs associated with unstable prices seem to be located in the productive sector of the economy, in principle producer prices should matter more than consumer prices. On the other hand, it would appear that the CPI is superior in terms of visibility and accuracy. With regard to the former, headline CPI movements attract the highest degree of press attention as they affect the position of all agents (individuals, private firms and government). Also, since the calculation of the CPI typically involves fewer items than those involved in the calculation of the RPI, the importance of biases due to measurement errors is expected to be more limited. Finally, (Mayes and Chappler, 1995) suggest that the CPI is the index whose movements provide better information for monetary policy assessment purposes since it places a higher weight on imported goods (whose prices are affected by monetary policy more directly and more quickly due to the fact that the latter has a strong impact on the exchange rate)[30]. All in all, the balance of arguments referring to comprehensiveness, visibility and accuracy turns in favour of a target for the rate of growth of the Greek CPI.

A fourth issue related to the adoption of inflation target by the BoG refers to the choice between a point versus a range inflation target. Cukierman (1994b) argues that the distinction between point and range targets is one of secondary importance when agents form rational expectations. The reason is that under such circumstances economic agents perceive that the monetary authorities can only achieve a certain inflation range even when they announce a point target because of their limited control over inflation. However, most of the countries which have adopted an inflation-targeting regime set targets in terms of ranges. This practice is usually explained on the following grounds: First, in most countries, including Greece, the exact nature of the relationships which link monetary instruments with actual inflation is usually unknown, therefore it would be almost impossible to meet a specific point target[31]. That would put the monetary authorities in the unpleasant

[30] Before closing this section, it might be useful to mention that a number of observers (e.g. Yates, 1995) have suggested that the choice of index is not very important in the long-run, if the alternative indices exhibit common long-run trends, i.e. if they cointegrate. Indeed, in the case of Greece recent empirical evidence suggests that a number of price indices do cointegrate (see Papapetrou and Hondrogiannis, 1997). However, the existence of cointegration does not exclude the possibility that there will be short-run divergence between the series. Such short-run divergence may be enough to affect inflationary expectations and reduce the probability of meeting the target (or, perhaps more importantly, increase the costs of achieving it).

[31] Moschos (1995) found that over the period January 1975-June 1994, changes in the weighted exchange rate of the drachma vis-à-vis a basket of 19 currencies and the broad money supply have had a certain impact on the rate of growth of the Greek CPI. According to his results, each of the two variables explains 8-10% of the variance of inflation forecasting error, i.e. a total of 16-20%. Although this is not a negligible percentage, it is

position of having to provide explanations as to why the target was not met (Goodhart and Vinals, 1994). Second, a rigid point target does not allow any flexibility in monetary policy, a fact which may introduce elements of instability into the economy (Brunila and Lahdenpera, 1995). If, based on the above, a range inflation target is to be preferred, the next question is what its width should be[32]. The main issue here is the trade-off between increased feasibility, i.e. the probability to stay within the range target, and the usefulness of a wide range target as a nominal anchor for inflation expectations. Feasibility would be inversely related to the difference between the initial level of inflation and the upper and lower limits of the range. In addition, the wider the width of the target range is, the higher is the probability that the target will be met (even in the event of a non-monetary shock). But, on the other hand, the wider the range is, the less useful is the target in changing the behaviour of agents through a reduction in inflation expectations, not least because "agents often perceive the upper limit of any range to be the effective target for policy, thereby imbuing inflation expectations with an inflation bias" (see Haldane, 1995a p. 7)[33].

Finally, the fifth issue to be addressed by the BoG before setting an inflation target refers to the selection of the optimal periods over which the inflation targets will have to be met. The time horizon of inflation targets is conditional upon the lag effects present in monetary policy, that is upon a number of relationships which link the movements of monetary instruments and inflation indicators with the movements of actual inflation. Nevertheless, it would appear that the time horizon of inflation targets should be set neither too short nor too long. Too short intervals would not allow time for the rate of inflation to adjust to the movements of the instruments to be chosen for meeting the targets set; would deprive the central bank of one of the advantages of inflation targets vis-à-vis intermediate monetary targets, i.e. a higher degree of flexibility in the conduct of monetary policy; and would also create the danger of overreaction at the first sign of inflationary pressures. On the other hand, too long intervals would deprive the officials of the central bank, the government and private agents of the opportunity to assess the degree of success of monetary policy in achieving the targets (see Laidler and Robson 1993).

---

not high either. Furthermore, his results suggest that change caused by an increase in the exchange rate is completed within a period of 15 months, whereas the first effect of a monetary shock on inflation appears with a time lag of at least 12 months.

[32] In relation to this, another interesting question is whether the authorities should select a target range centered around the optimal rate of inflation (whatever that rate might be) or should have it skewed to one side or the other. For an interesting discussion on this point see Yates (1995).

[33] Finally, the choice of the width is related to the initial level of inflation and the nature of the targeted index. Ben-Bassat (1995) argues that the volatility of inflation is positively correlated with its level, therefore the reduction in inflation allows the selection of a narrower width; and that excluding items whose prices are quite volatile allows the selection of a narrower band.

All in all, on the basis of our previous discussion and having in mind credibility considerations, we propose a four-year (1998-2001) monetary strategy involving range targets for the rate of growth of the Greek consumer price index. The justification for the last three components of our proposal (range, growth rate, CPI inflation targets) appears above. The rationale behind the idea of introducing a rolling inflation targets strategy has as follows: In Greece, a country whose current inflation rate is three times higher than the EU average, the rate of change of prices is influenced by the following factors: (a) imported inflation; (b) the standard cyclical demand pressure in the goods market and the cost-push effects in the labour market; (c) structural weaknesses in the supply side of the economy reflecting out of date institutional features in the goods and labour market; (d) a weak fiscal position predominantly expressed by a high level of public debt; and (e) a widely spread inflation psychology embedded into the decisions of individual agents, private firms and the government. As far as point (a) is concerned, by the end of 1997 imported inflation in Greece had declined substantially, therefore the potential for further reduction is rather limited. With regard to (b), over the last three years or so economic activity in Greece has shown signs of a modest recovery which is projected to continue in the near future. As a result, the effect of the cyclical demand pressure on prices is not expected to contribute to any reduction in prices. A substantial reduction in the existing rate of inflation is conditional upon the reduction in the existing distortions in the markets of goods, services and labour as well as upon the pursuit of a disciplined fiscal policy. However, it is quite clear that even if the Greek authorities proceed to an immediate, full implementation of measures which were announced along with the recent devaluation, any beneficial effect on inflation will take some time to appear as structural adjustments do not take place instantly. In the absence of a deliberate suppression of aggregate demand, it would be over-optimistic to expect a rapid deceleration of inflation in the near future. Setting an inflation target equal to the EU average would most probably not constitute a feasible objective and the credibility of such an inflation target may be doubted by the markets. Furthermore, under the present circumstances such an inflation target would almost certainly "condemn" Greece to higher than otherwise long-term real interest rates, at least for a painfully long time until the commitment were to become fully credible.

In the light of the above, a monetary strategy involving rolling inflation targets would have three considerable advantages. First, and fairly obvious, due to the existence of the "higher" component, it would increase the chances of the BoG meeting the target. Second, due to the "gradually converging" component, it would signal the commitment of Greece to pursue EMU participation in a consistent way and would not undermine markets' expectation on this issue. Third, as a result of its gradual character, such a monetary strategy would imply a lower output (and employment loss). In other words, it would ensure that further reduction in inflation would not necessitate large swings in economic activity and/or instrument instability in the conduct of monetary policy, e.g. abrupt and large swings in interest rates and exchange rates, elements which could create or intensify the short-run trade-off between inflation and output variance (see Archer, 1995). As a result, it would appear that if Greece is to join the EMU on 1 January 2002, i.e. the date of the replacement of national currencies with the euro, she could now introduce a four-year monetary programme (1998-2001) involving annual inflation targets gradually converging to the EU average. Starting from an inflation rate of 6% at the beginning of 1998, the programme could aim at an annual reduction in the inflation rate by approximately 1.5 percentage points per year. In that case, the corresponding range targets could be set as follows: 1998: 6% to 4.5%, 1999: 4.5% to 3.0%, and from 2000 onwards 3% to 2%. In our view, these ranges are narrow enough for influencing private sector's expectations but also wide enough so that hitting the range target will be a feasible objective. Provided that the government would introduce the promised structural reforms necessary in the goods and labour markets, such a monetary strategy could establish a downward path for inflation targets which would not be so steep as to appear impossible but sufficiently steep to show a clear downward trend for inflation. To that end, in an effort to enhance further the credibility of the new policy regime during the transition period between the introduction of inflation targets and the accession of Greece to the EU, the BoG could seek the approval of the ECB for the actual level of inflation targets in the same way as Greek governments acquire the approval of the European Commission for the rest of the economic policies which they apply.

5.4.2.2. Operation of inflation targets

The first issue to be addressed here is directly related to the political credibility of the new monetary regime. More specifically, it refers to the selection of the body which should be responsible for the setting of the inflation targets. The countries which have adopted an inflation-targeting regime have chosen different practices on this issue. For example, in the UK the inflation target is set by the government whereas elsewhere, (e.g. in New Zealand and Canada), the target is jointly agreed by the central bank and the government[34]. The rationale behind the choices of these countries is that a government which has had a say in the setting of an inflation target is unlikely to criticize publicly this target later, therefore it cannot undermine its credibility. But, on the other hand, it might well be the case (see Goodhart and Vinals, 1994) that a political party in opposition which criticizes the governmental economic policy in general, could also criticize the target jointly agreed by the government and the central bank. Under such circumstances, the credibility of the target might be doubted if agents perceive a substantial probability of a change of the party in office.

In Greece, where monetary policy has been subject to the political business cycle bias (see Alogoskoufis and Philipopoulos, 1992) and the government has a long-standing reputation of interference in as many fields of economic life as possible, it would

[34] Of course, in all countries the responsibility for meeting the target is left to the central bank.

appear that an inflation-targeting regime would be regarded as politically credible only if it the targets are set by an *independent* Bank of Greece. Of course, the BoG would have to discuss its intentions with the government before announcing the target in order to ensure the coordination of monetary, fiscal and incomes policies. However, by leaving the final decisions regarding the inflation targets to the BoG only, one would exclude the possibility of partisan political business cycles effects in the field of monetary policy (see also next chapter). Finally, one might argue that in the context of a democratic political system, the government has to maintain an escape mechanism, i.e. the right to override the targets set by the central bank, in order to cope with adverse economic circumstances. Indeed, such escape clauses are in existence in other inflation-targeting economies (e.g. New Zealand, United Kingdom). Thus, if unanticipated real shocks ever hit the economy, an escape clause put in place would allow the government with the approval of the Parliament to override the targets set by the BoG by choosing higher temporary inflation targets. However, it would be important to take all the necessary steps to ensure that the government will not make use of such an escape mechanism too often. Furthermore, if the necessity arises, the Parliament should publicly explain the rationale behind its decision to override the targets and define a relatively short-run, clear-cut transition period for the return to the *status quo ante.*

The second issue related to the operation of inflation targets refers to the policy instruments to be used by the BoG in order to achieve the meeting of the inflation targets. As earlier argued, the main policy instruments used by countries which have adopted formal inflation targets is the short-term interest rate and the same could also be true tin Greece. On the other hand, a vital element for the success of an inflation-targeting regime in delivering price stability is the selection of an appropriate set of indicators as guides for the conduct of monetary policy. Indicators are those variables which can capture information about inflation and inflationary expectations because they have shown predictive power for inflation in the past. By following closely the movements of such variables, the central bank makes its assessment regarding the future movements of inflation and judges accordingly whether and how it should intervene in order to ensure that the inflation targets are met. Policy indicators currently in use in inflation-targeting countries include monetary variables, such as the rate of growth of various monetary aggregates, the rate of growth of credit provided by commercial banks and other credit institutions[35], spot and forward exchange rates, the movements of

[35] Credit developments in particular are considered to be of great importance within the framework of an inflation-targeting regime. The underlying argument is that in the short and medium-term time horizon, changes in money supply do not respond perfectly to changes in money demand. As a result, if the rate of growth of money supply is higher than the rate of growth of agents' money demand, expenditure would increase so that money holdings would remain at the desired level. Under such conditions, excessive credit creation (caused, for example, by a surge in consumers' confidence) could lead to increased expenditure which in turn could build up inflationary pressures. By following developments in the field of credit creation, the central bank has the ability to intervene in due course, either by means of

the price indices which are not targeted (e.g. PPI, GDP deflator etc.), the rate of growth of equity prices, the shape of the yield curve (i.e. forward interest rates) and prices in the housing market (a fairly credible reflector of general demand conditions); activity variables such as trends in consumer spending, factory production and the divergence of actual production from its potential level (i.e. the output gap); variables referring to labour market conditions such as the rates of growth of nominal unit labour costs and nominal wages and the percentage of unemployment; fiscal indicators such as such the rate of growth of government spending and the size of the budget deficit; and survey data on price expectations. All or some of the above could be included in the BoG's policy indicators agenda.

A third issue associated with the operation of inflation targets refers to the handling of strong unanticipated shocks such as an oil crisis or a sudden increase in indirect taxes (not a rare phenomenon in the case of Greece) which may render the meeting of the inflation target either very difficult or very costly in terms of welfare loss. Stevens and Debelle (1995) argue that monetary authorities should not be particularly worried about demand shocks as under such circumstances there may be relatively little real conflict between the price and output objectives[36]. However, the problem seems to be more complicated when the unanticipated shock comes from the supply side. In this scenario, monetary policy can reduce price variability only by increasing short-term output variability (see Andersson and Berg, 1995). Therefore, the question is how inflation targets can be selected so that the short-term price-output trade-off will not undermine the political credibility of the monetary framework. To that end, the choice of target ranges rather than target values discussed above is an obvious precautionary step so that, if the necessity arises, there will be some room for easing monetary policy without redefining the inflation targets. However, if the shock is a severe one, this may not be enough. For such occasions, a common practice, which can certainly be adopted by Greece, is to exclude from the targeted index a number of items whose prices are thought to be directly influenced by external shocks[37].

---

increasing interest rates or by means of other measures (e.g. increasing the reserves ratio, conducting open market operations etc.).

[36] Take for example the scenario of a positive demand shock which creates a positive output gap. Increased demand would result in inflation pressures which would appear in the movements of the policy indicators. The central bank could then adjust short-term interest rates in due course and in such a way that these inflationary pressures will neither give rise to a higher level of actual inflation nor destabilize long-term inflation expectations.

[37] Items which are usually excluded from the targeted index include energy and food prices, changes in indirect taxes, local authorities levies and changes in mortgage and other interest rates. As short-run interest rates are regarded as the main instrument of monetary policy, interest rate changes are often excluded from the targeted index so that authorities can use this instrument to suppress inflationary pressures without increasing the measured rate of inflation. A similar argument can be made for changes in indirect taxes in the sense that these can be used for a reduction in the budget deficit which is thought to influence inflationary expectations. The string attached to such practices is that if the targeted index excludes a large number of items, it could destabilize inflation expectations in the sense that it could mitigate

Another practice which could be adopted is to allow the government to ask the central bank to override the inflation target set in the event of serious, unforeseen circumstances such as a natural disaster or large terms of trade shocks[38]. However, if the government is allowed to override the inflation target, that could undermine the credibility of the monetary framework by leaving room for external interventions in the conduct of monetary policy. As a result, in some of the countries where inflation targets have been adopted (e.g. New Zealand), the government is institutionally bound to explain publicly the reasons behind its decision to override the target. Such an arrangement should also be adopted in the case of Greece.

Finally, another key element for the successful operation of an inflation-targeting regime in Greece would be the regular publication of a report presenting the independent assessment of the BoG regarding the inflation situation, its future prospects and the policies which the bank believes to be necessary for the meeting of the targets set. A typical Inflation Report (e.g. the Inflation Report published by the Bank of England) should include a detailed analysis regarding the movements of the variables thought to influence inflation and presents probabilistic forecasts reflecting the projections of the central bank for the movements of inflation for a period up to two years ahead, i.e. the horizon over which a change in monetary policy is believed to have its greatest effect on the price level. The usefulness of this form of communication between the monetary authority and the public is that it increases the degree of transparency and public understanding of the objectives and macroeconomic implications of monetary policy because it obliges the central bank to publish its objectives, explain its actions towards meeting its targets and justify its future inflation projections. In that respect, the Inflation Report increases the motivation of the central bank to deliver price stability by means of increasing the degree of accountability of the central bank towards the public. The latter will judge the professional competence of the bank on the basis of the relevance of the views and the accuracy of the projections previously recorded in the Report. The Report enhances public debate on the bank's views and monetary policy in general, a fact which increases the knowledge of the public about the potential (but also the limits) of monetary policy; and provides the basis for the provision of feedback communication from the public to the bank regarding the latter's views and policies (see Bank of England, 1996). This point is particularly relevant in the case of Greece, a country where the existing information flow from the Bank of Greece to the general public is rather poor, and this is an issue that calls urgently for improvement. However, a vital element for the proper functioning of the Inflation Report in Greece would be to exclude any possibility that the views expressed in it will not represent

---

one of the main merits of inflation-targeting, i.e. its advantage of being unambiguous and well understood by the public.

[38] Haldane (1995a, p. 10) justifies these practices on the grounds that "supply shocks shift the equilibrium price level but should not, of themselves, affect underlying inflation (at least in terms of first-round effects). Their effect is therefore legitimately accommodated in the setting of monetary policy (though there is a need to be mindful of potential second-round effects)".

the independent assessment of the BoG regarding the future prospects of inflation. In order to avoid such a danger, some further elements of the existing British practice can be adopted. According to the present monetary arrangements in Britain, government officials are not allowed to see the text of the Inflation Report before the latter it is being published. This practice, together with the rather speedy (within six weeks) publication of the minutes of the monthly meeting of the Governor of the Bank of England with the Chancellor of the Exchequer, could serve a twofold purpose: first, they ensure the independence of the views expressed in the Inflation Report; second, they oblige the government to rationalize assessments and policies which deviate from those expressed and recommended by the Bank.

Chapter 6

AN INDEPENDENT BANK OF GREECE: an idea whose time has come

6.1. Introduction

The Bank of Greece (BoG) was founded in 1928 with a mandate to safeguard the value of the national currency. Before that, the National Bank of Greece, the largest commercial bank of the country was also performing the main functions of a central bank. The first appointed Governor of the Bank of Greece was A. Diomides who stayed in office for about three years. Generally speaking, during its first twenty years or so the BoG enjoyed a significant degree of independence.

However all that changed in 1946 with the establishment of the powerful Monetary Committee. The BoG's autonomy was systematically undermined by the Monetary Committee which was now effectively in charge of monetary policy. Since then, the BoG was the monetary branch of the government. This is manifested from the two main goals of monetary policy during the period until the abolition of the Monetary Committee in 1982, namely the financing of the needs of the public sector (which resulted in the steady monetization of government deficits) and also the provision of cheap credit to preferred public and private borrowers[1]. Not surprisingly, the Bank of Greece is classified in empirical studies as the most dependent, together with that of Portugal, among those of the OECD countries (at least until 1989). The steady money financing of budget deficits during the 1970s and 1980s has undoubtedly contributed to the two-digit inflation rates in that period. In fact, the dramatic deterioration of inflation in the 1980s has been well documented. While inflation in Greece was only slightly higher than the average of the EEC countries during the 1970s, it was as much as three times higher than the average of the EEC countries during the 1980s.

In Greece, the debate about an independent Bank of Greece has been associated with the Maastricht Treaty which requires from governments of the member-states to grant independence to their Central Banks during the second stage towards the Economic and Monetary Union. Thus, the first official reference to the issue of making the Bank of Greece independent was made in the Greek Convergence Programme 1993-1998. In the monetary policy section, one reads that "the government intends to enact

---

[1] See Halikias (1978).

the independence of the Bank of Greece during 1993 in an attempt to strengthen the effectiveness of monetary policy and also to make easier the participation of Greece to the EMS and in general to the process towards the Economic and Monetary Union". In fact, in August 1993, the government was about to pass a bill to the Greek parliament granting constitutional independence to the Bank of Greece. But certain events of political nature (mainly related to intragovernmental disagreements on issues of foreign policy) took place that time which led to the downfall of the government and to the announcement of early elections. As a result, the issue of independence was put aside for quite some time.

In August 1994 and during a parliamentary debate, Yannos Papantoniou, the Minister of National Economy, referred to the government's intention to grant independence to the Bank of Greece in the near future. In the (revised) Greek Convergence Programme 1994-1999 of the Pasok government, an explicit reference (though quite brief) was made to the forthcoming independence of the Bank of Greece and to the resulting increase in the credibility and effectiveness of Greek monetary policy. It is also encouraging that there was a broad consensus, in principle, among the major political parties in Greece on the issue of independence. In addition to the government, the opposition party is also in favour of an independent Bank of Greece. The Programme for the National Economy (February 1995) of the New Democracy party included an extensive paragraph on the issue of making the Bank of Greece independent from the government. In light of the government's commitment and general support from all major political parties in Greece, as well as the time constraint imposed by the Maastricht Treaty, the enactment of a Bill that would grant independence to the Bank of Greece should be only a matter of time[2].

Our objective in this chapter is to examine thoroughly the important issue of how much independence should be granted to the Bank of Greece, how a venture like that could be implemented and what would be its practical implications for the conduct of Greek monetary policy. Before embarking on that, we take a look at the theories which make the case for central bank independence. We then look briefly at the empirical research which classifies central banks from a large number of countries, including Greece, according to their independence based on various criteria. In section 6.4 we consider the question of how much independence should be given to the Bank of Greece. In section 6.5 we examine what changes (if any) should be made in a number of associated functions of the Bank of Greece in order to avoid any conflict with the main function of monetary policy independence. In the last section (6.6) we explain how this independence could actually be implemented. We further examine the consequences for the democratic accountability of an independent monetary policy in Greece and we propose a number of practical arrangements which, in principle, should safeguard that monetary policy be conducted by an

[2] As a matter of fact, in December 1997 the Greek government granted independence to the BoG (see below).

independent BoG is subject to democratic control.

6.2. Central bank independence: A brief review of theories

In the last ten years there has been a growing interest in the possibility of promoting price stability through the establishment of independent central banks. Since the late 1980s, countries in all parts of the world such as Chile, Venezuela, Mexico, Argentina, New Zealand, South Africa as well as former communist states like Poland, have implemented or are considering changes in legislation that would grant the central bank constitutional independence from the executive branch of government. In the European Union, the Maastricht Treaty requires the national central banks to become independent before the start of the third stage of Economic and Monetary Union, and in the light of this France and Spain in 1994 granted independence to the Banque de France and the Banco de Espana respectively. A further requirement of the Maastricht Treaty is that the European Central Bank be independent too. Last, but not least, the new Labour Government in the UK has granted instrument independence to the Bank of England in May 1997.

6.2.1. The prototype model and some extensions

The theoretical case for central bank independence has been made within the game-theoretic approach to economic policy that considers monetary policy endogenously determined by the strategic interaction of different players in the economy.[3] The seminal paper on central bank independence (hereafter referred to as CBI) is due to Thompson (1981) and has been further developed by Rogoff (1985). Rogoff, within a simple stochastic macroeconomic model, has investigated the effects of delegating monetary policy to an independent authority. By "independent", it is meant that the central banker has distorted preferences relative to those of the government and in particular it is required that she places a greater weight on inflation stabilization than the government does. Delegation of monetary policy to an authority with such preferences reduces the inflation bias that arises under discretion at the cost of responding suboptimally to supply shocks (the trade-off between credibility and flexibility). Quite interestingly, the net outcome is beneficial to a society with targets over output and inflation. What is important to note however, is that it is optimal for the government (and society) to choose an agent to head the central bank who places a moderately but not infinitely greater, weight on inflation stabilization than the government does[4].

---

[3] Earlier policy models considered monetary policy as given exogenously and hence they were not very helpful in addressing questions of institutional reforms like that of central bank independence.

[4] Broadbent and Barro (1997) have recently provided empirical evidence for this result. They

The Rogoff model has been quite influential as is evidenced by the large number of researchers who have used it to investigate further the macroeconomic effects of delegating monetary policy to an independent authority. For instance, Lohmann (1992) proposes a richer institutional arrangement that takes into account extreme circumstances like stock-market crashes, oil shocks, etc. In Rogoff's model, the moderately conservative central banker achieves a lower time consistent inflation rate at the cost of a distorted response to output shocks. This cost is higher for extreme shocks. Lohmann developed a model of delegation in which the central bank sets the inflation rate while allowing for a flexible escape clause implemented in such situations. Specifically, the government pays an extra cost when it overrides the central bank's monetary policy decision ex post to stabilize the extreme shock. Lohmann shows formally that the optimal strategy for the central bank is to avoid being overridden by announcing an inflation rate that makes the government indifferent between overriding the central bank and not doing so. The larger the output shock, the more the central bank is forced to accommodate that shock. The main contribution of Lohmann's paper is to show that delegating monetary policy to the central bank combined with the government's option to override the central bank's decision when it is needed, dominates the central bank arrangement proposed by Rogoff. Lohmann's analysis provides a neat and rather realistic design where normally the central bank sets independently the inflation rate except of extreme situations where it implements a flexible escape clause. In that sense, Lohmann's central bank framework implies a less conservative central banker than in Rogoff's model.

In the Rogoff model, the government's loss function represents the preferences of a homogeneous population. Society is homogeneous and as a result there is no disagreement over the policies followed by the central banker. Consequently, the choice of the central banker is no subject of partisan politics. Waller (1992) addresses the following question: What is the optimal choice of a conservative central banker when the economy is characterized by heterogeneity? In his model heterogeneity comes from a two-sector labour market structure: a competitive sector and a noncompetitive sector characterized by nominal wage rigidities. Although the loss functions in the two sectors are identical, output variability, due to nominal wage rigidities is higher, in the non-competitive sector than in the competitive sector. Thus, a central banker, optimally chosen to minimize the social loss function defined as a weighted average of the two sectors loss functions, may not be optimal for either of the two sectors. If the non-competitive sector were allowed to choose the central banker, it would choose a less inflation-averse central banker relative to the competitive sector's choice, since it suffers more in output variability than the competitive sector. In the same line of reasoning, the competitive sector would be

---

have estimated (using US data and for the period 1954-1994) that the relative weight on inflation stabilization takes a value of 3, which implies that the (absolute) percentage weight on output stablization takes a value of 0.25 and hence the percentage weight on inflation stabilization is 0.75.

willing to accept a more conservative central banker than it is socially optimal. Thus, in an economy with more than one sector and with political parties representing these sectors, the choice of a conservative central banker may be subject to partisan influences. This point has been made also by Alesina and Grilli (1992) within the context of a monetary union in Europe and the establishment of a European Central Bank. They showed how different member countries may disagree over the conduct of the European monetary policy formulated by a common central bank. Specifically, during the transition to a political union, different countries will have their own national loss functions and the effects of the common monetary policy will be evaluated on the basis of these national loss functions. Thus, a policy optimally chosen by a common central banker to stabilize the variance of European output, may not be optimal for a country with a larger variance of national output. For such a member country, the European central bank will be "too" conservative in the sense that it is not stabilizing enough. This may give rise to disagreement over the choice of the governor of the European Central Bank

Another extension of the Rogoff model has been provided by Mourmouras (1997a) who introduces Gray-Fischer type indexed labour contracts into the Rogoff set-up. His main result is that increased wage indexation makes the government choose a less conservative central banker to fight inflation. Wage indexation makes inflation easier to live with and this reduces the will of a government to fight inflation. This result might explain why economies with widespread escalator clauses experience chronic inflation rates even in the absence of shocks.[5]

6.2.2. An optimal contract for the governor?

One of the most prominent contributions to the literature on central bank independence has been made recently by Carl Walsh (1995). His main innovation is to adopt a principal-agent framework in an attempt to analyze the incentives a central banker may face in the standard monetary policy game. Walsh argues that the trade-off between credibility and flexibility or between price stability and output stabilization, simply reflects the sub-optimal incentives faced by the central banker. Under an optimal contract this trade-off disappears, and credibility and flexibility are simultaneously achieved. Walsh shows that the government can offer a contract to the governor of the central bank that eliminates the inflationary bias of discretionary policy while still ensuring that inflation responds optimally to supply shocks. In contrast to the Rogoff's approach of viewing the central banker as more inflation averse than the rest of society, in Walsh's model the government offers the central bank governor a state-contingent wage contract. His objective is to maximize the

[5]See also Mourmouras (1993). In a subsequent paper, Mourmouras (1997b) has also shown that delegating monetary policy to a conservative central banker may reduce the alleged social inefficiency of equilibrium wage indexation that arises in models of discretionary policy.

budget transfer from the government which in turn depends on inflation and unemployment. As Walsh himself has pointed out, the New Zealand Reserve Bank Act of 1989 had actually offered the governor of the central bank a contract that shares the basic features of the optimal incentive contract briefly presented above.

Lars Svensson (1997a) argues that the trade-off between average inflation and output variability in the Rogoff model follows from a particular parametrization of preferences. Svensson shows that an alternative way to model central bank independence is to assume that the central banker has a lower inflation target than the rest of society. Inflation then can be reduced without an increase in output variability, a result that makes the economic case for central bank independence even stronger.

6.2.3. Other recent contributions

6.2.3.1. Central bank independence in a public finance framework

In a more general public finance framework, van der Ploeg (1992) argues for delegating monetary policy to an ultra-conservative independent central banker who cares only about price stability. Monetary policy discretion results in an inflation bias and a sub-optimal government revenue mix that relies too much on seigniorage and too little on conventional taxes[6]. Van der Ploeg shows that a fully independent central bank committed to price stability yields a higher welfare than a dependent central bank. An independent central banker leads to zero inflation and seigniorage revenue and this forces the government to raise taxes in order to finance government spending. Van der Ploeg also shows that a fully independent central banker is more likely to be preferred when the stock of outstanding nominal government debt is high, when a large proportion of wages is not indexed and when the extent of the shadow economy and the collection costs of conventional taxes are insignificant.

Similar results are obtained by Cukierman (1994b), who also emphasizes the role of an independent central banker in reducing inflation expectations and which in turn reduces nominal interest rates and interest payments for servicing the government debt. Mourmouras and Su (1995a) adopt a public debt-stabilization framework and focus on the strategic interactions between the central bank and the government in a continuous-time dynamic game. They build upon Dornbusch's (1991) theory of credibility and stabilization according to which a stabilization plan can be seen as an asset with uncertain return. The main finding is that central bank independence promotes fiscal discipline and the likelihood of a successful public debt stabilization plan[7]. They also show that despite the larger burden it places on the government, an

---

[6]For empirical evidence on the role of fiscal policy in determining monetary policy, particular with respect to government deficits, see Demopoulos, Katsimbris and Miller (1987), Burdenkin (1987,1988) and Ahking and Miller (1985), etc.

[7] The same point had been made by Fratianni and von Hagen (1993).

independent central banker makes the government itself better off. This is important because it suggests that, in a public debt stabilization programme, a government could benefit[8] by delegating monetary policy to an authority with a preference for low inflation rates despite the resultant loss of seigniorage revenue.

6.2.3.2. Central bank independence, money financing and long-run growth

A large body of the literature has considered the benefits from having an independent central banker in charge of monetary policy in models with fixed output. An obvious question that arises is what is the role of an independent central banker in an economy with capital accumulation. Do countries with more inflation averse central bankers experience higher growth rates? Traditional growth theory considers monetary policy as exogenous[9] and hence is not very helpful in addressing questions of institutional reforms. Mourmouras and Ghosh (1998, 99) introduce endogenous monetary policy in a monetary endogenous growth model in which monetary behaviour reflects the government's desire for inflationary financing of budget deficits. The monetary authority chooses the money stock to minimize the costs of inflation subject to private sector's expectations, the government budget constraint and the capital accumulation equation. With endogenous monetary policy, both the inflation rate and long-run growth rate are determined endogenously. The authors characterize the Markov-perfect equilibrium in which the equilibrium paths for capital and real money balances reflect the strategic interactions between the monetary authority, the government and the private sector. Delegation of monetary policy to an inflation averse central banker results in lower inflation rate and higher growth rate. The intuition is that a more inflation averse central banker achieves lower inflation and smaller seigniorage revenues and hence less money financing of government consumption. This in turn implies that more resources are available for capital accumulation. This might provide some theoretical underpinnings to the evidence reported by Cukierman *et al.*(1992, 93), namely that central bank independence has a positive effect on growth in less-developed countries (LDCs) and no effect on growth in industrial countries.

6.2.4. Some critical comments

It appears from the above discussion that macroeconomic theory provides us with a number of arguments in support of delegating monetary policy to a central bank that

---

[8] Mourmouras and Su (1995a) define and characterize the closed-loop Nash equilibrium. Mourmouras and Su (1995b,1995c) show that this result is robust to alternative assumptions about the type of strategies and information sets available to the players in the economy.

[9] This is true in both the old and new growth theory. For instance, this is the case in Tobin (1965), Sidrauski (1967a, 1967b), Fischer (1979), Aghevli (1977), Cohen (1985), but also in the most recent endogenous growth literature with money, e.g. in van der Ploeg and Alogoskoufis (1994), Roubini and Sala-i-Martin (1992).

enjoys large freedom in pursuing its anti-inflationary policies. We turn now to discuss a number of critical comments on the literature.
Some authors have argued that the problem of time inconsistency in monetary policy is actually less serious than it is often claimed. For instance, Minford (1995) argues that in democracies it can be solved by taking into account the electorate's behaviour. Voters set incentives subject to which the government maximizes its own chances of getting re-elected to office. In essence, this implies an additional constraint to the government. The result is that even if the government has unlimited discretionary powers, it chooses the precommitment solution with an optimal response to shocks. We find this argument persuasive.

Along the same lines, Goodhart and Huang (1995) question the empirical significance of the inflationary bias, given the long and variable lags in the effects of monetary policy. More precisely, since monetary policy instruments operate with considerable lags (quite often up to two years), a rational public will observe them and anticipate inflation correctly. Hence once again the time inconsistency problem may be less serious in practice.

The contracting approach, though promising, has been criticised on the grounds that such contracts are not feasible in practice. In fact, political unfeasibility may well be the reason we do not observe this type of institutional arrangement in the real world. Even more importantly, McCallum (1995, p.210) convincingly argues, "such a device does not actually overcome the motivation for dynamic inconsistency; it merely relocates it". His point is that under the performance contracts arrangement, the government has to enforce the contract, but the government may still have the incentive not to do so. For instance, this may well be the case when output is too low, in which case the government may try to induce the central banker to be more expansionary by devising extra types of financial rewards for the central bank if it accommodates. Or in the case where the central bank has failed to achieve the requirements of the contract, and instead has generated too much inflation, the government would have little incentive to enforce the contract. It could well be advantageous for both the government and the central bank to ignore the breach of the contract and continue the principal-agent relationship.

McCallum (1997) argues that assuming that a central bank optimises period by period may be wrong. A central bank in charge of monetary policy may ignore the short term gains of inflation (if any at all) and concentrate on achieving the optimal policy rule. If this is the case, then the concept of an independent central bank is perhaps quite meaningless.

But even if one accepts the period by period optimization framework, there are still some questionable assumptions in the prototype CBI model. For example, the assumption that the target output is invariant to supply shocks. As Driffill (1997) puts it: "In the context of a real business cycle model, productivity shocks drive cyclical fluctuations in equilibrium GDP and labour supply. The fluctuations in GDP are equilibrium phenomena, and do not imply a need for government intervention or smoothing...Consequently, it is not clear that a government should wish to stabilise the level of GDP against all supply shocks".

An argument that has been put up against independence of a central bank has to do with the possible conflicts between an independent central banker's monetary policy and other areas of economic policy, such as fiscal policy, an issue that is best known as the co-ordination problem of monetary and fiscal policies. At the heart of the issue of policy co-ordination is the premise that the credibility of monetary policy, sometimes, does not depend upon monetary policy alone, but rather upon the whole macroeconomic policy framework in its entirety.[10] For instance, if there exist co-ordination problems or conflicts between the monetary and the fiscal arms of the government, this may generate uncertainty and speculation over how and when the conflicts will be solved. In this framework, Alesina and Tabellini (1987) consider a model with three players, namely the government, the central bank and the private sector. The government plays a non-cooperative game with the central bank over the revenue mix for financing government expenditure. A lower inflation rate reduces seigniorage revenue and forces the government to raise distortionary taxes which is costly. On the other hand, the central bank plays also the standard policy game with the private sector (i.e. output is too low and this generates incentives for surprise inflation). Alesina and Tabellini show that it is still beneficial to have an independent central bank in charge of monetary policy. Equally interesting is their finding that the standard result that rules are better than discretion does not necessarily follow when there are policy co-ordination problems.

Goodhart (1995) goes one step further and argues that the issue of co-ordination may be seen as an argument for rather than against central bank independence. The point of his argument is that the issue is not really co-ordination, but which policy instrument should move first. With an independent central bank, monetary policy is aimed at achieving low inflation. The government can still vary fiscal policy. But while with a dependent central bank the government can assume that interest rates do not respond to fiscal policy, with an independent central bank this is no longer the case. For example, an expansionary fiscal policy will be followed by the central bank's reaction to raise interest rates. Goodhart argues that it is one of the advantages of an independent central bank that once the government looses control over short-term monetary policy, fiscal policy itself becomes more disciplined[11].

---

[10]Quite relevant on this point about the unity of macroeconomic policy is Arthur Okun's (1972) view that "whether good fiscal policy is more or less effective than good monetary policy for stabilization purposes is like the question of whether good headlights are more or less important than good breaks for night driving. Fortunately, neither the stabilization policy maker nor the driver has to make such a choice."(p.125).

[11]A quite different dimension to the issue of monetary and fiscal policy co-ordination has been given by a well known policy-maker some years ago. Arthur Burns (1978, p.381), a former

Another objection to an independent central bank concerns the accountability of an independent central banker. Delegating authority to an independent central banker naturally raises the question of the degree to which a central bank explains or makes visible its policies to the government, the parliament and the public. The point is that since an independent central banker is granted independence on the grounds that he will promote price stability for the benefit of the general public, the public has to have some degree of reassurance that an independent central bank is in fact motivated to achieve that objective. This requires that the public is able to monitor the performance of the central bank and hold accountable the governor who is in charge of formulating and implementing monetary policy. Our personal view regarding the issue of democratic accountability is that this is a very important subject that needs serious consideration. We believe that the question of democratic accountability is closely linked to the relevant issue of how much independence should be given to a central bank. Our view is that there are no general answers to these two interrelated issues; rather, both the independence and accountability issues are country specific, in the sense that they depend upon the monetary history and culture of each country[12]. Certainly, as Goodhart (1995) argues, an independent central bank will fail and be rejected, unless it can establish broadly-based public support for its policies. The educational and presentational skills of an independent central bank will be as important as its technical and operational capabilities. To succeed it has to establish a broad constituency.

6.3. The Bank of Greece: Past experience and current regime

There now exists a large amount of empirical work which directly tests and lends support to the proposition that countries with independent central banks tend to deliver lower rates of inflation. In contrast, there seems to be no inevitable cost in terms of lower growth. The most well known study in the field is that by Alesina and Summers (1993). The two authors use data from the period 1955-1988 to confirm that central banks that are free from government interference do indeed deliver better inflation outcomes. In addition, countries with independent central banks do not, on average, have higher unemployment rates than others; in fact many have less. Their main findings are summarised in Figure 6.1 below. Their index of central bank independence is based on such factors as whether or not the governor and the bank's board are appointed by the government, the length of their appointments, whether government representatives sit on the board of the bank, the extent to which the central bank monetizes government deficits and so on. Parts (a) and (b) of Figure 6.1

Fed Chairman has advocated independence of the Federal Reserve System on the grounds of *dispersion of power*. His point is that " a fragmentation of decision making power... introduces *competition* among the different arms of the policy making administration... and this may produce a better political and economic outcome".

[12]We return to the issue of independence versus accountability in section 6.6. below.

Figure 6.1

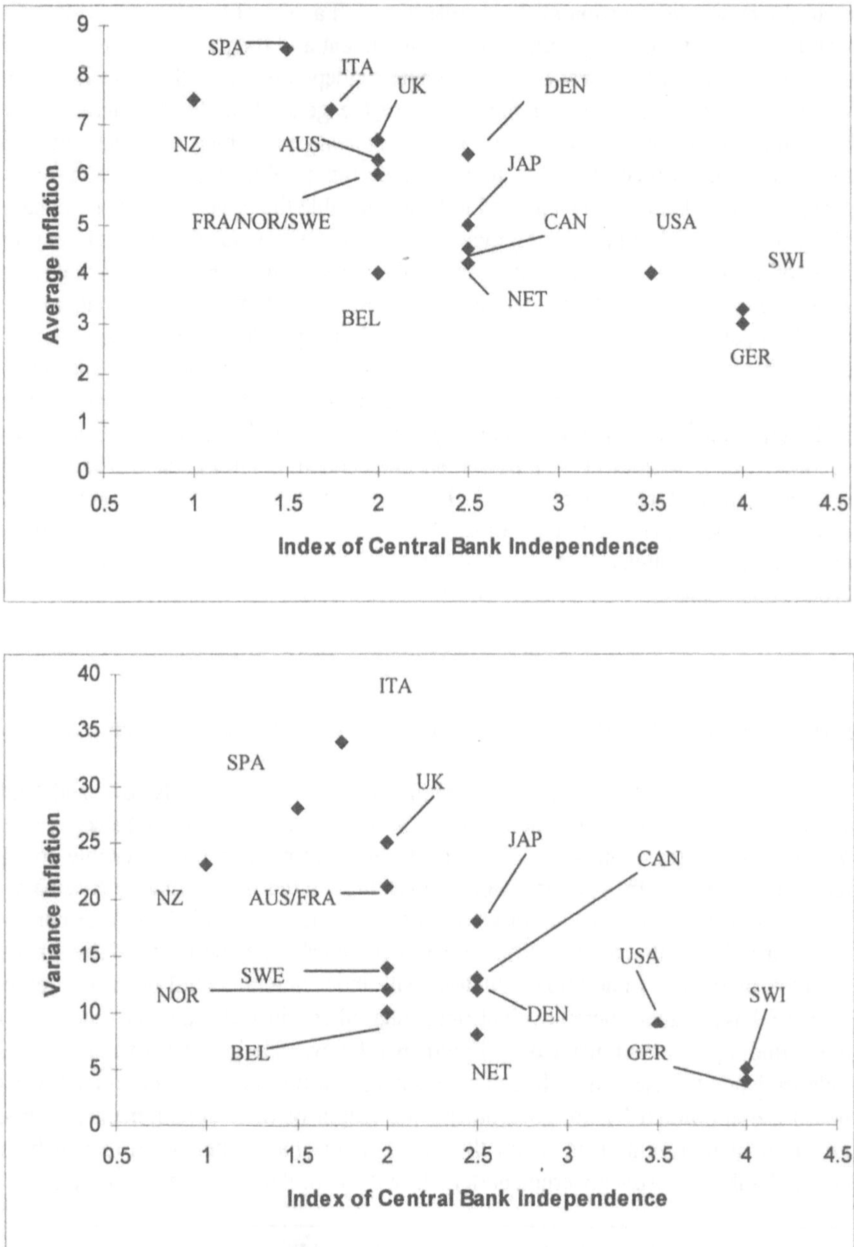

Central bank independence and inflation performance, 1955-88
Source: Alesina and Summers, (1993)

Table 6.1

	Appointments				Relationship with government		Constitution		Index of political independence
Countries	(1)	(2)	(3)	(4)	(5)	(6)	(7)	(8)	(9)
Australia		*					*	*	3
Austria						*	*	*	3
Belgium				*					1
Canada	*	*					*	*	4
Denmark		*				*	*		3
France		*		*					2
Germany		*		*	*	*	*	*	6
Greece			*					*	2
Ireland		*				*	*		3
Italy	*	*	*		*				4
Japan							*		1
Netherlands		*		*	*	*	*	*	6
New Zealand									0
Portugal					*				1
Spain				*	*				2
Switzerland		*			*	*	*	*	5
UK					*				1
US				*	*	*	*	*	5

Political independence of central banks
Source: Grilli, Masciandaro and Tabellini, 1991, p. 368

Notes: (1) Governor *not* appointed by government; (2) Governor appointed for > 5 years; (3) *All* the Board *not* appointed by government (4) Board appointed for > years; (5) No mandatory participation of government representative in the Board; (6) No government approval of monetary policy formulation is required; (7) Statutory requirements that central bank pursues monetary stability amongst its goals; (8) Legal provisions that strengthen the central bank's position in conflicts with the government are present; (9) Overall index of political independence, constructed as the sum of the asterisks in each row.

indicate a strong negative relationship between central bank independence and the level and variability of inflation. Alesina and Summers also examine the relationship between central bank independence and the level and variability of economic growth in a set of countries[13]. They find that central bank independence has neither huge benefits nor costs in terms of real macroeconomic performance. Switzerland, which has a highly independent central bank, shows much lower and variable growth than the average country in the sample, while Germany which has also a very independent central bank has good economic performance.

Greece was not included in the Alesina and Summers study. Grilli *et al* .(1991) obtained similar results for a sample of countries which includes Greece. The interesting feature in the Grilli *et al.* study is that it distinguishes carefully between *political* and *economic* independence of the central bank. Political independence (or goal independence) refers to the autonomy of the central bank to choose the final goals of monetary policy such as price stability. Economic independence (or instrument independence) refers to the autonomy of the central bank to choose the instruments with which to pursue these goals. Table 6.1 (taken from Grilli *et al.*, 1991) measures the overall degree of central bank political independence in 18 OECD countries. Columns (1) to (8) refer to different attributes. An asterisk indicates that the central bank of the country in question possesses that attribute. The last column is the sum of the asterisks in each row and it is a measure of political independence. A major determinant of the index of political independence is the extent to which the central bank governor (and the executive board) are political appointees. According to Table 6.1, Germany and the Netherlands (both score 6 out of 8) with Switzerland and the US (both score 5 out of 8) also enjoying the highest degree of political independence. Greece scores 2 points out of 8 which in relative terms implies that the Bank of Greece is among the most politically dependent central banks in the OECD.

Table 6.2 measures the economic independence of central bank in the same sample of countries. The index of economic independence is determined by the access the government has to central bank credit as well as the nature of the monetary instruments under the direct control of the central bank and the bank's involvement in the overall banking supervision. The last column, again, is the sum of the asterisks in each row and is an overall index of economic independence. Economic independence is high in Canada, Germany, Switzerland and US (they all score 7 out 8). Greece scores 2 out 8 which implies that the Bank of Greece is among the most economically dependent central banks in the OECD during the period under consideration.

Figure 6.2 below summarizes Tables 6.1. and 6.2, showing the degree of political and

---

[13] The countries considered in Figure 6.1 are the following: Australia (AUS), Belgium (BEL), Canada (CAN), Denmark (DEN), France (FRA), Germany (GER), Italy (ITA), Japan (JAP), Netherlands (NET), Norway (NOR), New Zealand (NZ), Spain (SPA), Sweden (SWE), United Kingdom (UK) and United States (USA).

Table 6.2

	Monetary financing of budget deficit					Monetary instruments		Index of economic independence
Countries	(1)	(2)	(3)	(4)	(5)	(6)	(7)	(8)
Australia	*	*	*	*	*	*		6
Austria			*	*	*	*	**	6
Belgium		*		*	*	*	**	6
Canada	*	*	*	*		*	**	7
Denmark		*			*	*	**	5
France				*	*	*	**	5
Germany	*	*	*	*	*	*	*	7
Greece				*		*		2
Ireland		*	*	*		*		4
Italy				*				1
Japan	*		*		*	*	*	5
Netherlands			*	*	*	*		4
New Zealand			*	*		*		3
Portugal				*		*		2
Spain			*	*			*	3
Switzerland		*	*	*	*	*	**	7
UK	*	*	*	*		*		5
US	*	*	*	*	*	*	*	7

Economic independence of central banks
Source: Grilli, Masciandaro, Tabellini, 1991, p. 369

Notes: (1) Direct credit facility: not automatic; (2) Direct credit facility: market interest rates; (3) Direct credit facility: temporary; (4) Direct credit facility: limited amount; (5) Central bank does not participate in primary market for public debt; (6) Discount rate set by central bank; (7) Banking supervision *not* entrusted to the central bank (**) or not entrusted to the central bank alone (*); (8) overall index of economic independence (being the sum of the asterisks in columns 1-7).

Figure 6.2

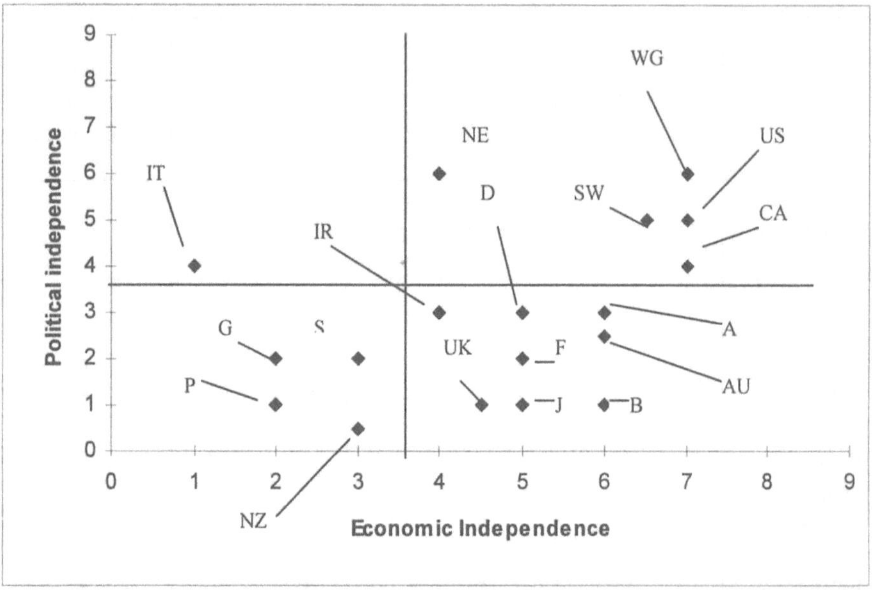

Political and economic independence of central banks
Source: Grilli, Masciandaro, Tabellini , 1991, p. 371

A= Australia, AU = Austria, B = Belgium, CA= Canada, D = Denmark, F = France, WG = West Germany, G = Greece, IR = Ireland, IT = Italy, J = Japan, NE = Netherlands, NZ = New Zealand, P = Portugal, S = Spain, SW = Switzerland, UK = United Kingdom, US = United States

economic independence of central banks in the 18 countries under consideration. One can see that Greece belongs to a group of four countries which are all in the lower-left quadrant (the other three countries are Portugal, Spain and New Zealand before the reforms) all of whom have the most dependent central banks both politically and economically.

The classification of the Bank of Greece as one of the most dependent central banks has also also been confirmed by Healey *et al.* (1995). According to their study, the Bank of Greece scores 3 points out of 9 on the index of political independence, while on the degree of economic independence the Bank of Greece does even worse; it gets just 1 point out of a possible 10.

An obvious question then is what are the main factors behind the high degree of dependence of the Bank of Greece? Let us consider first the political dependence

Table 6.3

	Vulnerability Index (V_i)	Political transitions	Central Bank Turnovers	
			Total	Non-political
Australia	0.000	3	3	3
Austria	0.000	2	3	3
Belgium	0.167	6	3	2
Canada	0.000	4	2	2
Denmark	0.000	4	0	0
France	0.500	2	4	3
Germany	0.000	2	2	2
Greece	0.250	8	5	3
Ireland	0.286	7	3	1
Italy	0.077	13	2	1
Japan	0.222	9	4	2
Netherlands	0.000	3	1	1
New Zealand	0.000	5	4	4
Portugal	0.385	13	7	2
Spain	0.167	6	3	2
Switzerland	0.167	6	3	2
UK	0.000	3	2	2
USA	0.000	4	3	3

$$V_i = \frac{\text{Number of replacements of the governor within i months}}{\text{number of political transitions}}$$

Political vulnerability of central banks, 1972-1989
Source: Cukierman et al., (1992)

of the Bank of Greece. As we noted above, a major determinant of central bank's political dependence is the extent to which the central bank governor (and the executive board) are political appointees and more generally how large the political influence on the central bank is. Cukierman *et al.* (1992) construct an index of political vulnerability of the central bank, a rather robust measure of political influence on the central bank, by looking at the probability that a central bank governor will be replaced shortly after a political change in government. The sample in the Cukierman *et al.* (1992) study consists of 67 countries. Table 6.3

compares the results for the group of countries in the Grilli *et al.*(1991) study. One can see clearly that Greece had one of the highest index of political vulnerability of the central bank during the period 1972-1989 and deteriorates even further in the period up to 1996. Since 1974 it has become common practice in Greece for a new party in government to appoint a new governor of the Bank of Greece.

During the period 1953-1974 the Greek drachma was pegged to the US Dollar ($=30 GRD). This implied a considerable loss of monetary autonomy since monetary policy was dictated by the Fed. The fixed exchange rate regime of the Bretton Woods served as a pre-commitment device for Greek policy-makers since it tied their hands to low inflation policies. In fact, during the period 1954-1973, Greece experienced an average inflation rate of only 4%. In other words, before 1974 the issue of an independent Bank of Greece did not really matter too much as Greek monetary policy was "buying" credibility from the low inflation fixed exchange rate system of Bretton Woods. Following the collapse of the Bretton Woods regime in 1971, Greece adopted (in 1974) a managed floating exchange rate policy which provided the Greek monetary authorities with sufficient autonomy to formulate and conduct an independent monetary policy. For twenty years after 1974, Greece experienced a high and persistent inflation rate, on average more than 18% annually. Thus, since 1974 the issue of independence and the related issue of the political vulnerability of the Bank of Greece and its effects upon the outcome of monetary policy have become much more relevant and important.

In recent Greek monetary history, the most striking example of a political change of the governor following the election of a new party in office is that which followed the October 1981 elections, when the conservatives were ousted by the socialists after ruling for almost eight years. The new government removed the long-serving governor Professor Xenophon Zolotas, *the* guru of post-war Greek monetary affairs. Prime Minister Andreas Papandreou justified the turnover at the Bank of Greece on the grounds that he simply wanted his own man at the central bank since this would help him to implement his government's economic agenda more effectively. The pattern was repeated in the aftermath of the 1990 elections when the conservatives came back into power and appointed their own man at the Bank of Greece, and the same happened in the general elections of 1993 in which the socialists took office and, once more, a political appointee was soon made governor of the Bank of Greece.[14]

Turning our attention now to the low levels of economic independence of the Bank of Greece for the period 1950-1989, this is attributed largely to the steady money financing of budget deficits. As we noted above, the central bank's credit to the

---

[14] The average (actual) tenure of Governors of the Bank of Greece during the period 1950-89 was about 5.5 years. This compares with an average tenure of 20 years for Holland, 10 years for Germany and the UK, 7.5 years for the US and 6.5 years for France. If we extend the period to 1996, the average tenure of office for Greek Governors is even lower.

government is one of the key economic data used in the construction of the index of central bank economic independence. Thus, while the central bank's credit to government as a percentage of the central bank's total credit in countries like Germany is 0.025%, in Netherlands is 0.02% and generally in almost every developed economy is below 1%, in Greece the average figure in the 1970s was 26% and during the 1980s it has reached the record figure of 56% ! More generally, in Greece the monetization of government deficits has taken place through the extended banking system which is strictly controlled by the government. To give one example, until 1993 commercial banks were obliged to keep a fixed percentage (up to 40%) of their new deposits in the form of government bonds in order to finance budget deficits. However, since 1st January 1994, and in accordance with the Maastricht Treaty requirements, the money financing of budget deficits has stopped, and this has obviously increased the economic independence of the Bank of Greece. Even before that, the reforms that took place in 1987 (following the recommendations of the Committee on the Reform and Modernisation of Greece's Banking System) had already increased the economic independence of the Bank of Greece. These reforms concentrated mainly on interest rate deregulation, which in practice meant that the Bank of Greece could now influence market interest rates, the gradual abolition of secondary reserve requirements, and finally the Bank of Greece's involvement in repurchase agreements and Treasury bills auctions, which extended its monetary policy instruments and enhanced its role in the implementation of monetary policy.

As a result of the 1987 and 1994 reforms, the Bank of Greece enjoys today a higher level of economic independence than ever before. From Table 6.2 above, if one takes into account the changes regarding the money financing of budget deficits, one can argue that the Bank of Greece now scores 6 points out of 8 on the central bank economic independence index. In theory and according to Table 6.2, what is left to attain full economic independence is for the Bank of Greece to give up her responsibility of banking supervision since the latter facilitates the financing of government borrowing by administratively increasing the private demand for government bonds.[15] Thus, as one can also see from Tables A.6.1 and A.6.2 in the Appendix, in theory at least, the Bank of Greece shares today a lot of similar institutional features with other central banks in the European Union. From the same Tables in the Appendix one can see that the Bank of Greece is today less economically independent than the Bundesbank only because of the supervision of financial institutions. However, one should take the information reported in these tables with a pinch of salt, since as we are going to argue in the next section, the claim, for instance, that the change in key interest rates in Greece is the central bank's responsibility alone is not always true. We proceed now to the next section to make a case for granting political and economic independence to the Bank of Greece.

---

[15] We return to the important issue of supervision and regulation of the banking system in section 6.5.1 below.

6.4. How independent should the Bank of Greece be?

Our proposal regarding the degree of independence which should be granted to the Bank of Greece is influenced to a great extent by the monetary history and inflation culture of the country. It appears that there are no general answers to the question of how much independence should be given to a central bank, the answer to such a question is essentially country-specific. Different countries have different monetary and inflation cultures which will reflect in different degrees of independence of their central banks.

Grilli *et al.* (1991) have suggested that political independence of the central bank can be identified with the autonomy to pursue the ultimate objective of price stability. Effectively this means that the central bank is free to formulate the goals of monetary policy either in terms of intermediate monetary targets (a two-stage monetary strategy) or in terms of formal inflation targets (a one-stage strategy). In Greece, until very recently monetary and exchange rate policy was formulated by the Cabinet and conducted by the Bank of Greece (Bill 1866/82). There was no such statutory requirement that the Bank of Greece should pursue the goal of price stability. As we argued in the previous section, following the reforms of 1987 and 1994, the Bank of Greece now enjoys high levels of economic independence but very low levels of political independence. Thus the question regarding the independence of the Bank of Greece today is essentially about the political independence of the Bank of Greece. Should the Bank of Greece be given full political independence, namely the capacity to choose as its final goal price stability? In the rest of this section we argue that a strong case can be made in the case of Greece for an affirmative answer. Later on, in section 6.5.2. we spell out the main ingredients (including the necessary legal steps) that would guarantee the successful transition to a monetary policy independence regime.

Political independence

The main ingredients of our argument can be found by looking at Greece's post-1974 inflation history which suggests the existence of a *partisan political business cycle.* Before 1974, the Greek currency was pegged to the US dollar and as a result the country experienced low inflation rates. Since 1974, the Greek monetary authorities followed a crawling peg exchange rate policy that allowed them to exercise discretionary monetary policy, which, in the end, has resulted in high and persistent double digit inflation rates. Moreover, Greece has had a polarised political system in which the ideological differences (as these have been manifested in actual economic policy-making) between the conservative party (New Democracy) and the socialist party (Pasok) have been rather deep over the past twenty years. Following the restoration of democracy in July 1974, New Democracy won a clear victory in the November 1974 elections and remained in power until October 1981. In the October

1981 elections, Pasok scored a landslide victory and stayed in power until June 1989, after also winning the elections of June 1985. New Democracy came back to power in April 1990 with a slim majority (after a number of elections which led to two hang parliaments and two short lived governments, a right-left coalition and a national unity government), but were ousted by the socialist party in the October 1993 elections. The latter managed to stay in power in the last general election in 1996. While it is true that since 1990 both parties have tried to reduce inflation as part of the country's obligations to meet the Maastricht criteria, it is evident that for the period of 1974-1989, inflation under socialist administrations was higher on average by as much as 8 percentage points than under conservative administrations.[16] With the same, more or less, level of polarisation of the political system in the 1990s, there is no guarantee that history will not repeat itself in the near future, especially during pre-election periods. Socialist governments, with their higher tolerance of inflation, have generated higher inflation rates than the conservatives, yet they failed to translate this into lower unemployment, verifying the predictions of the partisan theory on political business cycles. In other words, it appears that the preferences of political parties are quite important when looking at actual outcomes for inflation in Greece.

This point has serious implications for the desired degree of political independence for the Bank of Greece, and more specifically for the following important question: who should set the inflation target in Greece: the government or the central bank? Granting full political independence to the Bank of Greece would imply that the inflation target is chosen by the central bank, irrespective of the party in power and its preferences for low or high inflation. Otherwise, the alternation of parties in power[17] would imply different inflation targets each time, with the central bank just left to implement these different inflation targets. The result of this would be that monetary policy in Greece would not be able to escape from the partisan political business cycle from which it seems to suffer, and the whole idea of an independent Bank of Greece would remain, at best, doubtful. Allowing the government to set (or even jointly with the central bank) the inflation target is a scenario that suits countries like the United Kingdom, or Germany, in which an anti-inflationary psychology is embedded in the behaviour of government and trade unions. In a country like Greece

[16] See the evidence reported in Alogoskoufis and Philippopoulos (1992) and Kapopoulos (1995).

[17] Recently Alesina and Gatti (1995) have extended the Rogoff model on central bank independence to incorporate electoral uncertainty, in which case two competing parties have different preferences. In their framework, output variability can be decomposed in two parts. The first one is the "economic" variability that is due to nominal and real shocks, and the second part is "political" that is due to electoral uncertainty. An independent central bank in such a framework not only reduces the inflationary bias, but also eliminates political induced output variability since monetary policy is not under the direct control of governments with different preferences. This strengthens the case for political central bank independence, especially in countries experiencing partisan political business cycles. The relevance of the above argument to the Greek case is more than obvious.

with its well known polarised political system and powerful trade unions, granting economic yet no political independence would not bring the desired results. Only a Bank of Greece which independently sets and implements an inflation target would be capable of keeping inflationary expectations low and hence being in a position to deliver low inflation rates.[18]

Economic independence

We turn now to the second part of our policy proposal, namely that the Bank of Greece should be given statutory (qualified) economic independence. According to the definition proposed by Grilli *et al.* (1991), economic independence gives the Bank the capacity to choose the policy instruments with which to pursue the policy objectives. These authors suggest that economic independence can be identified with issues like the autonomy of the central bank in refusing to finance the budget deficit, the nature of monetary instruments under the control of the central bank and finally its role in supervising the banking sector.

Since 1st January 1994, the inhibition of monetary financing of budget deficits[19] is an undeniable fact and hence full economic independence should imply that the Bank of Greece is free to choose its monetary policy instruments. In practice this would mean that the Bank of Greece has the authority to change its key interest rate, the overnight interbank rate. In fact, it seems that this is true. One could argue that a piece of evidence for this fact is that the Bank of Greece in its daily intervention in the interbank money market offers a higher interest rate than the yield on government securities. However, this autonomy of the Bank of Greece to change its key interest rate is subject to the following two important qualifications.

First, as we have seen in chapter 4, following the deregulation of the Greek financial system and the liberalization of capital movements, the Bank of Greece has adopted the exchange rate as its principal intermediate target for monetary policy in recent years. The policy of a crawling peg (just 1% depreciation against the ECU for the year 1996) that only partially offsets the inflation differential with the European Union countries, requires high short term interest rates which implies that the degree of freedom for an independent monetary policy is rather limited. In practice, the support of an exchange rate target through high interest rates imposes a ceiling on the

---

[18] One perhaps could argue that a weakness of this argument is that a determined government could well change the legislation concerning central bank independence and pursue for instance inflationary policies. Theoretically this may be true, in practice, however, it is much more difficult to change the existing law from changing the inflation target which may be considered as just a policy announcement. In addition, the implied loss of credibility and the uncertainty regarding the reaction of the financial markets to such a move would force the government to think twice before changing the legislation on central bank independence.

[19] Although one should note that economic independence would also be enhanced if a number of loopholes in the legislation, like for instance the Bill 233/45 which allows the Bank of Greece to make advance payments to the government, are closed.

interest rate set by the Bank of Greece[20].

Second, the overall level of interest rates is influenced to a large extent by the interest rates on government securities[21] which do not always reflect fully the market conditions, and some analysts believe that they are still set by the Ministry of Finance. This imposes severe limits upon the conduct of monetary policy and upon the central bank's capacity to affect the level of interest rates in the economy. Indeed, this has given rise in recent times to a continuous row, which is regularly reported in the financial pages of Greek newspapers, between the governor of the Bank of Greece and Mr. Kyriazides, the deputy minister of Finance in charge of public debt management, who left the government in the 1996 reshuffle.

Granting statutory economic independence to the Bank of Greece, namely giving it formally the exclusive right to change the key interest rate, would increase the Bank's autonomy, reduce frictions with the fiscal authorities and it would make it more difficult for a government to intervene over the level and timing of changes in interest rates. Political intervention over the timing of changes in interest rates is always a likely event in Greece, especially during pre-election periods, where it is common practice for governments of all types to increase government spending for electoral purposes. A reduction in interest rates before an election would enable the government to economise a lot from the servicing of government debt[22] and spend these savings on more politically sensitive purposes. An independent central bank that refuses to reduce its key interest rate would make the government think twice before reducing interest rates on government securities.

6.5. Independence and other associated functions of the Bank of Greece

Of course, the design and conduct of monetary policy will be only one of the general functions of an independent Bank of Greece. Like many other central banks in the world, the Bank of Greece undertakes a number of other functions like the management of the currency issue, the banker's bank role, participating in the clearing and settlement systems, the holding and managing of international reserves, acting as the lender of last resort and supervising financial institutions, carrying out exchange rate policy, a direct involvement in the management of public debt, etc. Our focus, here, is on the last three functions of the Bank of Greece namely, banking supervision, exchange rate policy and debt management.

---

[20] See also our analysis in chapter 5, section 5.4.1.

[21] See Papademos (1990), Georgoutsos and Karamouzis (1995).

[22] It is estimated that a reduction of 1% in the interest rates on government securities would save the government more than 200 billion drachmas (in 1995 prices).

6.5.1. Banking supervision

Traditionally, the Bank of Greece has had the sole responsibility for bank supervision. We explain here why in the new regime of central bank autonomy this function should remain with the Bank of Greece. We will argue that separating or even dividing the supervisory responsibilities with the government or any other independent body would be an unnecessary luxury.

As we shall shortly argue, the theoretical case for and against separation is rather balanced, a fact which is reflected in existing international practices. In the past, it was quite common for the two functions of monetary policy and banking supervision to be carried out by a single institution, namely the central bank. However, over the years, due to the forces of competition operating within the banking industry, this arrangement resulted in a situation where the exact nature of the operations of the banking system became rather unclear (in the sense that it became increasingly difficult to draw the dividing line between the operations of banks and other financial intermediaries). As a result, the ability of central banks to supervise effectively the banking system has been slipping. This, in turn, has resulted in attempts to shift the supervisory function from the central bank to an independent agency, which in most cases, is controlled by the government (see Goodhart and Schoenmaker, 1995, p.555). As one can see from Table 6.4 below, during the 1980s, in 13 countries out of a sample of 24, the macro function of monetary policy and the micro function of banking supervision were carried out by different institutions. The remaining 11 countries had a combined regime. Highly independent central banks like the Reserve Bank of New Zealand, the Banque de France, the Federal Reserve, the De Nederlandsche Bank and others, exercise either solely or partly a supervisory role. However, as Goodhart and Schoenmaker (1995, p.544) have pointed out: "...there is a tendency for more dependent central banks to have combined functions. This may be because in countries where the central bank was dependent on the government for monetary policy, central bank officials tended to give more weight to other fields in which they could still take the lead, often including more micro-level relationships with financial intermediaries." In which case, the question is how strong is the intellectual case for and against combining the two functions? Below, we attempt to discuss briefly the competing arguments.

Arguments against combining the two functions

The main argument for not combining monetary policy and banking supervision within a central bank is that of a possible conflict of interest. In its simplest form, a central bank acting as lender of last resort in trying to rescue a troubled bank, may inject large amounts of reserves into the banking system, which may undermine its anti-inflationary monetary policy. A second type of possible conflict and perhaps an even more convincing argument is the case where the central bank wants, on the one hand, to maintain high interest rates (in order, for instance, to support its currency in

Table 6.4

Country	Monetary agency	Supervisory agency
Australia	Reserve Bank of Australia (CB)	Reserve Bank of Australia (CB)
Austria	National Bank of Austria (CB)	Federal Ministry of Finance (MF)
Belgium	National Bank of Belgium (CB)	Banking and Finance Commission
Canada	Bank of Canada (CB)	Office of the Superintendent of Financial Institutions (MF)
Denmark	Denmarks Nationalbank (CB)	Finance Inspectorate (MI)
Finland	Bank of Finland (CB)	Bank Inspectorate (MF) and Bank of Finland (CB)
France	Banque de France (CB)	Banque de France (CB) Commission Bancaire
Germany	Deutsche Bundesbank (CB)	Federal Banking Supervisory Office Deutsche Bundesbank (CB)
Greece	Bank of Greece (CB)	Bank of Greece (CB)
Hong-Kong	Hone Kong Monetary Authority (CB)	Hone Kong Monetary Authority (CB)
Ireland	Central Bank of Ireland (CB)	Central Bank of Ireland (CB)
Italy	Banca d'Italia (CB)	Banca d'Italia (CB)
Japan	Bank of Japan (CB)	Ministry of Finance (MF), Bank of Japan (CB)
Luxembourg	Luxembourg Monetary Institute (CB)	Luxembourg Monetary Institute (CB)
Netherlands	De Nederlandsche Bank (CB)	De Nederlandsche Bank (CB)
New Zealand	Reserve Bank of New Zealand (CB)	Reserve Bank of New Zealand (CB)
Norway	Norges Bank (CB)	Banking, Insurance and Securities Commission (MF)
Portugal	Banco de Portugal (CB)	Banco de Portugal (CB)
Spain	Banco de Espana (CB)	Banco de Espana (CB)
Sweden	Sveriges Riksbank (CB)	Swedish Financial Supervisory Authority
Switzerland	Swiss National Bank (CB)	Federal Banking Commission
United Kingdom	Bank of England (CB)	Bank of England (CB)
United States	Federal Reserve Board (CB)	Ministry of Finance (MF), Federal Reserve Board (CB), State Governments, Federal Deposit Insurance Cooperation.
Venezuela	Banco Central de Venezuela (CB)	Superintendency of Banks

CB = Central Bank, MF = Ministry of Finance, MI = Ministry of Industry

Monetary and supervisory agencies
Source: Goodhart C.A.E. and Schoenmaker D. (1995).

foreign exchange markets) and, on the other hand, is aware that such high interest rates may have adverse effects on financial and banking institutions in terms of their profitability. While the first type of conflict may sound a bit unconvincing (for example, one can argue that a central bank can always find ways to neutralize such rescue cash injections through open market operations) the second type of conflict is quite plausible and realistic, especially when the central bank is independent. In addition, as Goodhart and Schoenmaker (1995, p. 547) have suggested, such a conflict of interest would be more intense and more likely to take place the greater the banking system "involves intermediaries financing maturity mis-match positions through wholesale markets in a competitive milieu."

A second argument against combining the two functions is that having the supervisory functions within the central bank might make the bank vulnerable to political pressures in the event, for example, of a bank failure, and in turn may have adverse effects on the independence of monetary policy. Furthermore, automatic monetary accommodation by the lender of last resort may involve problems of moral hazard: banks (in particular those controlled by the state) have little incentive to avoid losses and failures. A third and related argument is that bank failures and rescue operations can often be bad publicity for those involved and be quite damaging for the reputation of a central bank supervisor, who, therefore, may prefer to pass supervision to a different institution. A final argument for keeping supervision out of the central bank is that responsibility for bank supervision should go to the institution that pays in the end the bill. For example, when a bank failure occurs, to the extent that a rescue operation involves taxpayer's money (as it is often the case), then a government should play a major role in the supervisory function as "he who pays the piper calls the tune".

Arguments in favour of combining the two functions

The main argument in having the two functions under the same roof is that of enhancing the co-ordination between monetary policy and prudential control of the banking system. In fact, this argument could be regarded as a reversal of the conflict of interest argument discussed above. It states that the two functions of conduct of monetary policy and the search for price stability on the one hand and the preservation of financial stability on the other, are historically two inseparable functions. Long tradition of central banking has seen banking supervision as closely related to monetary control, essentially since it can reduce the possibility of an unexpected demand for the emergency issue of high-powered money. Co-ordination of the two functions increases efficiency through better dissemination of relevant information and avoidance of working at cross-purposes.

Another argument in favour of combining the two functions concerns the issue of monetary over-killing, namely the danger of a financial crisis if counter-inflationary policies are taken too far, especially in the case of an independent central bank. For instance, if the supply of credit is kept too tight over an extended period of time by a central bank which no longer regulates the financial system, then this could lead to a build-up of exposed positions for a significant number of financial institutions. A final argument is based on the fact that most central banks act as lender of last resort to the banking system, even though the final cost of a bank rescue is paid by the taxpayer's money. In fact, central banks often have a pivot role in bank rescue operations. Thus, the rescue and lender of last resort functions makes the central bank willing to assume also a definite role in the design and conduct of banking supervision.

Why the Bank of Greece should retain the supervisory function

What emerges from the above discussion is that in order to safeguard the independence of a central bank, certain functions which might give rise to conflicting objectives and undesirable political pressure should be avoided. Having said that, it appears that in the case of Greece taking the supervisory function away from the Bank of Greece may not be a wise act.

A key feature of the Greek economy and of public life more generally is the absence of credible and respectable institutions. The Bank of Greece, despite its governmental dependence, has managed to enjoy high levels of respectability from financial institutions, investors and the Greek public. On the other hand, it is also true that any newly-built institution in Greece would have to face a rather slow-moving public administration and bureaucracy and as a result it is not at all clear that another regulator would be more effective than the Bank of Greece in supervising the banking system. Although there is some recent evidence (i.e. the delay over the cleansing up of the failure of the Bank of Crete) which suggests that there is still room for improvement in this field, in general, it is widely accepted that the Bank of Greece is doing a fine job in her role as supervisor of the Greek financial system.[23] In fact, given the current state of affairs in Greece, it may be unwise to strip an independent Bank of Greece of its supervisory authority.

Note that although bank failures is a rather rare phenomenon in Greece (only one serious bank failure[24] in the last twenty years or so) the interconnected issue of bank failures and banking supervision is quite important in Greece for the years to come for one more reason. As a result of the forthcoming competition from the European banking system, a number of commercial banks, private and public, will be put under

---

[23] The recent Bill No. 2076/92 passed in the Greek parliament designed to modernize the banking system along the EU directives was a welcome step towards this direction. In 1995, the BoG also adopted the 92/30 EU directive for the supervision of the banking system on a unified basis.

[24] This is the case of the Bank of Crete, a small private bank owned by George Koskotas who embezzled 30bn drachmas of the funds of the Bank of Crete. The Bank of Greece guaranteed the bank's deposits and the bank's customers did not lose their savings.

a severe test in the years to come. In the new era of globalization, where the forces of international competition change conditions in domestic markets rapidly, a large number of small-size banks would have to merge with each other or with larger financial institutions in order to survive, or, in some cases, to discontinue their operations. In other words, the role of bank licensing and supervision of the banking system both in terms of assessing the banks' portfolios and their capital adequacy will become increasingly more significant in the years to come and perhaps there is little to be gained from these sort of experiments. In fact, given the current state of affairs in Greece, where the influence of politics over the economy is still evident, it may be unwise to strip an independent Bank of Greece of its supervisory authority. Note, also that given that there is no serious disagreement against the Bank of Greece remaining the lender-of-last-resort (L-O-L-R) to guarantee the liquidity of the banking system in moments of crisis, then perhaps he who pays should also have the supervisory responsibility.[25] In summary, given the institutional characteristics of the country, it may be hard to see, in the case of Greece, how the L-O-L-R and banking supervision functions can be meaningfully vested in separate bodies.

6.5.2. Debt management

The Bank of Greece has traditionally acted as the government's fiscal agent, advising on and implementing domestic and external public debt policy as well as the holding and managing foreign exchange reserves. In the new regime of independence which will set as an objective the divorce between the government and the Bank of Greece, such a central bank function should end immediately largely because the Bank's impartiality and independence on monetary policy would be limited by its preoccupation with the management of government debt. It is the government's debt after all, let the government be responsible for it.

In the new regime of independence, who then should be in charge of managing the country's debt? It appears that the answer to the above question (in paper so far) has been already given by the recent Bill 2343/95 on the internal re-organisation of the functions of the Ministry of Finance. More specifically, Article 5 of the above Bill opens the door for the establishment of an independent body in charge of public debt management. Such an organisation should be responsible for the management of both domestic and external public debt and be accountable to the Ministry of Finance. Its main objective should be the efficient service of government debt as well as the restructuring of its maturity. The experience from countries like Ireland, Portugal and Sweden which have recently established such independent public debt management agencies would be extremely helpful in designing a similar body in Greece. In addition, the accumulation of knowledge, practices and expertise in the body

[25] Of course there is an equally plausible counter-argument to that, namely that at the end it is the taxpayer who bears the costs of bank failures.

currently in charge of debt management (the so called International Borrowing Division in the Bank of Greece) could serve as a benchmark and provide the required continuity and stability in the management of the country's debt.

6.5.3. Exchange rate policy

The evidence from countries with highly independent central banks like Germany or the US suggests that control over exchange rate policies stays firmly with the government.[26] In Greece, the design and control of exchange rate policy is with the government (Bill No. 1866/82) while the Bank of Greece is responsible for the daily execution of the policy. In chapter 4 of this book we argued that the Greek government should not rush to join the ERM-II. We instead argued that the (overvalued) drachma should be left to find its equilibrium value. In such a case and during the transitional period towards the euro and the adoption of exchange rate practices by the European Central Bank, there is little significance on who should be in control of the exchange rate policy: the government or the Bank of Greece. Simply, the foreign exchange market should determine the exchange rate. Occasionally, the Bank of Greece with its complete autonomy over the short-term interest rate could influence the exchange rate for the purpose of achieving the inflation target in the medium term. Note that this is distinctly different from the current regime of exchange rate targeting, namely the change in the interest rate to pursue simultaneously and (quite often) incompatible domestic and external objectives. In brief, the sole pursuit of price stability is one objective, and the pursuit of price stability *conditional* on the exchange rate objective of the government is quite another. Finally, even in the new independence regime, the Bank of Greece would hold and manage the foreign exchange reserves and use these reserves in occasional intervention in the foreign exchange market on behalf of the government.[27]

6.6. An independent and accountable Bank of Greece

6.6.1. Independence versus accountability?

As we have seen in Section 6.2 one of the main counter-arguments against central bank autonomy, concerns the possible implications that independence might have on issues of democratic accountability. Those who oppose the idea of independence

[26] The German government's refusal to take the advice of the Bundesbank on the appropriate rate for unifying the Ostmark and the Deutschmark has been well documented.
[27] In the United Kingdom the Treasury holds the reserves and the newly independent Bank of England manages them, while in the US and New Zealand reserves are held by both the Treasury and the Central Bank (see e.g. Swinburne and Castello-Branco, 1991).

argue that central bank autonomy and more general, of socio-political institutions may reduce their accountability to a vanishing point. Before examining the validity of this argument, it is useful to understand its motivational force. Central bank independence implies in principle that it has sweeping statutory powers: In the pursuit of its single objective, namely price stability, the governor of the bank is expected to make decisions independently of political arrangements and influences. This has raised fears that such an institution, which allows no external intervention or the imposition of certain external qualitative constraints on its objectives and procedures, is bound to violate basic principles of democratic governing. In the following we explain how such a scenario can be, in fact, avoided. More specifically, we argue that independence and public accountability are not two antithetical or mutually exclusive concepts; consequently, whatever these two concepts profess can be complementary or reconcilable. In addition, since it is possible to travel on the joint path of accountability and independence, we must understand the demand for securing accountability not as a return to government interventionism but in terms of new and flexible types of public intervention or regulation. In this light, the compatibility of accountability and independence must be seen as relying on certain necessary conditions. We now consider these two points.

Our first consideration concerns the possibility of reconciliation between the demands of independence and those of democratic accountability. It is our firm view that the developments of any further arguments for the independence of a central bank must have as their starting point the unchallenged and unequivocal commitment to the need for democratic control. It is only from this initial standpoint that we can draw special attention to the need for proper implementation of any suggestion which speaks in favour of independence. In order to provide a constructive account of what a proper implementation actually involves, it is vital to convey some positive and more stimulative information about the concept of democratic accountability or democratic control. Reference to this, or to any other similar expression, assumes the existence of certain kinds of constraints imposed upon the actions of government, or of any other social institution. These may be "constitutional" constraints, in the sense that they appear in the form of legal rules or principles whose validity or legitimacy is predetermined by a democratically elected body. In this case any institution may be held accountable if it does not comply with these set of rules. Another sense of accountability appeals to the need for answerability: Any institution, the government for example, is in this sense accountable in as much as it responds to the needs, claims and interests of those who render its continuation in office possible. In this case, supporters of a government exercise a certain kind of power which forces the government to be open for criticism and (re)examination. In some political circumstances this sense of accountability may also involve what we usually mean with *popular mandate*: to the extent that the re-election of a government depends heavily upon the satisfaction of the claims of the electorate, it must procure such a result. In this particular case, the rights of the electorate constitute the basis of the government's obligations.

In the case of a central bank, the problem emerges strikingly more pressing because the whole point about central bank independence is that it is not democratically elected, namely, it is a non-majoritarian institution. Other examples of such types of institutions are various regulatory agencies which work, for example, for the protection of the environment, of consumers' rights, or rights to equal opportunities and least but not last the judiciary system, one of the pillars of modern society. Since we have accepted the need for public accountability, we must, therefore, assume the imposition of a new set of regulations or constraints on the performance of any non-majoritarian institution such as the central bank. The fact that a certain body or institution does not subscribe to the rules of the majority rule does not and should not entail that it remains essentially and inescapably free from all regulation and control. We have, simply, to assume that it is subject to a different type of regulation. We therefore come to a better understanding of this whole issue; the viability of any project which attempts to reconcile the demands of independence and public accountability or control can be tenable on the further assumption that we do accept the need to implement a different, richer and more suitable to the circumstances of a non-majoritarian institution, set of forms of control or regulation. This brings us to the next point.

This point suggests that the compatibility of independence and accountability should be better understood and appreciated from the standpoint of a new system of regulation. In particular, this system must involve: First, a clear definition of statutory prescriptions for monetary policy. In this case, any ambiguity in the definition of the institution's objectives must be avoided. Second, clarity in the definition of the measures for judging the performance of the independent agency or institution. Third, all the procedures in and through which the independent institution operates must be transparent and easily accessible to public knowledge, reflection and criticism. The idea in this particular point is that any "Machiavellian" or authoritarian tendencies would be avoided if the procedures of the institution are open to the public, or under the glare of publicity. It is only through this that both the rationality of the procedures is secured and public participation is rendered possible. Finally, professionalism and expertise are required because areas of monetary policy are often complex and they require specialised knowledge. In what follows, we shall look closer at the application of these conditions to the case of the Bank of Greece.

6.6.2. Institutional arrangements towards an independent Bank of Greece

To enhance and preserve the political and economic independence of the BoG, new legislation should guarantee the following three major changes in the statute of the BoG. Such legislation should take the form of a Bill passed in the Greek Parliament and which ideally, should have the support of all major political parties, something which seems feasible in Greece today.

A single statutory objective

As a result of the Policy Ineffectiveness Proposition it is now widely accepted that active monetary policy cannot achieve sustainable real output effects. On the other hand, it is also widely recognised that price stability is a necessary (though not sufficient) condition for long term economic growth, while sound and stable monetary policy is a precondition for such price stability. In addition, as we have already argued (also see below), central bank independence requires a transparent monetary policy. With more than one macroeconomic objective, such transparency would tend to be reduced since quite often policy failures with respect to one objective can be too easily excused by reference to one of the other objectives. This would effectively weaken the accountability and independence of the BoG. The Bank of Greece should concentrate on achieving and maintaining price stability, yet ensuring that price stability is the sole objective of monetary policy.

In the case of Greece with its poor inflation record, it is imperative that this single objective takes an explicit form. We propose this to be an explicit and formal target for inflation of 2-3% annual rate. As a safety valve, the new statute should also make the provision for an overriding mechanism in case of unexpected shocks (broadly defined). More precisely, the government with the approval of Parliament should be able to suspend the price stability objective although for a limited period only.[28]

Statutory responsibility for monetary policy

The new statute of the BoG should also state clear that the BoG should have the sole power to design the monetary policy framework in terms of both targets and monetary instruments; to be able to set both the single objective and to choose the right instruments in the daily conduct of monetary policy. This will enhance both the goal and instrument independence of the BoG.

In principle, such an inflation target should be agreed in consultation with the government. It would be a highly desirable development in the case of Greece for a scenario in which the introduction of the inflation targeting regime which specifies a time path for price reductions enjoys a joint commitment between the BoG and the government. However, in case of disagreement or conflict it would be the BoG's view that would prevail. To safeguard this, the new legislation should make an explicit statutory statement that the BoG sets exclusively the inflation target. This is quite important in the case of Greece because of the inflationary psychology which has been built up during the last twenty years or so. Inflation targets are after all policy announcements which (at least at the early stages of their introduction) will inevitably be faced with scepticism amongst the public. In fact, legislation would guarantee the

[28] We return to the issue of overriding later on in our discussion of democratic control and accountability. See also our discussion in chapter 5.

long-term nature of such policy announcements, but needless to say policy announcements do matter only if they are credible. Inflation targets set exclusively by the BoG would enhance the credibility of monetary policy. This credibility in turn would help reduce inflation expectations because it would remove the partisan political business cycle that is evident from the recent monetary history of the country. Credibility is a rather overused term in both the recent academic literature and actual policy making. Yet, what is undeniably true, is that credibility is gained rather slowly and policy announcements alone are not always helpful. Actions are also necessary, especially during the early days of a new policy regime. An inflation target set *solely* by an independent BoG is just such an action that would convince the markets and more generally enhance the credibility and transparency of monetary policy.

The composition of the Board of the Bank of Greece

An equally significant institutional arrangement and practical in its nature, guaranteeing the independence of the BoG would be a major restructuring in the governing bodies of the Bank. The objective of such venture should be clear enough, namely to eliminate any political pressure from the design and conduct of monetary policy. This is an issue of great importance given the proposed political and economic independence. Monetary policy decisions have quite often had a direct impact on the economic welfare of current and future generations, hence the whole thing becomes even more delicate when such decisions are taken by unelected officials.

Our own proposal is for a two-tier board structure. Although in daily practises, economic agents identify the central bank with the Governor, it would be rather risky both in political and economic terms to empower a single individual with the huge responsibility of price stability, not to mention the other associated functions of a central bank. Decentralization of power and duties within the BoG seems to us the only sensible arrangement given the new regime of political and economic independence.

Moreover, this should be recognised in the statutes by a detailed description of powers and responsibilities. In brief, the two-tier board structure established by legislation should have one supervisory level, the Board of Governors, and an executive body, the Monetary Policy Committee. This is similar to the board structure of successful independent central banks like in the US and Germany (see Table 6.5). In most cases, the government appoints the majority of the members in the governing bodies and the same should also be true in the Greek case. For instance, in the US, Board members are appointed by the President, subject to Senate approval and for a lengthy term of 14 years. The president of the regional Reserve Banks (appointed by the regional Bank Boards) together with the Board of the

Table 6.5

United States	Members of Federal Reserve Board appointed by US President, subject to Senate approval for 14-year term; Fed Chairman and Vice Chairman by same procedure from among ranks of Board for 4-year term.Open Market Committee comprises Board and Presidents of regional Reserve Banks, appointed by regional Bank Boards for 5 years with possible reappointment, but approved by Fed Board itself. Regional Boards have 9 Directors, 6 elected locally and 3 appointed by Fed Board. Neither Executive or Legislature has any input in appointment of regional Presidents.
Germany	Bundesbank Council comprises Presidents of Land Central Banks and their Directorate, all appointed by Federal President, for 8-year term with possible reappointment. Director nominated by Federal government, after consulting the Council; Presidents of LCBs nominated by Bundesrat, the upper Federal chamber, based on recommendations from Lander governments.
New Zealand	Formal powers vested in Governor. Board of 7-10 Directors charged to monitor on behalf of Finance Minister the performance of Governor in relation to targets and objectives. 4-7 of Board are non-executives, and required to be a majority of any meeting. Board appointments effectively by Finance Minister, but Governor's appointment must satisfy both Board and Minister (double veto). Deputy appointed by Board on recommendation of Governor.
Switzerland	Executive Board, a directorate of 3, nominated by 40-member Council, the supervisory body appointed by government (Bundesrat) for 6 years; eligible for re-election.
Holland	Governing Board +12-member Supervisory Board and 17-member Council that advises minister of guidelines that Bank should follow in policy. Governing board (President, Secretary and 3-5 others) appointed by the Crown for renewable term of 7-years; nomination by government on basis of list; prepared by Governing Board, containing 2 names for President and the Secretary and 3 names for the other members.
Canada	Board comprises Governor, Senior Deputy Governor, 12 Directors and Deputy Finance Minister (who has no vote). Directors appointed for 3-year terms by Finance Minister. All provinces represented on Board.
ESCB	Decision-making council to comprise Governors of national central banks and members of executive board of European Central Bank. That Board comprises President, Vice-President and up to 4 others. All Board members appointed by EC Council (heads of government) for non-renewable 8-year term. Heads of national central banks to have term of at least 5 years, with possible reappointment.

Board structures in some independent central banks

Source: Begg et al. (1993), p. 27

Governors constitute the executive body, the FOMC. In the case of Greece, the Board of Governors (the supervisory body) should have representatives (up to nine) from all parts of society (e.g. from the industry, the banking and financial sector, trade unions etc.) so that the BoG has a broad constituency. The Board of Governors should have a staggered 8-10 years tenure. Their collective expertise and professional experience would safeguard the independence and accountability of the BoG. The Governor and the two (or three) Deputy-Governors should have five-year fixed but renewable contracts (which is longer compared to the electoral cycle but equal to the length of the Greek President's term). The Monetary Policy Committee (the executive body) should consist of the Governor, the Deputy-Governors, the Bank's Chief Economic Advisor plus 3-4 individuals outside the Bank. Those individuals should be widely accepted experts in the fields of money, banking and/or finance and should have staggered four-year terms. In both bodies, decisions should be taken on a simple majoritarian basis.

6.6.3. How to secure the democratic control of an independent Bank of Greece

As we have argued in section 6.6.1, democratic control over an independent central bank requires in practice the existence of certain constraints in the form of legal rules imposed upon the BoG. These rules should take the form of statutory prescriptions which will make the procedures in which the independent BoG operates more transparent and hence more accountable. In the following, we identify a number of changes we believe would have to be made in order to safeguard the democratic control of an independent BoG.

First, the existing legal status of the BoG would have to change. Strictly speaking, the legal status of the BoG right now is quite similar to any other state commercial bank's with its stock of shares traded daily on the Athens Stock Exchange. This is rather bizarre, and almost a Greek world exclusive[29]! The implication of this is that the Governor of the BoG is accountable in the first place to the General Meeting of shareholders and then to the government or Parliament. This rather peculiar legal status should stop immediately and be replaced by the board structure described in the previous section.

A significant and quite common accountability mechanism that should allow an improvement in the transparency of monetary policy should be the regular appearance of the Governor of the BoG before the Parliamentary Committee on Monetary Affairs. This would make the BoG directly accountable to the Greek Parliament. Such a Parliamentary Committee should monitor the performance of the BoG and make publicly available any reservations about the course of monetary policy to which the BoG should reply in public. Equally important, the BoG should

[29] A similar practice exists in Switzerland.

publish a quarterly Inflation Report (see chapter 5) in which a detailed description of inflation developments should be given. The Inflation Report should also spell out the Bank's short-run measures and the time required in achieving (and maintaining) the inflation target. The Inflation Report, together with the publication of the minutes of the meetings of the Monetary Policy Committee, and occasional Bank statements in the national press would improve the level of public awareness and understanding of monetary policy.

Finally, an appropriate escape clause put in place should help avoid any monetary over-killing in the case of a large unexpected inflationary shock. The government (only with the approval of the Parliament) could suspend in principle the price stability mandate although, only for a specified period. During this period the BoG should retain its instrument independence. Such a form of overriding procedure would help in further increasing the transparency as well as securing the accountability of an independent Bank of Greece.

Annex: Assessing the recent Bill 2548/97

In December 1997 and after a four-year delay (!), the government finally enacted legislation (Bill 2548/97) granting statutory independence to the Bank of Greece. It appears that there was no significant reason behind this long delay, but anyhow what matters really is that the independence of the Bank of Greece is now a legislative Act. Given that this last chapter of the present book has been written time ago, we restrict ourselves here to a few points about the recent Bill and which we believe deserve further commentary.

Undoubtedly, Bill 2548/97 is the most important institutional change in the monetary affairs of Greece during the last fifty years. It signifies the irreversible divorce of the Bank of Greece from the government and as such it is a major step towards the right direction. It is, however, far from perfect. There are both positive and negative elements in the 14-article Bill. On the positive side, one has to make a reference to Article 2 (par. 1.a) that entrusts the Bank of Greece with the design and conduct of monetary policy (see also section 6.6.2 above). The same Article 2 (par. 1.b) entrusts the BoG with the execution of exchange rate policy, while its ultimate design is being left with the government (see also section 6.5.3 above). Article 2 (par. 1.d) empowers the BoG with the sole responsibility for banking and financial supervision (see also section 6.5.1 above). In addition, there is no reference to the management of the government's debt and this is also a positive development (see section 6.5.2. above). The legislator was also wise enough (Article 12, par. 17) to leave the door open for further changes in the Bank's statute in connection with the BoG's role as an integral part of the system of European central banks (ESCB). To give one example, current Article 2 (par. 1.c) of Bill 2548/97 entrusts the BoG with the management of foreign exchange reserves. When Greece fully adopts the *euro*, the above paragraph will have to be removed or altered as the great majority of foreign exchange reserves of the country would have to be transferred to the European Central Bank in Frankfurt, since the latter will be then in charge of the daily conduct of the (European) exchange rate policy (and hence Article 2, par. 1b of Bill 2548/97 would also have to be removed).

Turning now to the shortcomings of the Bill, one has to mention the no-change in the legal status of the BoG (see section 6.6.3 above) and that there is no requirement that appointments at the Board level should have the approvement of the Parliament. In addition, although there are explicit references to independence (more precisely in Article 1 that states that the Bank's single objective is to maintain price stability, in Article 2 on the exclusive responsibility for the design and conduct of monetary policy, and in Article 3 that states that the Bank does not seek or take any instructions from the government or any other body) in a country like Greece this is not perhaps sufficient. There should be an explicit statutory reference to this single objective in terms of a formal target for inflation (see section 6.6.2 above). Finally, the proposed structure of the governing bodies of the Bank (Articles 5 and 6) may also be questioned, in the sense that too much power is concentrated on the hands of only one man -- the Governor of the Bank. Article 5 of Bill 2548/97 enacts the establishment of a six-member Monetary Policy Council with six-year terms in office (only governmental approval is required for the choice of the members of the Council). We believe that the revised structure board is rather too centralised and with too many powers left with the Governor. In section 6.6.2 above we propose instead a more decentralised two-tier board structure.

Chapter 7

SUMMARY AND LESSONS FOR EU CANDIDATES

Our principal objective in this book was to address the European dimension of the Greek economy and Greek monetary policy on the road to the euro. Apart from providing an evaluation of recent monetary policies in Greece, we expose a number of weaknesses of the current monetary strategy (ERM participation). The obvious rationale behind the participation in the ERM-II is that if Greece's ultimate objective is to become a full member of the EMU it has to display a pro-European face and joining the ERM-II is a good opportunity of doing so. In addition, there is also the standard argument that the shadowing of the euro will be a commitment to low inflation. This might sound good, but, as we argued in this book, there is a number of problems at both the theoretical and practical level with participation in the ERM-II.

At first place, a fairly obvious question that arises is the following: the ERM after a long period of turbulence, did eventually collapse in 1993; so, why history might not repeat itself ? Speaking in general terms, any new ERM arrangement (especially one with narrow bands) could suffer from all the drawbacks characterizing a near fixed exchange rate regime, namely that there are limits regarding the efficiency of such a regime in a world of high capital mobility, fiscal imbalances and asymmetric shocks. It is of course, true that some of the soft European currencies did survive within the ERM for a number of years but what people often tend to forget is the fact that this has been achieved under two special conditions: capital controls and compulsory central bank intervention. Neither of the two conditions is any longer met today, making any participation of countries with fiscal imbalances in a new ERM at least questionable.

More specifically now, there exists a number of good reasons which all in all make a good case in arguing against ERM-II participation. In chapter 4 we provide a thorough treatment of the subject; here we restrict ourselves to a brief summary of the main points. The recent participation of the drachma in the ERM has undoubtedly increased the international exposure of the Greek currency. This in turn implies that the probability of speculative attacks against the drachma will be higher compared to the past, especially if the drachma enters the ERM-II with an overvalued central rate against the euro and/or there is no swift progress in the field of fiscal consolidation and structural reforms. In other words, as recent experience has shown, in an environment with high capital mobility, international investors appear to be extremely sensitive to movements in the fundamentals of the economies and they stand ready to "punish" countries which appear unwilling to improve their macroeconomic imbalances. The above argument becomes more acute in the light of the following three eventualities: Firstly, the BoG recently announced that exchange rate movements against the ECU will be restricted to a narrow (±2.5%) range around the present central rate, and this will continue even when drachma participates in the ERM-II. This might be potentially dangerous as the adoption of a narrow band could create problems similar to those created by the strong drachma policy which led eventually to drachma's devaluation (e.g. a loss in competitiveness, which in turn may soon vanish the gains from the recent devaluation and cause problems arising from the increase in liquidity). Secondly, there is the prospect of an increasingly appreciating euro during the early stages of its launch. This together with the equally plausible scenario of loose national fiscal policies after 1999, would lead to an increase in interest rates in the euroland (as it happened in the case of US dollar in the early 1980s due to a combination of a tight monetary policy and a lax fiscal policy). A drachma that would shadow closely the euro would lead possibly to higher and higher interest rates in Greece, a tale that would resemble the sterling pound's experience in the ERM during the period 1990-92 (when high interest rates in Germany as a result of the 1990 re-unification, led to as high as 15% interest rates in Britain and eventually to the forced exit of the pound in 1992). In the light of the above, the future of the drachma within the ERM-II after 1999 is rather uncertain, as it is expected that international financial markets would follow closely the developments in the Greek economy. In brief, it appears that given :

- the inherent deficiencies of an ERM arrangement
- the recent 3-year experience of drachma's close shadowing of the DM that led to the March 1998 (effectively forced) devaluation.
- that fiscal imbalances still remain and structural reforms proceed with the speed of a turtle
- the commitment of the Bank of Greece to a narrow band of fluctuation against the euro
- the prospect of a strong euro

the participation of the drachma in the ERM-II may not stand the test of time.

In the third part of the book (chapters 5 and 6) we made a case for an alternative credible strategy to that of participation in the ERM-II. We argue that the drachma should be left without any intervention from the BoG to find its equilibrium value. In addition we argue that the adoption of explicit and formal *inflation targets* together with granting *political and economic* independence to the Bank of Greece may be proved a better way, overall, in reducing and maintaining a low inflation rate and in providing credibility to monetary policy than the nominal anchor of the new ERM. Direct inflation targeting is not just an anti-inflationary policy in the sense this latter term is used in the theory and practice of stabilization programmes. It is rather a unified monetary policy regime defined in terms of final objectives, targets, instruments and indicators.

There are both good theoretical and practical, general and country-specific reasons behind our proposal for the introduction of a direct inflation targeting regime in Greece. Inflation targets imply a more open and transparent monetary policy framework as they are better understood by the public. Inflation targets can also provide the monetary authority with a superior structure of incentives to deliver price stability, and incentives do matter, after all economics is all about incentives. Inflation targets can serve as a better anchor for expectations than intermediate targets. They can reduce the inflationary bias inherent in monetary policy without increasing output variability. They can also provide the monetary authorities with additional degrees of freedom in the conduct of monetary policy. They allow the central bank to use all available information in the fight against inflation by choosing the policy instrument which is judged to be the most effective at any point in time.

Furthermore, in the case of Greece, an inflation targeting regime would result to a change in the existing policy mix in reducing inflation. The strong drachma policy has led over the years of its implementation to a lax fiscal policy (placing little emphasis in reducing budget deficits and government consumption). The introduction of formal inflation targets could result in a more disciplined fiscal policy because it would establish a non-cooperative game between the government and the Bank of Greece. An irresponsible government that follows an inconsistent to the inflation target fiscal policy, would face a determined BoG which would take all necessary steps to meet that target. For instance, it could increase the short-term interest rate and this would be costly for the government in at least two respects: firstly, it would increase the burden of servicing the government debt, a big constraint on the Greek government as the level of debt is more than 100% of GDP; secondly, it would result in an economic slowdown for which the public would most probably hold the government responsible for it. In other words, a direct inflation targeting would result to a more disciplined fiscal policy with the interest rate being the enforcement mechanism.

With the adoption of inflation targets the short term interest rate becomes the main policy instrument. This in turn implies that the central bank can have potentially a more effective control over the level of aggregate demand, mainly through the interest rate effects on the volume of non-traded goods and services (a large sector of the economy in a semi-industrialised country like Greece). After all, it is well known that the most effective way of reducing inflation is by means of controlling the level (and composition) of the aggregate demand in the economy. This compares favourably with the strong drachma policy. In an exchange rate targeting regime, the central bank looses control over the level of interest rates and effectively the only way the central bank can affect the level of macroeconomic aggregate demand is through the volume of traded goods.

Finally, the conditions are now right for the implementation of this novel policy regime, as opposed to four years ago, since an inflation targeting regime is more likely to succeed in achieving and maintaining price stability when inflation is already low enough. Greece only recently managed to have single-digit inflation rates (6% in 1997 and 4.5% in 1998), and hence the timing for the introduction of inflation targets seems favourable. Recent experience from a number of countries in Europe (UK, Sweden, Finland) and elsewhere (Canada, New Zealand) which have adopted formal inflation targets is really encouraging. Inflation targets in these countries have been largely met and actual inflation has declined substantially. Credibility of monetary policy in these countries as it is implied by the convergence of long-term interest rates to German levels has also improved. This stock of knowledge and accumulated experience of the above countries can be a quite useful externality for Greece in terms of the implementation and operation of an inflation targeting regime.

We summarize below the principal features of adopting formal and explicit inflation targets in Greece.

- In accordance with economic theory, the final objective of monetary policy would be that of price stability.
- Visibility and accuracy considerations imply that the balance of arguments turns in favour of the adoption of targets for the rate of growth of CPI.
- Efficiency considerations suggest that short-term interest rates would be the main policy instrument.
- Feasibility and other considerations argue in favour of rolling, higher but gradually converging to the EMU average, range inflation targets.
- Country-specific considerations argue in favour of an independent BoG having the sole responsibility of setting the range of inflation targets, and also deciding on the timing and level of interest rates.
- Unforeseen adverse shocks and accountability considerations argue in favour of an appropriate escape clause put in place which would help in avoiding any monetary overkilling of the economy.

Finally, in the new regime of political and economic independence, and mainly for country-specific considerations, the following are also an integral part of our proposed strategy:

- It may be unwise to strip an independent BoG of its supervisory authority.
- An independent agency other than the BoG should be in charge of public debt management.
- There is no reason for any change in who has control over exchange rate policy.
- Decentralisation of power and duties within the BoG seems the only sensible arrangement regarding the institutional change of central bank independence.

The proposed monetary policy strategy in the present book is by no means country-specific. Other economies with similar structural features aiming at joining the EMU could well adopt, *mutandis mutandis,* the same policy strategy. For instance, a large number of Central and East European (CEE) countries have recently applied[1] for EU membership that could lead eventually to full EMU membership.

It is clear by now that Central and Eastern Europe will become a two-speed region as far as EU membership is concerned. A group of countries (the so called "first-round", i.e. the Czech Republic, Poland, Hungary, Slovenia and Estonia) could achieve EU membership within five years or so since they have already put in place the necessary reforms such as privatization, liberalization of the price and trade regime, strengthening of their banking systems, making labour practices more flexible, etc., have achieved sufficient macroeconomic stability and in general have reoriented their economies westwards. This contrasts with the "second-round" group of countries, (i.e. Romania, Bulgaria, Latvia, Lithuania, etc) which will continue to struggle with political and economic reforms and have no chance of getting into the EU before 2010.

Applicant countries in both groups will be called to undertake further reforms in preparing themselves for EU membership. In Copenhagen, in June 1993, a number of economic criteria (the so-called "Copenhagen criteria"), were laid down that CEE countries would need to satisfy in order to gain EU membership. These criteria were[2] the existence of a functioning market economy, the capacity to cope with competitive pressure within the EU and the ability to take on the obligations of membership, including adherence to the aims of EMU. The first of these criteria refers to issues like privatization, legal rules that guarantee property rights, price liberalization, a stable macroeconomic environment characterized by low inflation, low levels of budget deficit and government debt, reduced variability of the exchange rate and so on. The second criterion refers to all those elements needed for a country to integrate successfully in the Union's internal market and equally important to cope with increased competition at the level of an enlarged Union. These include an efficient public administration, a developed banking and financial sector, competitive markets, etc. The final criterion refers to the ability of each CEE country to adopt in full the Union's 80,000 page *acquis communautaire,* its body of law.

There is a number of lessons that can be drawn from Greece's experience on the road to EMU membership which could be useful to CEE countries - EU candidates. As a general comment, we note that EMU should not be a short-run

---

[1] This group of countries includes Hungary (31.3.1994) Poland (5.4.1994), Estonia (28.11.1995), Lithuania (8.12.1995) the Czech Republic (23.1.1996), Slovenia (11.6.1996), etc.

[2] See Bulletin of the European Communities (1993).

objective for these countries, mainly for three reasons. First, although sufficient work has still to be done to correct macroeconomic imbalances, it is even more important for CEE countries to remove the many distortions at the micro level, aiming at improving productivity levels and the competitiveness of their economies. Second, premature adoption of strict convergence stabilization programmes would be unduly harmful. Finally, it may prove difficult - in the sense that it may take really long time - for the majority of CEE countries to implement the *acquis* in the area of EMU, even as non-participating countries.

Turning now to the fields of monetary and exchange rate policies, most CEE countries have today sliding pegs against strong currencies (mainly the DM). Pegging to a hard currency is motivated by the need for an anchor, especially as new market -oriented Central Banks seek to establish their credibility. The sliding feature of the peg permits controlled devaluations against western currencies to allow for the effect of inflation rates which are still considerably higher than those in the EMU. Interestingly, some of the first-round countries have recently adopted inflation targets. For instance, Hungary has followed a narrow crawling peg against a basket consisting of 70% DM and 30% of US$ and is moving towards the adoption of an inflation targeting monetary policy regime. The Czech Republic abandoned its peg after the currency crisis in the spring of 1997 and has adopted recently (1.1.1998) inflation targets, while Poland after abandoning its peg against a basket of currencies, resorted to floating and since 1.1.1999 to the adoption of inflation targets. Estonia sticks to the currency board that it adopted early on and it has been joined by Bulgaria in 1997, while recently Lithuania successfully abandoned the currency board arrangement. Slovenia, Romania, Slovakia and Croatia all operate a managed float which roughly shadows the DM.

One clear lesson for CEE countries that emerges from our discussion in chapter 4 of this book is that it might be risky to switch to fixed exchange rates against the euro during the transition path to EMU. During the convergence period some flexibility in the exchange rate might be needed in the associated CEE countries. The catching-up process that is still needed in these transition economies would most likely imply inflationary pressures or an appreciating nominal exchange rate. A certain degree of currency depreciation might be needed to compensate for the competitiveness losses generated by higher inflation rates relative to the low-inflation euroland. On the other hand, given the productivity differentials and the macroeconomic imbalances characterizing most of the transition economies, fixed exchange rates (or even participation in the ERM-II with a narrow band) could well result to overvalued currencies, high interest rates, a rise of capital inflows, continued intervention in foreign exchange markets, international exposure, speculative attacks and, all in all, to failure regarding the objective of exchange rate stability. It is probably wiser for the second-round CEE countries to maintain some flexibility in the exchange rate. Given the long convergence process needed for these countries, their immediate priority should be rather all these - well known, but long delayed - structural reforms which are necessary conditions for the proper operation of a market economy than the stability of the exchange rate - just for the sake of it.

For the five countries in the leading pact to join Europe's economic club, an alternative strategy to ERM-II participation could well be that of inflation targeting along the lines proposed for the Greek case in Chapter 5 of the present book. Inflation in some of the first-round CEE applicant countries has gone down to single - digit rates and as a result, the timing for the introduction of inflation targets appears to be right. As in the case of Greece, the success of setting and achieving inflation targets in CEE countries would be facilitated through the implementation of medium-term monetary programmes involving rolling annual inflation targets gradually converging to the EMU average. The higher component of the targets vis-a-vis the EMU rate would reflect that inflation might still have "real" origins due to the catching up process, e.g. due to adjustments in the structure of relative prices. The gradually converging component would increase the chances of meeting the targets and at the same time would not make them unduly constraining in terms of output losses. The target ranges should be country-specific to reflect the inflation history and culture of each country, but on the other hand, they should be sufficiently narrow in order to have an effect upon the private sector's expectations. Such a monetary policy strategy would have a number of advantages discussed at length in chapter 5. For instance, the adoption of inflation targets would imply a more transparent monetary policy framework as they are better understood by the public, they could serve as a better anchor for agents' expectations than exchange-rate targets, provide the Central Bank with additional degrees of freedom in the conduct of monetary policy, result to a better overall control over the level of aggregate demand, and last but not least result to a more disciplined fiscal policy.

The adoption of inflation targets would be expected to have a significant effect upon inflationary expectations, which could be stronger, the more credible monetary policy is. Monetary policy credibility, in turn, would be enhanced if an independent Central Bank has the sole responsibility of setting the range of inflation targets. As we have argued in Chapters 5 and 6 of the present book, in countries with polarized political systems, where political interference is widespread in as many fields of economic policy as possible, an inflation - targeting regime would lack credibility if the targets were set only by the government. Nearly ten years into the transition process, most CEE countries are still regarded as infant rather than mature democracies. Due to polarization, ideological differences among political parties - which of course at the end are manifested in actual economic policy making - are rather deep. As a result, if inflation targets are set solely by the government, a political party in opposition would naturally criticize the performance of the government regarding the inflation targets. Under such circumstances, the credibility of the inflation target would be doubted if the markets perceive a substantial probability of a change in the party in office. Granting full independence to the Central Bank would imply that the inflation target is chosen solely by the Central Bank, irrespective of the party in power and its preferences for low or high inflation, and this would enhance the credibility of the entire monetary policy strategy. Otherwise, a newly elected government which most probably has been elected with a promise of a new policy agenda, would not hesitate to change its predecessor's inflation target. This would result to a partisan political business cycle, in which the alteration of parties in power would imply a different target for inflation each time, with the Central Bank just left to achieve these different inflation targets.

Recent experience shows that an increasing number of transition economies seem to have realized the advantages of an inflation targeting monetary policy regime. As a matter of fact, the Czech Republic was first to switch over to inflation targets on 1st January 1998. The Czech National Bank announced net[3] inflation targets, namely the achievement of net inflation within the range of 3.5-5.5% by the end of 2000. In one of the first Inflation Reports published (April 1998) by the Czech Central Bank, an attempt is made to justify the switch over to inflation targets mainly on the following grounds : (a) the need for a nominal anchor that would have an impact upon inflationary expectations. (b) the fact that in either a managed float or an exchange-rate targeting regime, the speed and timing of the disinflation process are not explicitly specified. By contrast, in an inflationary targeting regime, the Central Bank openly announces its disinflation intentions. (c) such a monetary policy strategy would make convergence of inflation with EMU inflation smoother. It is still early days to attempt any evaluation of this novel policy regime in the case of the Czech Republic. A number of obstacles have yet to ovecome, like, for example, institutional rigidities that limit the efficiency of monetary policy instruments, the strong cost pressure from the segment of regulated prices in net inflation, the coordination of monetary policy with fiscal and wages policy, the presence of political uncertainty and so on. Judging from its high quality Inflation Report, it is clear, at least, that the Czech Central Bank has both the right instincts and the expertise to achieve its policy objective.

Very recently also, the National Bank of Poland (NBP) announced through the introduction of the Medium-Term Monetary Policy Strategy 1999-2003 (MTMPS), the adoption of direct rolling inflation targets. The Monetary Policy Council has set that the target for 1999 falls within the range of 8% to 8.5% and that the medium term target should be a rate of inflation below 4% by the year 2003. Their aim is to target the core inflation index which eliminates the impact of the prices subject to strong seasonal variations, to administrative regulations or to temporary supply shocks. They justified their choice of this monetary policy

[3] Net inflation represents the movements of unregulated prices (i.e. the CPI adjusted for regulated prices) further adjusted for the effects of indirect taxes.

strategy on the following two main arguments : (a) the need for the breaking up of inflationary expectations which constitute one of the main obstacles in the process of steadily reducing inflation; (b) the transparency, single clear objective and openness of this strategy would limit the ability of monetary authorities to implement short-term real objectives. The Council concludes that "... comparing with alternative strategies, direct inflation targeting is the best policy approach at the time preceding Poland's accession to the EU and the EMU" (MTMPS, p.12).

Finally, regarding the issue of central bank independence in transition economies, it is true that an increasing number of them (e.g. all the first-round countries, Latvia, Armenia, Lithuania, etc.), following recent world practices, have taken steps towards granting autonomy to their central banks. Although this is a welcome development, it has to be emphasized that an institutional change like that of central bank independence would be of little benefit if the tools to perform the job are not available. The main question for CEE countries is whether an independent central bank implements reforms towards the establishment of an environment permitting the use of market-based monetary policy instruments, since persistent weaknesses in the banking and financial sector would continue to hinder the conduct of monetary policy.

Table 7.1 below classifies CEE countries according to the progress made in reforming the banking sector and the liberalization of interest rates during the period 1991-97. According to the Financial Development Index reported in Table 7.1, countries are rated from 1, indicating a country that has made little progress beyond the establishment of a two-tier banking system (i.e. the separation of the central bank from a network of commercial banks), to 4+, indicating an advanced reformer to the BIS standards. As it emerges from Table 7.1, the first-round applicant countries score reasonably well. However, much remains to be done to bring monetary operations, even in the first-round applicant CEE countries, to modern market standards. For instance, given the structural and liquidity problems in the banking system, central bank need to design L-O-L-R facilities (e.g. the establishment of a Lombard window). Central banks in transition countries need also to enhance the efficiency of existing monetary instruments by ensuring compliance with reserve requirements. In addition, progress in enhancing the liquidity of the money market, and in particular of the interbank market, is crucial to the development of market-based monetary instruments. Further reforms in public-debt management, government securities market and banking supervision, along the lines of chapter 6 above, are needed to ensure a market-based monetary management. Such reforms are required as much as the autonomy from political interference in making the design and conduct of monetary policy in transition economies both efficient and credible.

Table 7.1

Country	*Banking Reform and Interest Rate Liberalization Index*
Albania	2
Armenia	2+
Azerbaijan	2
Belarus	1
Bosnia-Herzegovina	2
Bulgaria	3-
Croatia	3-
Czech Republic	3
Estonia	3+
FYROM	3
Georgia	2+
Hungary	4
Kazakhstan	2+
Kyrgyzstan	3-
Latvia	3-
Lithuania	3
Moldova	2+
Poland	3+
Romania	2+
Russian Federation	2
Slovak Republic	3-
Slovenia	3
Tajikistan	1
Turkmenistan	1
Ukraine	2
Uzbekistan	2-

Progress towards banking reform and interest rate liberalization in transition economies

Source: European Bank of Reconstruction and Development (1998)

1 Little progress beyond establishment of a two-tier system.

2 Significant liberalization of interest rates and credit allocation, limited use of directed credit or interest rate liberalization ceilings.

3	Substantial progress in establishment of bank solvency and of a framework for prudential supervision and regulation, full interest rate liberalization with little preference access to cheap refinancing, significant lending to private enterprises and significant presence of private banks
4	Significant movement of banking laws and regulations towards BIS standards, well-functioning banking competition and effective prudential supervision, significant term lending to private enterprises, substantial financial deepening.
4+	Standard and performance norms of advanced industrial economies: full convergence of banking laws and regulation with BIS standards, provision of full set of competitive banking services.

Plus (+) and minus (-) signs indicate a borderline case between two rate groups

Table A.6.1

INSTITUTIONAL FEATURES OF CENTRAL BANKS IN THE EUROPEAN UNION

Item	NATIONAL BANK OF BELGIUM	DANMARKS NATIONAL BANK	DEUTCSHE BUNDESBANK	BANK OF GREECE	BANCO DE ESPANA	BANQUE DE FRANCE
PRINCIPLE STATUTORY OBJECTIVE	None, although safeguarding the currency implicit	To maintain a safe and secure currency system	To safeguard the currency	To control currency in circulation and credit	To achieve price stability	To assure price stability
LEGAL AUTHORITY FOR						
1 - Exchange Rate Regime	1-Government	1-Government	1-Government	1-Government	1-Government	1-Government
2 - Setting targets for monetary growth	2- Central Bank (no target set at present)	2- Central Bank (no target set at present)	2-Central Bank	2-Central Bank	2-Central Bank	2-Central Bank
3 - Changing key interest rates	3-Central Bank	3-Central Bank	3-Central Bank	3-Central Bank	3-Central Bank	3-Central Bank
RESPONSIBILITIES						
1 - Execution of monetary and exchange rate policy	1-Yes	1-Yes	1-Yes	1-Yes	1-Yes	1-Yes
2 - Issue of currency	2-Yes	2-Yes	2-Yes	2-Yes	2-Yes	2-Yes
3 - Payments system services	3-Yes	3-Yes	3-Yes	3-Yes	3-Yes	3-Yes
4 - Bank of banks and government	4-Yes	4-Yes	4-Yes	4-Yes	4-Yes	4-Yes
5 - Supervision of financial institutions	5-No	5-No	5-No	5-Yes	5-Yes	5-Yes
6 - Safeguard financial stability	6-Yes	6-Yes	6-Yes	6-Yes	6-Yes	6-Yes
7 - Official reserve management	7-Yes	7-Yes	7-Yes	7-Yes	7-Yes	7-Yes
GOVERNING BODIES	Governor Board of Directors Council of Regency Board of Censors General Council	Board of Governors Board of Directors Committee of Directors Royal Bank Commissioner	Central Bank Council Directorate Managing Director of Land Central Banks	General Council	Governor Deputy Governor Governing Council Executive Commission	Governor Deputy Governors (2) General Council Monetary Policy Council
APPOINTMENT OF GOVERNOR BY	Crown on proposal of the Government	Crown on proposal of the Government	Federal president on proposal of Federal Government after consultation of Central Bank Council	Government on proposal of General Council	Crown on proposal of President of Government	Council of Ministers
Term	5 years (renewable)	No fixed term	Normally 8 years minimum 2 years (renewable)	4 years (renewable)	6 years (non-renewable)	6 years (renewable)
RECENT AND/OR PLANNED CHANGES	Since March 1993, abolition of the previous "power of suspension and right to oppose" by the Government with respect to central bank's decisions and operations concerning its basic tasks.	None	None	Law of December 1997 increasing the independence of the Central Bank and introducing the provisions of the Maastricht Treaty relating to Central Banks	Autonomy Law of 1 June 1994, introducing all the provisions of the Maastricht Treaty relating to central banks	Law introducing all the provisions of the Maastricht Treaty relating to central banks enacted in December 1993.

Note: All the national legislations that so required were changed in 1993 to be consistent with the Maastricht Treaty prohibition of public sector financing by the central bank.

Source: Goodhart and Venuels (1994)

Table A.6.1 (continued)

INSTITUTIONAL FEATURES OF CENTRAL BANKS IN THE EUROPEAN UNION

Item	CENTRAL BANK OF IRELAND	BANCA D'ITALIA	INSTITUT MONETAIRE LUXEMBOURGEOISE	NEDERLANDSCHE BANK	BANCO DE PORTUGAL	BANK OF ENGLAND
PRINCIPLE STATUTORY OBJECTIVE	To safeguard the integrity of the currency	None, although safeguarding the currency implicit	To promote the stability of the currency	To safeguard the value of the currency	To maintain internal monetary stability and the external solvency of currency	None, although safeguarding the currency implicit
LEGAL AUTHORITY FOR						
1 - Exchange Rate Regime	1-Government	1-Government	1-Government	1-Government	1-Government	1-Government
2 - Setting targets for monetary growth	2- Central Bank (no target set at present)	2- Joint with government	2-Not applicable	2-Central Bank (no target set at present)	2-Central Bank (no target set at present)	2-Government
3 - Changing key interest rates	3-Central Bank	3-Central Bank	3-Not applicable	3-Central Bank	3-Central Bank	3-Central Bank
RESPONSIBILITIES						
1 - Execution of monetary and exchange rate policy	1-Yes	1-Yes	1-Yes	1-Yes	1-Yes	1-Yes
2 - Issue of currency	2-Yes	2-Yes	2-Yes	2-Yes	2-Yes	2-Yes
3 - Payments system services	3-Yes	3-Yes	3-No	3-Yes	3-Yes	3-Yes
4 - Bank of banks and government	4-Yes	4-Yes	4-Yes	4-Yes	4-Yes	4-Yes
5 - Supervision of financial institutions	5-Yes	5-Yes	5-Yes	5-Yes	5-Yes	5-Yes
6 - Safeguard financial stability	6-Yes	6-Yes	6-Yes	6-Yes	6-Yes	6-Yes
7 - Official reserve management	7-Yes	7-Yes (together with the Italian Exchange Office)	7-Yes	7-Yes	7-Yes	7-Yes (as agent for the Government)
GOVERNING BODIES	Board of Directors	Governor Director-General 2 Deputy Director-Generals (Directorate)	Management Council	Governing Board Supervisory Board	Governor Board of Directors Board of Auditors Advisory Board	Governor Monetary Policy Committee
APPOINTMENT OF GOVERNOR BY	President on proposal of the Government	Board of Directors with approval of Government	Grand-Duke on proposal of Council of Ministers.	Nominated by joint meeting of Governing Board and Supervisory Board and appointed by Crown on proposal of Council of Ministers.	Council of Ministers on proposal of Minister of Finance	Crown on proposal of Prime Minister
Term	7 years (renewable)	Life	6 years (renewable)	7 years (renewable)	5 years (renewable)	5 years (renewable)
RECENT AND/OR PLANNED CHANGES	Prospective bill to suppress the power of the Government to be consulted by the Bank regarding the latter's general function and duty. Other institutional changes are presently under discussion.	Recent changes introducing all the provisions of the Maastricht Treaty relating to central banks.	Institution changes introducing all the provisions of the Maastricht Treaty relating to central banks.		Amendment to prohibit the underwriting of Treasury Bills. Institution changes introducing all the provisions of the Maastricht Treaty relating to central banks.	Monetary arrangements of May 19971

1: for further details, see chapter 5

Note: All the national legislations that so required were changed in 1993 to be consistent with the Maastricht Treaty prohibition of public sector financing by the central bank.

Table A.6.2

MONETARY POLICY INSTRUMENTS AND PROCEDURES IN THE EUROPEAN UNION

Item	Belgium	Denmark	Germany	Greece	Spain	France	Ireland	Italy	Netherlands	Portugal	UK
PERMANENT RESERVE REQUIREMENTS FOR MONETARY POLICY PURPOSES	NO	NO	YES	YES	YES	YES	YES	YES	NO	YES	NO
1 - Size (% of GDP) (a)	N.A	N.A	2.7	3.9	2.0	0.1	1.8	8.0	N.A	16.1	N.A
2 - Remuneration	N.A	N.A	No	Partly	No	No	Below market rates	Partly	N.A	Partly	N.A
STANDING FACILITIES (b)											
1 - Lending facilities af below or close to market rates (rate)	□ (below market)	N.A	*	N.A	N.A	N.A	N.A	* (close to market)	x	N.A	N.A
2- Deposit facilities	□	□	N.A	N.A	N.A	N.A	*	N.A		N.A	N.A
3 - Marginal refinancing	□	N.A	□	*	□	□	*	*	N.A □	□	*
OPEN MARKET OPERATIONS											
1 - Types (b)											
Outright transactions (c)	□	x	□	*	N.A	*	N.A	*	□	x	x
Reserved transactions in domestic securities	x	x	x	□	x	x	x	x	x	*	*
Foreign currency swap transactions	*	□	□	□	□		x	*	□	□	N.A
2 - Frequency of operations (d)	x	*	□	*	*	*	x	*	□	*	x
3 - Auction procedures											
volume tender	x	x	□	N.A	□	N.A	N.A	N.A	x	*	N.A
interest rate tender	□	N.A	x	□	x	x	x	x	N.A	*	x

Notes: N.A: Not applicable or not used.

(a) Amount outstanding at the end of 1992

(b) Importance in providing (or withdrawing) liquidity to (or form) the market □ Low, * Intermediate, x high

(c) These include issues of certificates of deposit by the central bank in the cases of Denmark and Portugal, and unsecured overnight loans in Greece

(d) □ About once a week, * several times a week, x more than once a day.

Source: Goodhart and Vinals (1994)

LIST OF FIGURES

Figure 1	Greek economic performance at a glance	4
Figure 2	Current Account and EU Transfers in Greece (% of GDP)	6
Figure 1.1	Income convergence in the Cohesion countries	12
Figure 2.1	Real GDP- Annual growth rate	32
Figure 2.2	Gross fixed capital formation (% of GDP)	37
Figure 2.3	Current Account deficit (% of GDP)	37
Figure 2.4	CPI inflation and unemployment rate	38
Figure 2.5	Primary and total budget deficit (% of GDP)	39
Figure 2.6	Money supply (M3) and credit growth (annual % change)	39
Figure 2.7	Public debt (% of GDP)	41
Figure 2.8	Public investment as % of total public outlays	43
Figure 3.1	Narrow money supply (annual % change)	70
Figure 3.2	Broad money supply (annual % change)	71
Figure 3.3	Bank credit (annual % change)	72
Figure 3.4	Nominal interest rates in Greece	73
Figure 3.5	*Ex-post* real interest rates in Greece	74
Figure 3.6	Short-term nominal interest rates in Greece and the EU	75
Figure 3.7	Short-term real interest rates in Greece and the EU	76
Figure 3.8	Bank of Greece interest rates	76
Figure 3.9	Overnight interbank interest rate	77
Figure 3.10	Drachmas per US Dollar	78
Figure 3.11	Drachmas per ECU and Drachmas per DM	79
Figure 3.12	Nominal depreciation of the drachma against the ECU and the DM (annual % change)	80
Figure 4.1	Rate of growth of money supply: targets and outcomes	85
Figure 4.2	Rate of growth of bank credit: targets and outcomes	86
Figure 4.3	Credit to the public sector as % of total bank credit	87
Figure 4.4	Income velocity of narrow money supply in Greece	88
Figure 4.5	Income velocity of broad money supply in Greece	89
Figure 4.6	Annual percentage change of income velocity of money	90
Figure 4.7	Annual CPI inflation, inflation differential against the EU and nominal depreciation against the ECU	92
Figure 4.8	Domestic and imported inflation	93
Figure 4.9	Foreign exchange reserves minus gold	97
Figure 4.10	Intervention rate of the Bank of Greece in the interbank money market (monthly average)	99
Figure 4.11	The yield curve in Greece, June 1994-August 1997	102
Figure 5.1	Long-term interest rates in EU inflation-targeting countries: convergence with Germany	126
Figure 5.2	Inflation in Greece (average annual % change in CPI and PPI)	128

Figure 5.3	CPI inflation in Greece and the EU	129
Figure 5.4	Domestic and imported inflation (average annual % change)	132
Figure 5.5	Nominal depreciation against the ECU and CPI inflation	133
Figure 5.6	Wage inflation and productivity growth (annual % change)	136
Figure 6.1	Central bank independence and inflation performance, 1955-88	161
Figure 6.2	Political and economic independence of central banks	165

LIST OF TABLES

Table 1	Nominal convergence among EU Member States	2
Table 1.1	Gross Domestic Product at market prices per head of population (1996 figures, EU15=100)	11
Table 1.2	The EMU Ins: official bilateral conversion rates	22
Table 1.3	Monetary policy strategies in the European Union before the introduction of the euro	24
Table 1.4	CPI Inflation in the EMU Outs (% per annum)	28
Table 2.1	Main economic indicators in Greece	33
Table 2.2	The year 1993 performance of the Convergence Programme 1993-98	47
Table 2.3	The Revised Convergence Programme of Greece, 1994-99	49
Table 3.1	Money supply and bank credit growth in Greece, average annual % change, 1975-96	71
Table 3.2	Money supply and bank credit growth in Greece, 1975-96, correlation matrix	72
Table 3.3	Interest rates in Greece	75
Table 3.4	Nominal depreciation of the drachma	79
Table 4.1	Real appreciation (-)/depreciation (+) of the drachma against the ECU (annual % change)	95
Table 4.2	Inflation, labour cost, profitability and current account, 1988-97	96
Table 4.3	Spot and forward rates of EU currencies against the DM, March 4, 1998	103
Table 5.1	CPI Inflation in inflation-targeting countries	125
Table 5.2	Average inflation in Greece and Western countries	130
Table 5.3	Inflation projections and outcomes	131
Table 5.4	Inflation in the traded sector	134
Table 5.5	Inflation in the non-traded sector	135

Table 6.1	Political independence of central banks	162
Table 6.2	Economic independence of central banks	164
Table 6.3	Political vulnerability of central banks, 1972-1989	166
Table 6.4	Monetary and supervisory agencies	174
Table 6.5	Board structures in some independent central banks	183
Table 7.1	Progress towards banking reform and interest rate liberalization in transition economies	197
Table A.6.1	Institutional features of central banks in the European Union	199
Table A.6.2	Monetary policy instruments and procedures in the European Union	201

BIBLIOGRAPHY

AGHEVLI B. (1977), "Inflationary Finance and Growth", *Journal of Political Economy,* 85, pp. 1295-1307.

AHKING F. and MILLER S. (1985), "The relationship between government deficits, money growth and inflation", *Journal of Macroeconomics,* 7 pp. 447-467.

AKERHOLM J. and BRUNILA A. (1995), "Inflation Targeting: The Finnish Experience" in Leiderman L. and Svensson L.E.O. (eds.) *Inflation Targets*, Centre for Economic Policy Research, London.

ALESINA A. and GATTI R. (1995), "Independent Central Banks: Low Inflation at No Cost?", *American Economic Review Papers and Proceedings,* 85, pp. 196-200.

ALESINA A. and GRILLI V. (1992), "The European Central Bank: Reshaping Monetary Politics in Europe", in M.Canzoneri, V.Grilli and P.Masson (eds.) *Establishing a Central Bank: issues in Europe and lessons from the United States",* Cambridge University Press, Cambridge.

ALESINA A. and PEROTTI R. (1995), "Fiscal Expansions and Adjustments in OECD Countries", *Economic Policy* 20, pp. 207-248.

ALESINA A. and PEROTTI R. (1996), Fiscal Adjustments in OECD Countries: Composition and Macroeconomic Effects, NBER Working Paper No. 5730, Cambridge MA.

ALESINA A. and SUMMERS L.H. (1993), "Central Bank Independence and Macroeconomic Performance: Some Comparative Evidence", *Journal of Money, Credit and Banking,* 25 No 2, pp. 151-162.

ALESINA A. and TABELINI G. (1987), "Rules and Discretion with Non-Coordinated Monetary and Fiscal Policy", *Economic Inquiry* 25, pp. 619-630.

ALLSOPP C. and VINES D. (1996), " Fiscal policy and EMU", *National Institute Economic Review* 158 (October), pp. 91-107.

ALOGOSKOUFIS G. (1986), " On the Determinants of Consumer Price Inflation in Greece", *Greek Economic Review* 8, pp. 245-266.

ALOGOSKOUFIS G. (1990), "Competitiveness, Wage Adjustment and Macroeconomic Policy in the Dependent Economy. The Case of Greece", *Greek Economic Review* 12, *pp. 15-57.*

ALOGOSKOUFIS G. (1995), "The two faces of Janus: Institutions, Policy Regimes and Macroeconomic Performance in Greece", *Economic Policy* 20, pp. 149-192.

ALOGOSKOUFIS G. (1995), The crisis of economic policy, Kritiki, Athens (in Greek).

ALOGOSKOUFIS G. and CHRISTODOULAKIS N. (1991), "Fiscal deficits, seigniorage and external debt: the case of Greece", in G. Alogoskoufis, L. Papademos and R. Portes (eds.), *External constraints on macroeconomic policy: the European Experience,* Cambridge University Press, Cambridge.

ALOGOSKOUFIS G. and LAZARETOU S. (1997), The Drachma, *IMOΠ* (Foundation of Studies on Economic Policy), Athens (in Greek).
ALOGOSKOUFIS G. and PHILIPPOPOULOS A. (1992), "Inflationary Expectations, Political Parties and the Exchange Rate Regime: Greece, 1958-1989", *European Journal of Political Economy* 8, pp. 375-399.
ALOGOSKOUFIS G. and PRODROMIDIS K. (1995), Delors Package II and Real Convergence, Foundation of Economic and Industrial Research (IOBE), Athens, (in Greek).
ALOGOSKOUFIS G. and SMITH R. (1991), "The Phillips Curve, the Persistence of Inflation and the Lucas Critique: Evidence from Exchange Rate Regimes", *American Economic Review* 81, pp. 1254-1275.
ANDERSEN T. and SCHNEIDER F. (1985), "Coordination of Fiscal and Monetary Policies under different institutional arrangements", *European Journal of Political Economy* 2, pp. 169-191.
ANDERSSON K. and BERG C. (1995), "The inflation target in Sweden", in Haldane A.G. (ed.) *Targeting Inflation*, Bank of England, London.
ARCHER D. (1995), "Some reflections on inflation targets", in Haldane A.G. (ed.) *Targeting Inflation*, Bank of England, London.
ARGHYROU M.G. (1998), "Causal relationships between public expenditure, public receipts and Gross Domestic Product: Greece 1965-95", *Applied Economics Letters* 5, pp. 727-731.
ARGHYROU M.G (1999a), "Long-run output effects of fiscal police: evidence from Greece", paper presented in 3rd Conference on Macroeconomic Analysis and International Finance, University of Crete, May 1999.
ARGHYROU M.G. (1999b), "EU participation and the external trade of Greece: an appraisal of the evidence", forthcoming in *Applied Economics.*
ARGHYROU M.G. (1999c), "Strong currency policy and long-run PPP: the drachma devaluation of 1998", mimeo, Department of Economics and Finance, Brunel University.
ARGHYROU M.G. and MOURMOURAS I.A. (1999), "The EMU Ins, the EMU Outs and the European Central Bank", in Beber M. and Kinsella R. (eds.), *A Central Bank for Europe,* Lothian Foundation Press, London, forthcoming.
ARTIS M. (1996), "Alternative transitions to EMU", *The Economic Journal* 106, pp. 1005-15.
ARROWSMITH J. (1995), "Economic and Monetary Union in a Multi-Tier Europe", *National Institute Economic Review* 153 (May), pp. 76-97.
BANK OF ENGLAND, Evolution of the Monetary Framework, Loughborough University Banking Lecture given on 7 November 1996 by the Governor of the Bank of England.
BANK OF GREECE, Economic Bulletin, various editions.
BANK OF GREECE, Report of the Governor, various editions.
BANK OF POLAND (1998), Medium-Term Strategy of Monetary Policy, Warsaw.

BARRO R. (1974), "Are Government Bonds Net Wealth?", *Journal of Political Economy 82,* pp. 1095-1117.
BARRO R. (1995), Inflation and growth, NBER Working Paper No 5326, Cambridge MA.
BARRO R. and GORDON D. (1983), "A Positive Theory of Monetary Policy in a Natural Rate Model", *Journal of Political Economy* 91, pp. 589-610.
BATTEN D., BLACKWELL M., KIM Z., S. NOCERA and OZEKI Y., "The conduct of monetary policy in the major industrial countries: Instruments and operating procedures", Occasional Paper No 70, International Monetary Fund.
BAYOUMI T. and EICHENGREEN B. (1993), "Shocking aspects of European Monetary Integration", in F. Torres and F. Giavazzi (eds.) *Adjustment and Growth in the European Monetary Union,* Center for Economic Policy Research, London and Cambridge University Press, Cambridge.
BEAN C. (1998), "The New UK Monetary Arrangements: a View From the Literature", mimeo, Department of Economics, The London School of Economics.
BEGG D. (1993), Independent and Accountable: A New Mandate for the Bank of England, A Report of an Independent Panel Chaired by Eric Roll, Center for Economic Policy Research, London.
BEGG D. (1997), "Monetary policy during transition: progress and pitfalls in Central and Easter Europe, 1990-96", *Oxford Review of Economic Policy* 13, pp. 33-46.
BEGG D. and WYPLOSZ C. (1987), "Why the EMS ? Dynamic Games and the Equilibrium Policy Regime", in R. Bryant and R. Portes (eds.) *Global Macroeconomics: Policy Conflict and Cooperation,* New York, St. Martin's Press.
BEGG D., CHAPPORI P., GIAVAZZI F., MAYER C., NEVEN D., SPAVENTA L., VINES X., and WYPLOSZ C. (1991), Monitoring European Integration: The making of the Monetary Union, Center for Economic Policy Reserach, London.
BEN-BASSAT A. (1995), "The inflation target in Israel: policy and development", in Haldane A.G. (ed.) *Targeting Inflation,* Bank of England, London.
BERNANKE B.S. and MISHKIN F.S. (1997), "Inflation Targeting: a new framework for monetary policy?", NBER Working Paper No 5893, Cambridge MA.
BLINDER A.S. and SOLOW R.M. (1973), "Does fiscal policy matter?", *Journal of Public Economics* 2, pp. 319-337.
BOFINGER P. (1995), "The Political Economy of the Eastern Enlargement of the EU", CEPR Discussion Paper No 1234, London.
BOWEN A. (1995), "Inflation targetry in the United Kingdom", in Haldane A.G. (ed.) *Targeting Inflation,* Bank of England, London, pp. 59-74.
BRISSIMIS S. and GIBSON H. (1996), "Monetary Policy, Capital Flows and Greek Disinflation", *Bank of Greece, Economic Bulletin* 9, pp. 21-38.
BROADBENT B. and BARRO R. (1997), "Central Bank preferences and macroeconomic equilibrium", *Journal of Monetary Economics* 39. Pp. 17-43.

BRUNILA A. and LAHDENPERA (1995), "Inflation targets: principal issues and practical implementation", in Haldane A.G. (ed.) *Targeting Inflation,* Bank of England, London.
BUITER W. and KLETZER K. (1990), "Reflections on the Fiscal Implications of a Common Currency", CEPR Discussion Paper No 418, London.
BUITER W., CORSETTI G. and ROUBINI N. (1993), "Sense and Non-sense in the Treaty of Maastricht", *Economic Policy,* 16, pp. 57-100.
BULLETIN OF THE EUROPEAN COMMUNITIES (1993), 6
BURNS A. (1978), Reflections of an Economic Policymaker, Washington DC: American Enterprise Institute.
BURDERKIN R.. (1987), "Cross Country Evidence on the Relationship between Central Banks and Governments", *Journal of Macroeconomics* 9, pp. 391-405.
BURDERKIN R. (1988), "Interaction between Central Bank Behaviour and Fiscal Policy: The US case", *Applied Economics,* pp. 97-111.
CALVO G.A. *et al* (1993), "Financial Sector Reforms and Exchange Rate Arrangements in Easter Europe", IMF Occasional Paper No. 102.
CANZONERI M.B. and ROGERS C.A. (1990), "Is the European Community an Optimal Currency Area? Optimal Taxation Versus the Costs of Multiple Currencies", *American Economic Review* 80, pp. 419-433
CARLTON D.W. (1982), "The Disruptive Effects of Inflation on the Organization of Markets", in R.E. Hall (ed.), *Inflation: causes and effects,* pp. 139-152, Chicago University Press, Chicago
CHRISTODOULAKIS N. (1994), "Fiscal developments in Greece, 1980-93", *European Economy* 1994 No 3, pp. 99-134.
COHEN (1985), "Inflation, Wealth and Interest Rates in an Intertemporal Optimizing Model", *Journal of Monetary Economics* 16, pp. 73-85
COURAKIS A. (1981), "Financial structure and policy in Greece: Retrospect and prospect", *Greek Economic Review 3,* pp. 205-244.
COURAKIS A.S. and TAYLOR M.P. (eds.) (1990), Private behaviour and government policy in interdependent economies, Oxford University Press, Oxford.
CROCKETT A.D. (1994), "Rules versus Discretion in Monetary Policy", in J.A.H. de Beaufort Wijnholds, S.C.W. Eijffinger and L.H. Hoogduin (eds.), *A Framework for Monetary Stability,* Kluwer Academic Publishers, the Netherlands, pp. 165-184.
CUKIERMAN A. (1992), Central Bank Strategy, Credibility and Independence: Theory and Evidence, Cambridge, MA: MIT Press.
CUKIERMAN A. (1994a), "Central Bank Independence and Monetary Control", *The Economic Journal,* 104, No. 427 pp. 1437-1448.
CUKIERMAN A. (1994b), "Commitment Through Delegation, Political Influence and Central Bank Independence", in J.A.H. de Beaufort Wijnholds, S.C.W. Eijffinger and L.H. Hoogduin (eds.), *A Framework for Monetary Stability,* Kluwer Academic Publishers, the Netherlands.

CUKIERMAN A. (1995), "Towards a Systematic Comparison Between Inflation Targets and Monetary Targets", in Leiderman L. and Svensson L.E.O. (eds.) *Inflation Targets,* Centre for Economic Policy Research, London.

CUKIERMAN A., WEBB S., and NEYAPTI B. (1992), "Measuring the Independence of Central Banks and its Effects on Policy Outcomes", *World Bank Economic Review* 6, pp. 353-398.

CUKIERMAN A., KALAITZIDAKIS P., SUMMERS L. and WEBB S. (1993), "Central Bank Independence, Growth, Investment and Real Rates", *Carnegie-Rochester Conference Series on Public Policy* 39 pp. 95-140.

CZECH NATIONAL BANK (1998), Inflation Report, Prague.

DE GRAUWE P. (1994a), The Economics of Monetary Integration, second edition, Oxford University Press.

DE GRAUWE P. (1994b), Towards European Monetary Union without the EMS, *Economic Policy* 9, pp. 149-185.

DE GRAUWE P. (1994c), Discussion on Issing, 1994.

DE GRAUWE P. (1996a), How to fix Conversion Rates at the Start of EMU?, CEPR Discussion Paper No. 1530, London.

DE GRAUWE P. (1996b), Inflation Targeting to Achieve Inflation Convergence in the Transition Towards EMU, CEPR Discussion Paper, No. 1457, London.

DE GRAUWE P. and VANHAVERBEKE W. (1993), "Is Europe an Optimum Currency Area? Evidence from Regional Data", in P. Masson and M. Taylor (eds.), *Policy issues in the operation of Currency Unions,* Cambridge University Press, Cambridge.

DEMOPOULOS G. (1982), "Financial Markets and Institutions in Greece", *European Economy 5*, pp. 149-154.

DEMOPOULOS G., KATSIMBRIS G. and MILLER S. (1987), "Monetary Policy and Central Bank Financing of Government Budget Deficits: A Cross Country Comparison", *European Economic Review 31,* pp. 1023-1050.

DEWATRIPONT M., GIAVAZZI F., VON HAGEN J., HARDEN I., PERSSON T., ROLAND G., ROSENTHAL H., SAPIR A. and TABELLINI G., (1995), *Flexible Integration,* Center for Economic Policy Research, London.

DORNBUSCH R. (1991), "Credibility and Stabilization", *Quarterly Journal of Economics,* 106, pp. 837-850.

DORNBUSCH R. and GIOVANNINI A. (1990), "Monetary Policy in the open economy", in B. Friedman and F. Hahn (eds.), *Handbook of Monetary Economics,* vol. II, North-Holland, Amsterdam.

DRIFFILL J. (1994), comment on Freedman C., "Formal Targets for Inflation Reduction: the Canadian Experience", in J.A.H. de Beaufort Wijnholds, S.C.W. Eijffinger and L.H. Hoogduin (eds.), *A Framework for Monetary Stability,* Kluwer Academic Publishers, the Netherlands, pp. 17-29.

DRIFFILL J. (1997), "Institutions and Monetary Policy", *mimeo,* Department of Economics, University of Southampton.

DRIFFILL J., MIZON G. and ULPH A. (1990), "Costs of Inflation", in B. Friedman and F. Hahn (eds.) *Handbook of Monetary Economics,* Vol. II, North-Holland, Amsterdam.
EICHENGREEN B. (1990), Is Europe an Optimum Currency Area ?, CEPR Discussion Paper No 478, London.
EICHENGREEN B. (1993), "European Monetary Unification", *Journal of Economic Literature 16,* pp. 1321-1357.
EIJFFINGER S. and SCHALING E. (1993), "Central Bank Independence in Twelve Industrial Countries", *BNL Quarterly Review* 184, pp. 49-89.
ESTRELLA A. and HARDOUVELIS g. (1991), "Possible roles of the yield curve in monetary policy" in *Intermediate Targets and Indicators for Monetary Policy,* Federal Reserve Bank of New York, New York.
EUROPEAN BANK FOR RECONSTRUCTION AND DEVELOPMENT (1998), Annual Report , London.
EUROPEAN ECONOMY, Annual Economic Report on Greece, various editions.
EUROPEAN COMMISSION (1977), Report of the Study Group on the Role of Public Finance in European Integration, Brussels.
EUROPEAN COMMISSION (1990), "One Market, One Money", *European Economy* 44.
FELDSTEIN M. (1983), Inflation, Tax Rules and Capital Formation, Chicago University Press, Chicago.
FILIPPIDES A., KYRIAKOPOULOS P. and MOSCHOS D., (1995), "Monetary Policy Instruments used by the Bank of Greece", *Bank of Greece Economic Bulletin* 6, pp. 63-72.
FISCHER A. (1995), "New Zealand's Experience with Inflation Targets", in Leiderman L. and Svensson L.E.O. (eds.) *Inflation Targets,* Innocenzo Gasparini Institute for Economic Research, Opera, Milan and Centre for Economic Policy Research, London.
FISCHER S. (1979), "Capital Accumulation on the Transition Path in a Monetary Optimization Mode", *Econometrica* 47, pp. 1433-1439.
FISCHER S. (1990), "Rules versus Discretion in Monetary Policy", in B. Friedman and F. Hahn (eds.) *Handbook of Monetary Economics,* Vol. II, North-Holland, Amsterdam.
FISCHER S. (1991), "Growth, Macroeconomics and Development", NBER Macroeconomics Annual No 6, pp. 329-364.
FISCHER S. (1993), "The role of macroeconomic factors in growth", *Journal of Monetary Economics* 32, pp. 485-512.
FISCHER S. (1995), "Central Bank Independence Revisited", *American Economic Review Papers and Proceedings* 85, pp. 201-206.
FRATIANNI M. and VON HAGEN J. (1993), "European Monetary Union and Central Bank Independence", *Regional Science and Urban Economics* 23(3), pp. 401-425.
FREEDMAN C. (1991), "The goal of price stability: The debate in Canada", *Journal of Money, Credit and Banking* 23(3), pp. 613-618.

FREEDMAN C. (1994), "Formal Targets for Inflation Reduction: the Canadian Experience", in J.A.H. de Beaufort Wijnholds, S.C.W. Eijffinger and L.H. Hoogduin (eds.), *A Framework for Monetary Stability,* Kluwer Academic Publishers, the Netherlands, pp. 17-29.
FREEDMAN C. (1995), "The Canadian Experience with Targets for Reducing and Controlling Inflation", in Leiderman L. and Svensson L.E.O. (eds.) *Inflation Targets,* Centre for Economic Policy Research, London.
FREEDMAN C. (1995), Discussion on Ben-Bassat (1995) and Bowen (1995).
FRIEDMAN B. (1988), "Lessons on monetary policy from the 1980s", *Journal of Economic Perspectives* 2, pp. 51-72
FRIEDMAN B. (1975), "Targets, instruments and indicators of Monetary Policy", *Journal of Monetary Economics* 1, pp. 442-473.
FRIEDMAN B. (1990), "Targets and Instruments of Monetary Policy", in B. Friedman and F. Hahn (eds.) *Handbook of Monetary Economics,* Vol. II, North-Holland Publishing Co., Amsterdam.
FRIEDMAN M. (1959), A program for monetary stability, Fordham University Press, New York.
FRIEDMAN M. (1962), "Should There Be an Independent Monetary Authority?", in Yeager L. (ed.), *In Search of a Monetary Constitution,* Cambridge, Harvard University Press, pp. 219-243.
GARGANAS N.C. (1983), "An Evaluation of the Predictive Accuracy of the Bank of Greece Model of the Greek Economy", *Greek Economic Review* 5, pp. 101-122.
GARGANAS N.C. (1994), "Greek Monetary Policy: Issues and Experience", paper presented at the London School of Economics conference on *Greece, Prospects for Modernization,* 17-19 November 1994, London.
GEORGOUTSOS d. and KARAMOUZIS N. (1995), "Monetary Policy in Greece and Interbank Interest Rates in 1994", in G. Provopoulos (ed.), *The Greek financial System,* IOBE, Athens, pp. 101-134 (in Greek).
GIANNITSIS A. (1988), The accession to the European Community and the impact on industry and external commerce, Foundation for Mediterranean Studies, Athens, (in Greek).
GIANNITSIS A. (1993), " Integration in the international market and implications for the industrial and technological structure of the economy", in *Macroeconomic management and the development deadlock,* Gutenberg, Athens, (in Greek).
GIAVAZZI F. (1989), The exchange-rate question in Europe, CEPR Discussion paper No. 298, London.
GIAVAZZI F. and PAGANO M. (1988), "The advantage of tying one's hands: EMS discipline and Central Bank credibility", *European Economic Review* 32, pp. 1055-82.
GIAVAZZI F. and SPAVENTA L. (1990), "The New EMS", in P. De Grauwe and L. Papademos (eds.) *The European Monetary System in the 1990s,* London, Longman.

GIOVANNINI A. (1992), "Central Banking in a Monetary Union: Reflections on the proposed statute of the European Central Bank", CEPR Occasional Paper No 9, London.
GOODHART C.A.E. (1995), "Central Bank Independence" in his collection of essays *The Central Bank and the Financial System,* Basingstoke, Macmillan.
GOODHART C.A.E. and HUANG H. (1995), "What is the Central Bank's Game", LSE Financial Markets Group, Discussion Paper No. 222, London.
GOODHART C.A.E. and SCHOENMAKER D. (1995), "Should the functions of monetary policy and banking supervision be separated ?", *Oxford Economic Papers* 47, pp. 539-560.
GOODHART C.A.E. and VINALS J. (1994), Strategy and Tactics of Monetary Policy: Examples from Europe and the Antipodies, LSE Financial Markets Group, Special Paper No. 61.
GRAHL J. (1997), After Maastricht: a guide to European Monetary Union, Lawrence and Wishart, London.
GREEN J.H. (1996), "Inflation Targeting: Theory and Policy Implications", IMF Working paper No. 96/65
GRILLI V., MASCIANDARO D. and TABELLINI G. (1991), "Political and Monetary Institutions and Public Financial Policies in the Industrial Countries", *Economic Policy* 13, pp. 341-392.
GROS and THYGESEN (1992), European Monetary Integration , St. Martin's Press, New York.
HALDANE A.G. (1995a), Introduction in Haldane A.G. (ed.) *Targeting Inflation,* Bank of England, London.
HALDANE A.G. (1995b), "Three issues on inflation targets", in Haldane A.G. (ed.) *Targeting Inflation,* Bank of England, London.
HALIKIAS D. (1978), Money and Credit in a Developing Economy: The Greek Case, New York University Press, New York.
HALIKIAS D. (1987), Financial Reform and Problems of Monetary Policy: An Address, *Bank of Greece Papers and Lectures* No 59, Athens.
HALIKIAS D. (1993), "Economic Stabilization and Growth: The Case of Greece", *Greek Economic Review* 15, pp. 97-136.
HALIKIAS D. (1996), The way to the European Monetary Union, Foundation of Economic and Industrial Research (IOBE), Athens, (in Greek).
HEALEY *et al* (1995), "The political economy of an independent Central Bank" in D. Currie and J. Whitley (eds.), *European Monetary Union after Maastricht,* Lothian Foundation Press, London.
HOSKINS W.L. (1991), "Defending Zero Inflation: all for naught", *Federal Reserve Bank of Minneapolis Quarterly Review* 15(2), pp. 16-20.
ISSING O. (1993), "Central Bank Independence and Monetary Stability", Occasional Paper No. 89, Institute of Economic Affairs, London.
ISSING O. (1994), "Monetary Policy Strategy in the EMU", in J. Beaufort Wijnhold, S. Eiffinger, L,. Hoogduin. (eds.), *A Framework for Monetary Stability,* Kluwer Academic Publishers, the Netherlands pp. 135-155.

KANELLOPOULOS C. (1992), "The Underground Economy in Greece: What Official Data Show", *Greek Economic Review* 14, No 2, pp. 215-236.

KATSELI L. (1990), "Structural Adjustment of the Greek Economy", in C. Bliss and J.B. de Macedo (eds.*), Unity with Diversity in the European Economy: The Community's Southern Frontier,* Cambridge University Press, Cambridge.

KENEN P. (1995), Economic and Monetary Union in Europe, Cambridge University Press, Cambridge.

KING M. (1995), "Do Inflation Targets Work?", address delivered to the Center for Economic Policy Research, 26 September 1995, London.

KING M. (1997), "Changes in UK monetary policy: Rules and discretion in practice", *Journal of Monetary Economics* 39, pp. 81-97.

KAPOPOULOS P. (1995), "Disinflation and Credibility in Small Open Economies in the 1980s: Parties, Elections and the ERM", *European Journal of Political Economy* 11, pp. 157-170.

KARATZAS T. (1987), Report of the Committee for the Reform and Modernization of the Banking System, in *Epikaira Themata* 5, Athens (in Greek).

KOLLINTZAS T. and BITROS G. (eds.), (1992), Looking for hope for the Greek economy, Institute of Studies for Economic Policy (IMOP), Athens, (in Greek).

KORLIRAS P. (1984), Past Performance, Problems and Prospects of Monetary and Credit Policies in Greece, *Bank of Greece Papers and Lectures,* No. 49, Athens.

KORLIRAS P. (1985), The Greek Balance of Payments, *Bank of Greece Papers and Lectures,* No. 50, Athens.

KYDLAND F. and PRESCOTT E. (1977), "Rules versus Discretion: The Inconsistency of Optimal Plans", *Journal of Political Economy 85,* pp. 473-493.

KYDLAND F. and PRESCOTT E. (1982), "Time To Build and Aggregate Fluctuations", *Econometrica* 50, pp. 1345-1370.

LAMFALUSSY A. (1989), "Macro-coordination of fiscal policies in an Economic and Monetary Union", in Committee for the Study of Economic and Monetary Union, *Report on Economic and Monetary* Union (Delors Report), Luxembourg.

LAIDLER D. and ROBSON W. (1993), "The Great Canadian Disinflation: The economics and politics of monetary policy in Canada, 1988-93", *Policy Study* 19, Torònto: C.D. Howe Institute.

LARRE B. and TORRES R. (1991), " Is convergence a spontaneous process? The experience of Spain, Portugal and Greece", *OECD Economic Studies* 16, pp. 169-198.

LEIDERMAN L. and SVENSSON L.E.O. (1995), Introduction in Leiderman L. and Svensson L.E.O. (eds.) *Inflation Targets* Centre for Economic Policy Research, London.

LOHMANN S. (1992), "Optimal Commitment in Monetary Policy: Credibility versus Flexibility" *American Economic Review* 82, pp. 273-286.

McCALLUM B. (1989), Monetary Economics: theory and policy, Macmillan, New York.

McCALLUM B. (1990), Targets, Indicators and Instruments of Monetary Policy, IMF Working Paper No. 90/41

McCALLUM B. (1995), "Two Fallacies Concerning Central Bank Independence", *American Economic Review Papers and Proceedings 85,* pp. 207-211.

McCALLUM B. (1996), Inflation Targeting in Canada, New Zealand, Sweden the United Kingdom and in general, NBER Working Paper No 5579, Cambridge MA.

McCALLUM B. (1997), "Crucial issues concerning central bank independence", *Journal of Monetary Economics* 39, pp. 99-112.

MASSON P. (1996), "Fiscal dimensions of EMU", *The Economic Journal* 106, No. 437, pp. 996-1004.

MAYES D. and CHAPPLE B. (1995), "Defining an inflation target" in Haldane A.G. (ed.) *Targeting Inflation,* Bank of England, London.

MINFORD A.P.L. (1991a), The mess we are in because of the Exchange Rate Mechanism, The Bruges Group, London.

MINFORD A.P.L. (1991b), The supply side revolution in Britain, Edward Elgar/Institute of Economic Affairs, Aldershot

MINFORD A.P.L. (ed.) (1992), The cost of Europe, Manchester University Press, New York.

MINFORD A.P. L. (1995), "Time-inconsistency, Democracy and Optimal Contingent Rules", *Oxford Economic Papers 47*, pp. 195-210.

MINFORD A.P.L. (1996), "Notes on Monetary Union in Europe", *Economic Affairs,* 16, pp, 9-16.

MODIGLIANI F. and PAPADEMOS L. (1980), "The Structure of Financial Markets and the Monetary Mechanism", in *Controlling Monetary Aggregates III,* Federal Reserve Bank of Boston, Conference Series No. 23, pp. 111-115.

MONTICELLI C. and VINALS J. (1993), "European Monetary Policy in Stage Three: What are the Issues?", CEPR Occasional Paper No 12, London.

MOSCHOS D. (1995), "Targets and Indicators of Monetary Policy in Greece", in Provopoulos G. (ed.) *The Greek financial system: Trends and prospects,* Foundation for Economic and Industrial Research (IOBE), Athens (in Greek).

MOULTON B. (1996), "Bias in the Consumer Price Index: What is the Evidence?", *Journal of Economic Perspective* 10, pp. 159-77.

MOURMOURAS I.A. (1993), "Time Consistency, Indexation and the Costs of Inflation", *Economics Letters* 42, pp. 361-365.

MOURMOURAS I.A. (1994), "A New Role for the Bank of Greece" *To Vima,* 4 September 1994, pp. 24-25 (in Greek).

MOURMOURAS I.A. (1997a), "On Wage Indexing, Policy Credibility and Inflation", *Journal of Macroeconomics 19,* pp. 19-30.

MOURMOURAS I.A. (1997b), "Monetary Policy Delegation and Optimal Wage Indexation", *Bulletin of Economic Research* 49, pp. 303-307.

MOURMOURAS I.A. (1997c), "The Drachma, Exchange Rate Policy and the ERM 1-2", *Kyriakatiki Kathemerini,* 16 February 1997, p. 54, Athens, (in Greek).

MOURMOURAS I.A. and ARGHYROU M.G. (1997),Greece and the European Monetary Union: an explorative essay, Department of Economics, Queen Mary and Westfield College, University of London, Discussion Paper No 362.

MOURMOURAS I.A. and GHOSH S. (1998), "Endogenous Inflationary Finance and Long-run growth", *Journal of Economic Studies,* forthcoming.

MOURMOURAS I.A. and GHOSH S. (1999), "Decentralized Policy Making in a Game Theoretic Model with Capital Accumulation", *Bulletin of Economic Research,* forthcoming.

MOURMOURAS I.A. and SU D-M (1995a), "Central Bank Independence, Policy Reforms and the Credibility of Public Debt Stabilizations", *European Journal of Political Economy* 11, pp. 189-204.

MOURMOURAS I.A. and SU D-M (1995b), "Seignorage, Stabilization Plans and the Maastricht Fiscal Rules: A Case for an Independent Central Banker", in D.Currie and J. Whitley (eds.), *European Monetary Union after Maastricht,* Lothian Foundation Press, London.

MOURMOURAS I.A. and SU D-M (1995c), "On Stabilization Plans and Central Bank Independence", *Applied Economics 27*, pp. 967-971.

MUNDELL R. (1961), "A Theory of Optimal Currency Areas", *American Economic Review* 51, pp. 657-665.

NEGREPONDIS-DELIVANIS M. (1994), Greek Public Debt and Deficits, Sakkoulas, Thessaloniki.

OECD ECONOMIC OUTLOOK, Report on Greece, various editions.

OECD ECONOMIC SURVEY OF GREECE, various editions.

OKUN A. (1972), "Fiscal-Monetary Activism: Some Analytical Issues", *Brookings Papers on Economic Activity* 6 (1), pp. 123-172.

OKUN A.M. (1975), "Inflation: Its Mechanics and Welfare Costs", *Brooking Papers on Economic Activity No 2,* pp.351-390.

ORTEGA E. and BONILLA J.M. (1995), "Reasons for adopting an inflation target", in Haldane A.G. (ed.) *Targeting Inflation,* Bank of England, London.

PAPADEMOS L. (1990), "Greece and the EMS: issues, prospects and a framework for analysis", in P. De Grauwe and L. Papademos (eds.), *The European Monetary System in the 1990s,* Longmann, London.

PAPAPETROU E. and HONDROYIANNIS G. (1997), "The causal relationship between Consumer Price Index and Producer Price Index in Greece", *Bank of Greece Economic Bulletin* 10 pp. 131-143.

PAVLOPOULOS P. (1987), The Underground Economy in Greece, Institute of Economic and Industrial Studies (IOBE), Athens (in Greek).

PERSSON T. and TABELLINI G. (1990), Macroeconomic Policy, Credibility and Politics, Kingston-upon-Thames: Kluwer.

PERSSON T. and TABELLINI G. (1993), "Designing Institutions for Monetary Stability", Carnegie Rochester Conference Series on Public Policy, 39, pp. 53-84.

PERSSON T. and TABELLINI G. (1996), "Monetary Cohabitation in Europe", NBER Working Paper No. 5532, Cambridge MA.

POOLE W. (1970), "Optimal choice of monetary policy instruments in a simple stochastic macro model", *Quarterly Journal of Economics 84*, pp. 197-216.
POTERBA J. and SUMMERS L. (1987), "Finite Lifetimes and the Savings Effect of Budget Deficits", *Journal of Monetary Economics 20,* pp.729-752.
PROVOPOULOS G. (ED.) (1995), The Greek financial system: Trends and prospects, Foundation for Economic and Industrial Research (IOBE), Athens, (in Greek).
ROGOFF K. (1985), "The Optimal Degree of Commitment to an Intermediate Monetary Target", *Quarterly Journal of Economics* 100, pp. 1169-1190.
ROGOFF K. and SIBERT A. (1988), "Equilibrium Political Budget Cycles", *Review of Economic Studies* 55, pp. 1-16.
ROMER D. (1996), Advanced Macroeconomics, McGraw Hill, New York.
ROUBINI and SALA-I-MARTIN, A growth Model of Inflation, Tax Evasion and Financial Repression, NBER Working Paper No. 4062, Cambridge MA.
SAHAY R. and VEGH C. (1995), "Inflation and Stabilization in Transition Economies: A comparison with market economies", IMF Working Paper 95/8.
SARRIS A. and ZOGRAFAKIS S. (1993), "Changes in the structure and distribution of income in Greece in a period of structural changes", in T. Giannitsis (eds.), *Macroeconomic management and the development deadlock,* Institute of Studies for Economic Policy (IMOP), Athens, (in Greek).
SHAPIRO M. and WILCOX D. (1996), "Mismeasurement in the Consumer Price Index: an Evaluation", in B. Bernanke and J. Rotemberg (eds.), in *NBER Macroeconomics Annual* 1996, pp. 93-142.
SIDRAUSKI M. (1967a), "Rational Choice and Patterns of Growth in a Monetary Economy", *American Economic Review*57, pp. 534-544.
SIDRAUSKI M. (1967b), "Inflation and Economic Growth", *Journal of Political Economy* 75, pp. 796-810.
SOTIRIOU I. (1978), The first fifty years of the Bank of Greece, Bank of Greece, Athens (in Greek).
STEVENS G. and DEBELLE G. (1995), "Monetary policy goals for inflation in Australia", in Haldane A.G. (ed.) *Targeting Inflation,* Bank of England, London.
SVENSSON L.E.O. (1995), "The Swedish Experience of an Inflation Target", in Leiderman L. and Svensson L. (eds.) *Inflation Targets*, Centre for Economic Policy Research, London.
SVENSSON L.E.O. (1997a), "Optimal Inflation Targets, "Conservative" Central Banks and Linear Inflation Contracts", *American Economic Review* 87, pp. 98-114.
SVENSSON L.E.O. (1997b), "Inflation forecast targeting: Implementing and monitoring inflation targets", *European Economic Review* 41, pp. 1111-1146.
SWINBURNE M. and CASTELLO-BRANCO M. (1991), "Central Bank Independence: Issues and Experience", IMF Working Paper No. 91/58.
THOMPSON E. (1981), "Who Should Control the Money Supply?", *American Economic Review Papers and Proceedings 71,* pp. 356-361.

TOBIN J. (1965), "Money and Economic Growth", *Econometrica* 32, pp. 671-684.

TOBIN J. (1980), "Stabilization policy ten years after", *Brookings Papers of Economic Activity* 1, pp. 19-71.

TONIOLO G. (1988), Central Bank Independence in Historical Perspective, Walter de Geuyter & Co., New York.

TSOUKALIS L. (1993), "Country profiles: Greece", in *The New European Economy: The politics and Economics of Integration,* second edition, Oxford University Press, Oxford.

WENNINGER J. (1990), "Monetary aggregates as intermediate targets", in *Intermediate Targets and Indicators of Monetary Policy: A critical survey,* Federal Reserve Bank of New York, pp. 67-108.

WALLER C. (1992), "The Choice of a Conservative Central Banker in a Multisector Economy", *American Economic Review* 82, pp. 1006-1012.

WALSH C. (1995), "Optimal Contracts for Central Bankers", *American Economic Review* 85, pp. 150-167.

WYPLOSZ C. (1991), "Monetary Union and Fiscal Policy Discipline", in EC Commission, European Economy, Special Edition, 1.

VAITSOS K. (1993), "Central Axis of economic policy for an exit from the crisis", Chapter 8 in Macroeconomic management and the development deadlock, Gutenberg, Athens, (in Greek).

VAN DER PLOEG F. (1991), "Macroeconomic Policy Coordination during the various phases of Economic and Monetary Integration in Europe", in EC Commission, European Economy, Special Edition, 1.

VAN DER PLOEG F. (1992), "Political Economy of a Conservative Central Bank: Credibility and Public Finance", mimeo, Amsterdam University.

VAN DER PLOEG F. and ALOGOSKOUFIS G. (1994), "Money and Endogenous Growth", *Journal of Money Credit and Banking* 26, pp. 771-791.

VARDAS T.K. (1996), "On Stabilization and Growth", *Economicos Tachydromos,* 14 March 1996, pp. 36-38, Athens (in Greek).

VON HAGEN J. (1991), " A Note on the Empirical Effectiveness of Formal Fiscal Restraints", *Journal of Public Economics* 44, pp. 199-210.

VON HAGEN J. and FRATIANNI M. (1993), " The Transition to European Monetary Union and the European Monetary Institute", *Economics and Politics* 5, pp. 167-186.

VON HAGEN J. and EICHENGREEN B. (1996), "Federalism, Fiscal Restraints and European Monetary Union", *American Economic Review Papers and Proceedings,* May, pp. 134-138.

VON HAGEN J and NEWUMANN M. (1994), "Real Exchange Rates within and between Currency Areas: How far away is EMU?", *Review of Economics and Statistics* 76, pp. 236-244.

YATES A. (1995), "On the design of inflation targets", in Haldane A.G. (ed.) *Targeting Inflation,* Bank of England, London.

ZOLOTAS X. (1978), "Inflation and the Monetary Target in Greece", *Bank of Greece, Papers and Lectures* No 38, Athens.

FSC
www.fsc.org
MIX
Papier aus verantwortungsvollen Quellen
Paper from responsible sources
FSC® C105338

If you have any concerns about our products,
you can contact us on
ProductSafety@springernature.com

In case Publisher is established outside the EU,
the EU authorized representative is:
Springer Nature Customer Service Center GmbH
Europaplatz 3, 69115 Heidelberg, Germany

Printed by Libri Plureos GmbH
in Hamburg, Germany